The Social Subjects Within the Curriculum

115 – 121

0750703822

The Social Subjects Within the Curriculum
Children's Social Learning in the National Curriculum

Edited by

John Ahier and Alistair Ross

The Falmer Press
(A member of the Taylor & Francis Group)
London • Washington, D.C.

UK   The Falmer Press, 4 John Street, London WC1N 2ET
USA   The Falmer Press, Taylor & Francis Inc., 1900 Frost Road, Suite 101,
        Bristol, PA 19007

First published in 1995

**A catalogue record for this book is available from the British
Library**

**Library of Congress Cataloging-in-Publication Data are available on
request**

ISBN 0 7507 0381 4 cased
ISBN 0 7507 0382 2 paper

Jacket design by Caroline Archer

Typeset in 10/12 pt Times by
Graphicraft Typesetters Ltd., Hong Kong

*Printed in Great Britain by Burgess Science Press, Basingstoke on paper
which has a specified pH value on final paper manufacture of not less
than 7.5 and is therefore 'acid free'.*

Contents

Contents

List of Tables

Introduction

John Ahier and Alistair Ross

The curriculum of children up to the age of 14 has been a matter of debate for many years. Different models have coexisted in a creative tension: schools and teachers (and occasionally the wider community, including parents) constructed a curriculum that they judged to be most suited to meet the specific needs of their particular pupils and communities. They have done this by combining appropriate elements from different models, among which can be identified:

- the curriculum designed for cultural transmission, to pass on a received body of knowledge, usually in the form of traditional subjects (the 'academic' curriculum of Goodson (1987), or, in the primary school, perhaps the 'preparatory' model of Blyth (1969), leading to the traditional academic curriculum of the secondary phase);
- the curriculum designed to develop socially, economically or technologically desirable skills, as represented for example in TVEI (in Goodson's terms, a form of the 'utilitarian' curriculum, or the 'elementary' model, following Blyth);
- the curriculum designed to enable the development of a socially constructed understanding of the world, in which appropriate behaviour is developed (the 'pedagogic' curriculum of Goodson, or the 'developmental' curriculum of Blyth), sometimes designed to serve a child-centred, evolutionary view of child development.

These models have often been identified through criticisms made of their particular outcomes, or of the different social and economic preparation they provide for the pupil. Thus the cultural transmission model has been described and criticized by Wiener (1981), for example, while the utilitarian model has been attacked by neo-conservatives in the Black Papers (Cox and Dyson, 1969 and 1970), and the pedagogic model by a range of politicians (such as Callaghan, 1976). What we lack is an adequate description and analysis of the origins of the various potential elements of the curriculum, or of the mechanisms that have operated to select a curriculum from these. While many commentators have observed that any curriculum is necessarily a reflection of the social context within which it is constructed, the detailed examination of the pressures and forces that have shaped the formation of curriculum areas and subjects has not been greatly pursued: Whitty (1985)

1

explored the social sciences, and Goodson both geography (1987) and aspects of business studies (1994), but all of these focused very much on the secondary school curriculum.

This book is set in the context of the pressures and forces that shaped the social elements of the curriculum, particularly in the primary and middle school curriculum, and especially the processes of curriculum reconstruction that followed the 1988 Education Reform Act. The introduction of the National Curriculum swept away much of the earlier models, substituting a single transmission model of knowledge, using a traditional set of subject divisions. For many teachers this was seen as an attack on the social elements of the curriculum which they had previously been able to promote. It was difficult to see how such a National Curriculum, ordered and assessed according to directions from a body set up by central government, could be informed by local communities and the actual social life of children. Initially all the social aspects of the curriculum appeared to be marginalized, perhaps deliberately so.

However, this original exposition of the National Curriculum, as a set of discrete asocial subjects, did not hold for long. There was firstly a series of attempts by members of the profession to 'colonize' the subject working parties and the subsequent orders with representations of the social — for example, in English, and in history in the PESC model (in which the political, economic, social and cultural aspects of a topic had to be addressed). Secondly, the necessity for a 'whole' curriculum that was considerably larger than the National Curriculum was recognized, and the Education Reform Act included the requirement that schools provide a 'broad and balanced' curriculum.

The publication *Curriculum Guidance 3: The Whole Curriculum* (NCC, 1990a) described a curricular provision that incorporated both cross-curricular skills (a range of competencies that are inadequately described as skills of communication, numeracy, study, etc.) and cross-curricular themes (economic and industrial; health education; careers; environmental education; citizenship). The NCC published a series of Curriculum Guidance booklets in 1990, one for each of these five themes (NCC, 1990b–f). The review of the National Curriculum, under the chairmanship of Sir Ron Dearing (NCC/SEAC, 1993; SCAA, 1994a) has left the idea of the whole curriculum untouched. The draft proposals for the post-1995 National Curriculum are still compatible with the requirements of the 1988 Educational Reform Act for a broad and balanced curriculum, and the NCC's cross-curricular descriptions, in themes and skills, remain as the only official guidance on the nature of the whole curriculum.

It is possible to describe the relationship between the whole curriculum, the basic curriculum (defined in Education Reform Act) and the National Curriculum (foundation and core) as a series of concentric sets, and this seems to have been the formal explanation of the National Curriculum Council. On the other hand, many teachers tend to view the cross-curricular themes as foci running across the subjects at right angles, as warp to the weft of the subjects. (Many more teachers appear to ignore the cross-curricular themes, or to be ignorant of them (HMI, 1991).

Various contributors to this volume open up general issues that explore the continuities and discontinuities, the parallels and divergencies, in the construction of practices in social education. The National Curriculum has attempted to redirect the way teachers represent the nature of social life, and this in some ways confronts previous notions of a social education. It can be argued that it replaces some of these earlier approaches with a purely individualistic conception of education, or with a different set of ideas about the nature of the social. Moreover, if there is a redirection of social education implicit within the National Curriculum/Whole Curriculum, this must confront previous conceptions of the individually learning child, given the interdependence between notions of the self and society. It is claimed in some chapters that changes in the general economic and social context which would have, in any event, undermined the old models of social education. It is a further problem as to whether social and economic life is now so diverse and complex that previous models of the self and social education programmes are inappropriate.

Some initial critical reactions to the National Curriculum are represented here in attempts to relate its structure and content directly to the general political philosophy of the government from which it came. The suspicion is that 'the social' would somehow cease to be a focus for education. Given the public denials of the very existence of society by Margaret Thatcher, and the belief held by her, and other followers of Hayek, that society cannot be 'made' by political initiatives (or what they call state interference), then it is argued that the new curriculum is, in essence, more about individual competition and instrumental achievement than it is about social relationships.

But perhaps a National Curriculum can never be developed and presented in asocial terms. In fact, on the political right, there were other conceptions of the social which could gave a degree of justification and coherence to the plans for curriculum change. Johnson's exploration of New Right thinking shows that it did have a conception of the social, albeit very different from previous social ideas which had dominated education (Johnson, 1992). The focus was not on inequality and difference, but on tradition, authority, the family, the Nation and national culture. The language of the National Curriculum which speaks of 'core' and 'foundation' is concerned to reassert those disciplines which are thought to have been ennobled by tradition.

These ideas, most fully expressed by Scruton (1980), certainly constituted a direct assault on the previous development of social studies teaching and its essential interdisciplinary nature. But again, we should beware of seeing the political Right as too unified as a force, whether in its educational or other areas of influence. Throughout the last twenty years these traditional conservative thinkers have been in tension with what have been termed the conservative modernisers (Ball, 1990), who have tended to argue for a set of educational changes more suitable to what they see as a rapidly changing economy. They have been somewhat critical of the traditional, academic curriculum, and its limited pedagogy, and it is this which makes for a possible link between them and some professional progressive educators. It could be argued that the cross-curricular themes developed by the National

Curriculum Council, and their implicit conceptions of the self, owe their existence in part to this link.

The situation is therefore a very complex one. We cannot just locate the National Curriculum in its social context, because it cannot be seen as just a reflection of that context, however conceived. Instead, it may be more helpful to see it as a condensation of reactions to a variety of economic, political and social changes. Its traditional elements may be traced back to anxieties about a loss of national-social cohesion which many thought were first seen in the 'permissive 1960s'. On the other hand, some of its more contemporary features may derive from concerns with poor national economic performance and the sense of rapid economic transformation which requires a new and flexible workforce.

Standing further back from the obvious and immediate problems facing the British state, the English and Welsh educational system, and a ruling political party very much centred on London and the South of England, is it possible to see a set of more general cultural, economic and social changes which form the backdrop to curricular debate, not only here, but in other contemporary societies? Rob Gilbert points to a whole set of observations about the nature of societies which have been characterized as post-modern, and explores the implications of these observations for social education in general, and education for citizenship in particular.

The clear implication is that earlier attempts at promoting political and social membership and participation, if they ever were effective, are very unlikely to be so now. So much has changed — in the economy, the culture and the personal lives of young people — that teachers can no longer rely on rational abstractions or presumed personal or social unities to develop programmes of social education.

For some, all the apparent characteristics of young people's lives in contemporary society — their mobility, insecurity, fragmentation and diversity — make for a fearful desire to return to old ways and old disciplines. For others, the whole project concerned with any kind of social education seems doomed to failure, because it depends on the notion of the rational and integrated individual, inconceivable in contemporary conditions. Gilbert, however, explores another approach, looking for the positive possibilities in a culturally differentiated society and a different form of political life. He presents us with new ways of developing citizenship, which he sees as consistent with the actual lives of young people in post-modern cultures now, and very different from that represented in *Education for Citizenship* (NCC, 1990f).

Jeff Vass approaches this from a rather different position, as he problematizes the whole project of describing a rational social education. He argues that the attempt to construct parallel but related narratives from the diverse discourses of the social sciences and other curriculum areas makes the teacher's task of presenting an integrated and coherent syllabus near impossible. Social identities — an individual's 'self' — are constructed, he suggests, from varied and contextually diverse social practices, and these are never constant. Therefore there is no point in addressing a unified self, or trying to construct one through an 'integrated' curriculum. He seeks to show how the apparent rationality of the economic descriptors in *Education for Economic and Industrial Understanding* (NCC, 1990b) fail to encapsulate our local, fragmented and contingent 'feel' for contemporary economic experiences. Gilbert's preferred programme for citizenship education, on the other hand, attempts to recognize and take account of young people's feel for their experience, albeit local, fragmented and contingent. Taken together, the chapters presented by Gilbert and Vass are in some ways similar to the tension felt by many teachers struggling with social education, between attempting to show how 'things' relate together, but at the same time accepting diversity, difference and fragmentation.

In the second part of the book, we consider the evolution of social education over the past few years, or at least, changes in the social curriculum. Competing models of the curriculum, that define it, for example, variously as bodies of know-ledge, as socially or economically necessary competencies, or in terms of individual, community or national consciousness, can be related to alternative view of the nature and place of the social.

Various views of the nature of the curriculum have been expressed over the past two or three decades. These arguments are long-standing: here, Alistair Ross traces them from Plowden and the establishment of the Schools Council in the mid-1960s (of particular interest, given the current rhetoric concerning that decade), but principally focuses on the events from the Ruskin Speech to the present. As he points out, the move away from social studies, so marked in the activities of educational policymakers in this period, is strangely out of kilter with international trends. In so many of the countries that are currently cast in the role of our eco-nomic competitors, social studies assumed an increasing proportion of curricular time. But in Britain, the description and practice of the social elements of the curriculum went into decline. Although the cross-curricular themes which emerged may be seen as reincluding the social in the curriculum, it was a very different idea of the social to that which had developed and lost in the previous two decades.

This point is further elaborated in Ross's second contribution, within the context of the current debate on the relationship between the individual and society, and particularly the view of the individual as primarily responsible for ensuring their own well-being, and the reciprocal understanding that society and the state have minimal obligations to the individual. In that context, it is possible to view the five identified cross-curricular themes not just as the old social subjects creeping back on to the agenda (economic and industrial understanding equating to economics, citizenship equating to political science, etc.) but as a revision and redefinition of these areas. Each cross-curricular subject, particularly as they are described in the five *Curriculum Guidance* booklets, can be analyzed to show how stress has been placed on the need to develop the individual's capabilities in that particular area, so that the initiative and responsibility is shifted towards them, and away from any communal or social provision. For example, in the area of health education, there is more stress on the duty of the individual to 'behave responsibly', to take evasive action, to plan their life-style, diet, fitness regime, etc., in such a way that mini-mizes their future call on the community-provided services. The term and practice of 'care in the community' epitomizes this move — responsibility for some of the sick is shifted from the State (which curiously some decades ago used to be seen as the community in corporate form) and its institutions to individuals and families, who are rhetorically retitled as 'the community'. Similarly, the focus in careers education moves away from describing opportunities and possibilities, and towards the individual identifying their own strengths, preparing themselves for transition and change, and presenting themselves to advantage — and in so doing, shifting responsibility for the individual's eventual status as employed/non-employed from the state (or 'the community', or 'the economy') to the individual.

The final section of the book takes in a series of reactions to the various individual cross-curricular themes. As argued earlier, what the cross-curricular themes have in common is that they are all concerned with how individuals behave and act in society, rather than about particular knowledge. If the foundation subjects are traditional cultural-transmission machines, the cross-curricular themes are their antithesis — they are not merely devices to create thematic links across subjects, as seen in the worst excesses of topic work, or the bits left out or forgotten when the original curriculum was put together (although there are elements of that). Each theme is concerned with the relationships between the individual and a particular aspect of the community/society — its economy, its health, its environment, its employment possibilities and the nature of the state and society. And the language with which each theme is described has been very carefully selected before being published. 'Citizenship' seems a peculiarly English construction, for example, with quite different overtones from *citoyens*: citizenship is passive, and relates to obligations to the state, and is cognate with the term 'subject'.

This section draws together the previous themes through a number of studies focusing on particular cross-curricular themes. These themes could be viewed as simply the old social curriculum dressed up in some new garb of interdisciplinarity. Alternatively, they might be a potentially insidious and reactionary attempt to shift responsibility from the social to the individual. A third explanation might be that they are simply a necessary reorientation towards the practicalities of late twentieth century economic realism.

The first of Anna Craft's chapters in this section (chapter 5) develops the idea of the developmental or the pedagogic curriculum outlined at the beginning of this introduction, and relates the holistic and integrated view of the curriculum — so commonly described in descriptions of primary practice — to the development of the individual self. It is of particular interest that the cross-curricular themes have been described to teachers as offering possibilities of an integrative approach to curriculum planning, in the way that they cross-cut traditional discipline boundaries: this ought to be of particular appeal to those primary practitioners who are suspicious that the artificial boundaries between subjects may interfere with the learning patterns of young children. One of the strengths of the integrated curriculum, it is often argued, is that it allows the development of the individual. In the case of these cross-curricular themes, however, the whole notion of the individual may be suspected of having been reconstrued in new terms.

The concepts of indoctrination and empowerment are of critical importance in the analysis of these possible interpretations. Both words are susceptible to use as rhetorical and pejorative terms. The remaining chapters in the section variously address

- who is indoctrinating whom?
- who is empowering whom?
- what is being indoctrinated?
- what powers are being transferred?

Each of these four questions is, in various ways, put to each of the cross-curricular themes.

Keith Crawford raises suspicions about the guidance offered in Education for Citizenship. Despite the rhetoric of empowerment and the freedom of intellectual enquiry that the document implies, he sees it as narrowly prescriptive, and as insidious in its omissions. It offers, he argues, a view of the citizen as a part-player in a vast and homogeneous social equilibrium, and ignores the tensions and imbalances that are inherent in contemporary pluralistic society. John Ahier continues the argument, asking similar questions about the specific construction the documents place on economic and industrial awareness and environmental studies. These two themes conceal a wide range of controversial issues and approaches, that are barely alluded to. In particular, many of the concerns that are raised are unfairly depicted as the responsibility of the individual, when clearly the only effective actors must be operating at national or supra-national level.

Anna Craft's second chapter presents a more optimistic view of the social in the cross-curricular themes. She argues that it is the near-compulsory nature of the cross-curricular themes (and she argues that the whole curriculum paper is almost obligatory) that brighten the prospects of genuine empowerment. The earlier optional status within the curriculum given to the economic led to its devaluation as 'not a serious (examinable) subject': she argues that its status and esteem should rise now that it has such official approval.

In the final chapter, the team from the Centre for Health Education and Research (David Stears, Stephen Clift and Shane Blackman) consider aspects of health education. Sex education and drug education, on which they focus, are clearly social issues, but ones also that can be imbued with such moral overtones that make it impossible for neo-conservative politicians not to continually interfere in the area. Indoctrination meets empowerment head-on in this area. Given the politician's self-imposed choice between indoctrination into what they perceive as moral absolutes and the potential risks of empowering young people to make their own decisions, there is no contest: indoctrination wins out every time. This particular cross-curricular theme has the goal posts in a condition of perpetual motion, as orders, circulars and guidance stream out of Sanctuary Gardens and from the Department of Health.

One might also draw parallels between the use of some of the terms in curriculum development and their contemporary use in the description of educational administrative structures. For example, the word 'empowerment' has been used to justify recent changes in the administration of education. The language of government has been that if responsibility ('ownership') of the educational service is shifted to the schools, then this will empower the schools and the 'communities' which they serve (by which they mean parents and local employers), and reduce the possibilities of obfuscation by the LEAs. Of course, it could alternatively be argued that the sweeping away of the middle ground of the LEA in practice removes the possibility of effective community involvement (meaning here the whole local community, responsible through local government structures), and its control in education. Individual schools with grant maintained status will in future be far more susceptible, both to highly localized and sectarian pressure groups and (paradoxically) to central government control. There are parallels between this use of the word 'empowerment' and its use in terms of 'empowering' children to take control through the curriculum, and the cross-curricular themes in particular. It is also instructive to examine the shifting conception of what words like community and social mean, not only within the curriculum, but also in the management of education.

'Empowering' children through economic and industrial understanding, for example, may mean developing their 'enterprise skills', so that they are in theory able to recognize and develop their own job opportunities through self-employment. It could alternatively be construed as a means of indoctrinating the young to see themselves as victims of their own inadequacy, rather than victims of faults in the system: if they fail to find employment, or if their own self-employment fails to get off the ground or falters, then the responsibility for that failure can be shown to lie with the individual, whose enterprise skills are either inadequately developed or poorly used, and not with the economy or society at large.

This book does not attempt to persuade teachers and others to return to some earlier 'golden age' of curriculum practice and theory. Most educators would acknowledge that the social, cultural, economic and educational contexts are now significantly different from those of ten or more years ago, although they might not agree on the terms to identify such changes. For some, the cultural conditions identified by the term post-modernism may seem significant; for others, the political conception of post-Thatcherism may seem more informative. Yet however we interpret or evaluate them, social changes necessarily influence curriculum construction, and many teachers continue and will continue to be committed to giving their pupils some form of explicit social education. It is hoped that this book will help explore the possibilities and constraints in attempting to do this in the mid-1990s.

Part 1

The Contemporary Context for the Social Subjects

Chapter 1

Education for Citizenship and the Problem of Identity in Post-modern Political Culture

Rob Gilbert

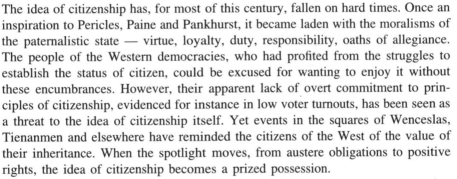

This quote seems to suggest.

Our society is passing through a period of change and we are concerned that without our realizing it, we could lose some of the benefits of living in the relatively free and open society which we have inherited. (Commission on Citizenship, 1990, p. xv)

The idea of citizenship has, for most of this century, fallen on hard times. Once an inspiration to Pericles, Paine and Pankhurst, it became laden with the moralisms of the paternalistic state — virtue, loyalty, duty, responsibility, oaths of allegiance. The people of the Western democracies, who had profited from the struggles to establish the status of citizen, could be excused for wanting to enjoy it without these encumbrances. However, their apparent lack of overt commitment to principles of citizenship, evidenced for instance in low voter turnouts, has been seen as a threat to the idea of citizenship itself. Yet events in the squares of Wenceslas, Tienanmen and elsewhere have reminded the citizens of the West of the value of their inheritance. When the spotlight moves, from austere obligations to positive rights, the idea of citizenship becomes a prized possession.

Schools have long been charged with the task, usually thankless, of promoting the citizenship ideal as an inheritance of the culture, and of showing new generations why they should prize it and how they might maintain it. Government interest in education for citizenship over the past decade has given new life to this important area and is therefore welcome. However, this revival is not a simple matter of injecting new enthusiasm and resources into established ideas and practice. Important changes in ways of thinking about citizenship, and in society itself, create the need for some basic rethinking about what education for citizenship entails.

Citizenship is a contested term whose meanings and contents are subject to debate and change (Leca, 1992; Oldfield, 1990). For some, citizenship is primarily about the broad range of entitlements which accrue to citizens. Here the chief concerns relate to the equitable distribution of access to normally expected levels of well-being. Surveys show that British citizens place these social rights to minimum standards of living, medical care, work and education at the forefront of the rights of citizenship (Johnston Conover, Crewe and Searing, quoted in Commission on Citizenship, 1990, p. 6).

A second emphasis focuses on citizenship as a set of moral and social virtues required for practising and sustaining a democratic ideal. Both these views are based on a substantive concern for the nature of citizens and society and the outcomes of citizenship. Citizenship in a democratic society is judged by the distribution of entitlements or the nature of its citizens.

Other views give more emphasis to the processes of citizenship. For instance, for a third group of commentators, citizenship implies membership of a community entailing a juridical status, which confers formal rights and obligations, such as equality under the law, the right to vote, paying taxes or otherwise contributing to the social and economic welfare of the community. The concern is for the extent to which these are safeguarded in law and government, and whether citizens practice these formally established rights and obligations.

A fourth view emphasizes participation in the legal/political system but also in the broader civil spheres of society. The chief concern is with citizens' decision making role in a civic culture. In both these views, citizenship in a democratic society is judged by the openness of the formal procedures governing legal, political and civil decision-making, and the extent to which citizens can and do participate in them. The procedural emphasis of the third and fourth views is echoed in the Commission on Citizenship's statement that 'We consider that citizenship involves the perception and maintenance of an agreed framework of rules or guiding principles, rather than shared values' (*ibid.*, p. 13).

There are two problems with these views of citizenship which are important for those with an educational interest. The first is their abstractness from the complex experiences of everyday life. The first approach usually deals with generalized distributions of material entitlements over populations, often neglecting the personal dimension of injustice which produces the subjective experiences of alienation or exclusion (Young, 1990). The second approach emphasizes abstract ideals to which people are to be committed in their public role as citizens, again overlooking the significance of these at the level of everyday personal experience. The third and fourth approaches are illustrated in the Commission on Citizenship's theme of citizenship as 'the separate role of individuals as citizens within the political or public community, and the rules that govern it' (1990, p. xv). This definition leads the Commission expressly to exclude the economy and the family as spheres of relations and experiences relevant to citizenship, and to focus on rules (rather than experience, practice or well being) as the essence of citizenship.

The great gap in these views is the lack of systematic attention to people's personal experience in their everyday lives, including the work place and private life, and how the abstract elements of citizenship are related to these spheres. If people are told that citizenship is unrelated to work, family and other elements of their everyday experience as persons, they might justifiably doubt its value. Similarly, if educators try to promote citizenship ideals and involvement without considering its personal significance for people in their everyday lives, students are unlikely to accept them.

The second issue with the conventional views of citizenship is that their value will depend very much on our analysis of the contemporary world and the concept of citizenship most appropriate to it. As the opening statement from the Commission on Citizenship notes, the Western world is in a process of fundamental change which goes to the heart of the individual-society relationship in which the concept of citizenship has developed. Generally described as a move from a modern to a post-modern society, this change provides the background to any discussion of the relationship between citizenship and personal experience, and will be taken up here.

Post-modern Society

Discussions of social change have pointed to changes in a range of elements of contemporary society. Hassan (1985) refers to 'a number of related cultural tendencies, a constellation of values, a repertoire of procedures and attitudes' (p. 119), while Huyssen (1986) refers to 'a noticeable shift in sensibility, practices, and discourse formations which distinguishes a post-modern set of assumptions, experiences, and propositions from that of a preceding period' (p. 181). By its very nature talk of social change on such a grand scale is imprecise, even speculative. However, there is sufficient evidence to suggest that the changes which underlie the concept of post-modernity are real, and that while it is difficult to gauge their extent and their future, they are more likely to continue than not. While these shifts have been noted in a range of social spheres, of most interest here are four dimensions of change which have particular importance for education for citizenship: the economy, informationalism, knowledge, and moral action.

A Post-industrial Economy

Changes in economic relations and organization have been labelled post-industrialism, post-Fordism and disorganized capitalism, terms signalling the move from the standardization, specialization and economies of scale of traditional industry to the innovation and multifaceted integration of flexible production and retailing which characterize current economic practice. As a result of increased corporatism, European union and economic globalization, the power of ownership has in many cases become further removed from the site of production, even as flexible production and franchising may devolve other decisions to the workplace (Murray, 1989).

The consequences for employment, regional economies and labour/management relations are in the direction of less stability over time, greater movement over space, and a general threatening of the old certainties of the economic system. The precariousness of the cults of the market and individual enterprise can be seen as a threat to any historic compromise or social contract between citizens and the economy.

The post-modern economy has fragmented the experience of production, and at the same time heightened the significance of consumption. While politics has in the past relied on a formal public rationality, 'the new consumerism on the other hand is all about floating visual images, pleasures and impossible dreams' (Mort, 1989, p. 169) — emphasizing a private sphere in which people find solace and satisfaction in getting and spending. Citizenship as entitlement becomes central to this issue, as does the relationship between civil and political rights on the one hand and social welfare rights on the other, since the principles of equality which drive political citizenship raise challenging questions when applied to the economic sphere.

This economic change has considerable impact on young people. Part-time work among school students is extensive, and is often concentrated in mass retailing outlets where these forms of economic relations are well established. Not yet citizens, but no longer children in this context, their status is ambiguous, and we know very little about how they see their entitlements, or what they learn about the place of the worker in the broader system. In addition, the post-industrial society calls on skills which increasingly bring the economy and the school closer together, with school-work transition, economic and industrial understanding, and school enterprises evidence of the link between knowledge and the economy. We know also that students' future career histories will involve much more job mobility than that of preceding generations. The post-industrial economy has a more direct impact on youth and schools than its predecessor, and education for citizenship needs to consider what this might imply.

The Information Society

Related to these changes is the growth of the information society. The information revolution is among the most pervasive forms of social change experienced by the present generation. In the advanced capitalist economies, information workers (including computer manufacturing, telecommunications, mass media, advertising, publishing, accounting) comprise more than half the workforce. Even more widespread is the involvement of computerization in all facets of life. As Chesnaux (1987) points out,

> Working in a factory, playing with one's children, planning one's leisure activities, following developments in macro-economics, creating works of musical or pictorial art — all these diverse activities are now capable of being carried out with the same methods of operation, by following the same logical processes, by making use of the same sort of abstract coding. (p. 27)

The characteristic organizational form of this computerized processing of information is a flatter, less hierarchical (though not necessarily less centralized) structure. Fragmentation, decentralization, and proliferating networks in the circulation of information parallel those of the economy (and are of course part of it). The speed and fragmentation of the reporting of events changes the nature of our observations of the world. Where once time and place provided a tangible distance and ordering of our observations, live global broadcasts and instant replays can depict the world as an ever present instant reality. In addition, new possibilities and problems arise in the fields of privacy, control, organizational structure, surveillance and planning.

These information forms permeate the media, industry and the bureaucracy, enabling symbolic hegemony among an apparent diversity of messages and channels. They are 'the organizing concepts of a post-modern *administrative control apparatus*, a social practice in a society that is semiotic at the cultural-consumption level, informational-production level, and at the communicative regulative or power level' (Wexler, 1987, p. 157).

Youth at the end of the twentieth century live in a world where events are constantly mediated by computerized and visual images, where electronic information is an ever present medium in which they live out their lives, where their schooling is increasingly administered, monitored and even provided by computerized and other forms of electronic device. The organizational forms of the information society go to the heart of the life experiences of young people, and to the extent that they are relevant to the nature and practice of citizenship, they are a force whose power needs to be appreciated.

Knowledge and Grand Narratives

Not only have the means of knowledge production and dissemination changed through the information revolution; so also, it is argued, have the forms and criteria of knowledge itself. Post-modernism is seen as having an epistemological effect of profound importance for the way in which knowledge is implicated in society.

In his study *The Post-modern condition: A Report on Knowledge* Lyotard (1984) argues that modern thought since the enlightenment has legitimated itself in terms of 'metanarratives' such as 'the dialectics of the Spirit, the hermeneutics of meaning, the emancipation of the rational or working subject, or the creation of wealth' (p. xxiii). These grand narratives have sought to ground knowledge in some fundamental unity, a privileged position of authority from which all knowledge could be categorized and assessed. Scientific knowledge, for instance, became most powerful when it connected into a single explanatory system the disparate discourses of our experience of the world.

However, these metanarratives are not universal but finite. They are produced by identifiable groups for particular purposes, times and audiences, and combining them into a unified whole becomes an impossible dream. In the case of the major social narrative of democracy, this totalizing logic lies in placing 'humanity as the hero of liberty' in the position of the main protagonist, the subject of history, a concept which constructs a legitimating consensus among 'the people'. However, the 'people' is a term in a metanarrative which subverts the democratic ideal, a self defeating contradiction in that it obliterates the reality of division and difference which is the dynamic of the events being described.

Lyotard's example comes from education, where 'the State resorts to the narrative of freedom every time it assumes direct control over the training of the "people", under the name of the "nation", in order to point them down the path of progress' (*ibid.*, p. 32). For Lyotard, the dangerous search for the grand narrative has failed. In the quest for alternatives, post-modernism, which he defines as 'incredulity to metanarratives' (*ibid.*, p. xxiv), sets the criteria which a revised knowledge must meet.

This view has particular significance for schooling, for as Lyotard observes, education for citizenship has historically been built on a consensual grand narrative of the rise of democracy as an inexorable progress from hierarchical to egalitarian social arrangements and from authoritarian to representative governments. This narrative has been constructed in such a way as to exclude its gaps and contradictions, and present the ideal of progress as a universal and natural force (Gilbert, 1984). Yet whether this progress has profited all citizens equally, and how we assess the extent of it, will be influenced by the perspective we take and therefore the social and historical milieu in which we are positioned. Lyotard's critique has much to say about education for citizenship.

Morality and Political Action

One consequence of this destabilizing of grand narratives, and the fourth problem to be raised, lies in the threat to the possibilities of a discourse of morality and concerted political action, for both require some sense of shared values and a common vision.

> With the development of mass consumption and mass systems of information, social styles and cultural practices become mixed into an indefinite medley of tastes and outlooks. With this fragmentation of culture there also goes a fragmentation of sensibilities, a mixing of lifestyles and the erosion of any sense of a cogent political project or coherent political programme, as the lives of individuals become increasingly merely a collection of discontinuous happenings. (Turner, 1989, p. 212)

The moral response to these circumstances will vary. Some commentators point to potential nihilism on the grounds that 'a coherent system of values . . . presupposes a relatively coherent community as the underlying social fabric of moral systems and ethical arguments', observing that contemporary society lacks the necessary 'underlying communal reality of values' (Stauth and Turner, 1988, p. 509). Others see narcissism as the typical outcome, where 'image systems, value codes, knowledge bases, and information networks' ground an inner directed consumption focused on 'personal fulfilment, physical fitness, self-actualisation, and spiritual awakening' (Luke and White, 1985, p. 35).

While the Commission on Citizenship has rejected shared values as a basis for citizenship, this view is not universally shared. Others argue that values of loyalty and commitment to certain rights and obligations are necessary to citizenship (Heater,

1990). Even the Commission's emphasis on agreed rules would require certain shared values before rules could be agreed and willingly followed. The importance for citizenship of morality and shared values cannot be so easily dismissed, but nor can they be easily established if the fragmentation of culture is as significant as the prophets of post-modernity claim.

Post-modern Political Culture

Economic relations, information, knowledge and morality are concepts at the heart of politics, and the changes reviewed here are pervasively political. Gibbins (1989) lists the characteristics of post-modern political culture which result from these changes, creating new forms and issues for political activity:

- an affluent 'postmaterialist' middle class has created new alliances around environmental, peace and feminist issues, and new forms of political expression in symbolic and life style politics;
- political order and legitimacy are threatened as objectivity, commensurability, unity and the integrated self are deconstructed, and replaced by relativity, pluralism, fragmentation and polyculturalism;
- post-modernism signifies discontinuity among economy, society and polity; an information and consumer economy coincides with heightened conflict between public and private spheres, growing distrust of government, and realignments of party and class allegiances;
- an eclectic and amorphous culture of plurality and mixed lifestyles is combined with an emphasis on leisure and consumption, and freedom, spontaneity and gratification take precedence over discipline, authority and predictability;
- the emerging character of contemporary political culture is pluralistic, anarchic, disorganised, rhetorical, stylised, and ironic.

Gibbins (1989) warns that this construction can be exaggerated, but points to signs that the trend is to:

> a world full of 'designer cultures' created for the needs of groups, presented by media persons, film and pop stars, advertisers, sportsmen, evangelists and millionaires, to fill the cultural void left by the collapse of cultural traditions. Political culture in a post-modern world may become more like a script and less an inherited narrative for life. (p. 24)

The overwhelming conclusion of the analysts of post-modernism is that it poses a threat to important and long-standing features of democratic life. However, these negative assessments are countered by others. For there are positive possibilities in the differentiation and proliferation of contacts and experience flowing from the diversification of social worlds which constitute the post-modern experience. Hall (1989) notes that each of these worlds has 'its own codes of behaviour, its "scenes" and "economies", and . . . "pleasures" ' (p. 129), and for those who have access to them they do provide space in which to assert some choice and control over everyday life '. . . to "play" with its more expressive dimensions. This "pluralization" of social life expands the positionalities and identities available to ordinary people (at least in the industrialized world) in their everyday working, social, familial and sexual lives'.

The question then becomes one of how people respond to the changes of post-modernity, how they see their desires and their options, whether they are able to coopt the diverse opportunities of fragmentation and change to their own benefit. This is very much a matter of the power they have to deal with change, precariousness and uncertainty. This in turn depends on how they see themselves as members of a community, and whether they see this membership as offering solidarity in the face of fragmentation, stability in the face of change, and security in the face of precariousness. How people see themselves in terms of their community is at the core of the issue of identity, and it is to the implications of post-modernity for identity and citizenship that we now turn.

The Problem of Identity

Participation in the political project of citizenship requires some recognition of common interests and values derived from shared past experience, as well as a desirable future sufficiently general as to have a broad appeal. If life in the West is increasingly characterized by precarious economic relations, the instantaneous seriality of electronic information, and by views of knowledge which dissolve history's grand narratives, how can a common base for such a general vision be found? This problem constructs itself around the notion of identity. Harvey (1989) sees the validity of the concept of post-modernism as depending on 'a particular way of experiencing, interpreting, and being in the world' (p. 53). The importance of post-modernity lies not in the objective forms of media, technology, or information, but in how they are appropriated into new modes of experience and expression — how they shape identity.

For post-modernism, fragmentation and instability of discourses are mirrored in personality, and schizophrenia displaces alienation as the analytical metaphor. Jameson points out that if personal identity is found in the 'unification of the past and future with the present before me', and if this unification requires a consensual narrative and stability of meaning, then it is impossible in a post-modern world: like the schizophrenic, we are 'reduced to an experience of pure material Signifiers, or in other words of a series of pure and unrelated presents in time' (Jameson, 1984, p. 72). Harvey (1989) concludes 'The immediacy of events, the sensationalism of the spectacle (political, scientific, military, as well as those of entertainment), become the stuff of which consciousness is forged' (p. 54).

Some commentators see this as a major threat to democracy itself. For instance, Wexler argues that the post-modern decline of independent universal standards of judgment deprives the individual of autonomy by dissolving the ground for a unified self. Lacking an autonomous moral discourse comparable to religious or cultural tradition, individuals can no longer centre their actions in a stable morality. Individual identity is decentred, diffused and fragmented. Since societies are equally fragmented, the base for the individual-society contractual relation (on which citizenship has been said to depend), no longer exists. The capacity of the individual mind to locate itself in history is lost, replaced by the mass media and its images, especially television, which now constructs the network for social relations, but in a form much less stable than before. Wexler quotes Baudrillard's (1983) metaphor of society as 'a random gravitational field, magnetized by the constant circulations and the thousands of tactical combinations which electrify them', and his view that 'the rational sociality of the contract . . . gives way to the sociality of contact' (p. 83).

There is much that is recognizable in this picture of late twentieth century life: telepolitics and network news, mass audience soaps, consumerism, the production of demand through the manipulation and consumption of images, increasingly fragmented occupational structures and work patterns — these are conspicuous and inescapable features of the information and consumer societies. Wexler (1990) takes up the implications of this 'semiotic society' for individual identity, since 'identity dynamics, like knowledge, are different in the semiotic society', and if citizenship is to survive as a meaningful term, 'it will have to be recreated within this new social, class, and psychological reality' (p. 171).

> In the absence of collective memory of traditions, in conditions of simultaneous demand for orderly, serial practice — the administered world of modern corporatism — and flexible response to destabilising sign circulation, the burden of identity labour falls toward the personal, narrative construction of a fictitious self order. Socialization is desocialized, deregulated, and like the more visible institutional apparatuses of the phase of industrial welfarism in decline, self-constructive practices are reprivatized. (*ibid.*, p. 172)

Wexler is pessimistic about how this trend can be reversed, what possible alternatives can arrest the power of the semiotic society. Others see in these political and social forms the possibility of a new kind of political identity — the rise of identity politics.

> Identity politics expresses the notion that individual and collective identities — race, gender, sexual preference, class background, and so forth — thoroughly infuse all political preferences and visions. . . . subject positions take precedent over, say, ethics in giving form to political beliefs. As such, they fundamentally depart from the universalizing tendencies of citizenship-based politics; for practitioners of identity politics, particularities not only matter, they are the stuff of which political thought is made. (Kauffman, 1990, p. 10)

19

Identity politics sees the socially-defined personal and interpersonal realms as the most important site of power relations ('the personal is political'), and its practitioners 'tend to focus more heavily on individual and group self-transformation than on engaging with the state' (*ibid.*). In this sense, identity politics is the direct opposite to the Commission on Citizenship's focus on rules. In identity politics the concern is much more for how people experience power relations in their everyday lives, and how their sense of themselves and their relations with others is given meaning. Taking political action, participating in the political process in all its diversity, becomes a matter of self-construction, reflection and expression.

> The starting point I'd suggest for any politics of identity is the issue of 'representation': both how our identities are represented in and through the culture and assigned particular categories; and also who or what politically represents us, speaks and acts on our behalf. These two senses of 'representation' alert us to the whole areas of culture and ideology as we live it and as it is lived and directly experienced by us. They help us think how we both 'make sense' of the world and get a sense of our 'place' in it — a place of many, and increasing, identities. (Brunt, 1989, p. 152)

Making sense of the world and our place in it is not achieved through rational abstract ideas of the state, but by reflecting on the realm of everyday experience and how it constructs our sense of ourselves. If schools wish to find the answer to the motivations of young people towards participation, not to mention the broader notion of citizenship, then they need to understand how the experiences of the young and their social location are represented to them by the cultures in which they live and those which they construct themselves.

The Classical View

A traditional approach to this issue has been to construct identity through a narrative of national formation. An interesting example is Heater's proposal of a concept of citizenship in the classical tradition. For Heater (1990), 'citizens' need to understand that their role entails status, loyalty, duties and rights 'not primarily in relation to another human being, but in relation to an abstract concept, the state' (p. 2). He carefully traces the idea and practice of citizenship from its origins in the Greek city state through its manifestations in the age of revolutions, nineteenth century nationalism, liberalism and socialism, to its consolidation in the modern nation state. This grand narrative, notwithstanding its diverse episodes and tenuous continuity, is held together by the idea of citizenship, a concept whose power derives from 'identity and virtue' (*ibid.*, p. 182).

This identity is based on social reciprocity and common interests, which may themselves be based on a sense of tradition, ethnicity or way of life, and heightened by systems of beliefs, ceremonies and symbols. Citizenship is one amongst many identities an individual will feel, but it is distinguished by being necessary for moral maturity, and by its potential to moderate the divisiveness of other identity feelings — gender, religion, race, class and nation: 'citizenship helps to tame the divisive passions of other identities' (*ibid.*, p. 184). In Heater's view, history, 'a society's collective memory' (*ibid.*), plays a special role in citizenship identity, along with nationality and fraternity. Equally, the cultural togetherness of nationality and the collaborative sense of purpose in fraternity bind people to a common identity.

However, Heater acknowledges that this commonness is threatened by a series of tensions: the division between an emphasis on individual freedom and social duties and obligations; the antithesis between the private and the public citizen; the difficulties of incorporating a complex society into a coherent relationship with a unitary polity; and the conflicting demands of state and world citizenship (*ibid.*, p. 284).

In his view, to rescue citizenship we need to liberate ourselves from the 'obsession' of the nation-state, for just as nationalism emerged as social and demographic mobility made local loyalty seem obsolete, similar trends now threaten nationalism itself. We have seen 'so much more mobility, communication and education as to render identity entirely determined by the nation-state similarly obsolete' (*ibid.*, p. 323). Heater's response is to continue to posit identity and virtue as the essence of citizenship, but to apply them at various levels, from the local through the national and continental to the global, to acknowledge the tension in the nation state and its challenge from both local and cosmopolitan tendencies. This will be achieved through the transfer of national powers to provincial and supranational organizations, both governmental and non-governmental.

While such a move seems ambitious in the present context of national power, it retains the conventional view of the nature of citizenship itself. The privileged position granted to citizenship over other identities remains, as does the essentialism of identity and virtue, and the aim for a universal basis of attachment through international organisations. 'The truly good citizen, then, is he [*sic*] who perceives this sense of multiple identity most lucidly and who strives most ardently in his public life to achieve the closest concordance possible between the policies and goals of the several civic levels of which he is a member' (*ibid.*, p. 326).

Heater's analysis is a useful contribution to our understanding of the problems of citizenship and their connection with nationhood and identity, but it hardly seems a promising response to the threats of post-modernity. If young people have difficulty in relating to national governments will they not have even more with international organizations? How will Heater generate commitment, not to another person, but to the abstract state and to the rational promotion of this commitment over others? This idealist approach to identity is typical of a traditional educational strategy in which the young are exhorted to commit themselves to an abstraction, and, by rational examination of the historical narrative constructed for them, to accept it as the template through which they are to understand their identity.

Such an approach misses important elements of post-modern political culture, with its growing cultural dimension, and lifestyle and identity politics. Its essential focus on formal entities also omits the experience of power relations in the private sphere, but also in the public sphere of the economy, a crucial dimension of people's experience of rights and obligations, entitlements and injustice.

Education, Citizenship and Identity

On balance, the reality of contemporary citizenship, the entitlements of the status of citizen, are contingent on power relationships played out in class, race, gender and international politics, but the maintenance and extension of citizenship rights will increasingly rest on the struggle for control over forms of power characteristic of the semiotic society. Since much of this power is symbolic, the cultural arena is a necessary site for political activity. Political struggle over the means and substance of cultural expression is crucial to power relations. Feminist politics is a powerful demonstration of this, in which the struggle of women 'over the gendered meanings, representations, and ideologies in popular cultural forms is nothing less than a struggle to understand and hopefully transform the historical contradictions of becoming feminine within the contexts of conflicting sets of power relations' (Roman, Christian-Smith and Ellsworth, 1988, p. 4).

Giroux (1989) discusses the elements of the critical concept of culture implied here: that culture is deeply implicated in the way social relations of dependency are structured within class, gender and other formations; that culture is analyzed not only as a form of life, but also as a form of production by which dominant and subordinate groups struggle to define and realize their aspirations through the production, legitimation and circulation of particular forms of meaning.

The political importance of the cultural lies in its increasing dominance as the mode of existence in the semiotic society, but for educators it also has a special significance for the clients of schooling: the cultural sphere is the sphere of the young. The youth culture industries are among the most widely penetrated by the semiotic society and its media forms. For some, this is a threat to the nation. For others, it offers new possibilities for a politics based in these cultural forms themselves.

Willis (1990) for instance, argues that what organization and protest has been generated by youth has drawn from 'an enormous reservoir of informal passion and energy and a sensuous hunger for access to and control of usable symbolic materials, their means of production and reproduction, as well as cultural assets and spaces necessary for their exercise' (p. 144). The 'proto-communities' that result from the serial and random contacts of popular culture do have the capacity to identify the influences that shape their private powers and those of others, a consciousness of a common culture as an arena of choice and control. 'The possibility of connecting with these, and interconnecting them is the promise of the politics of the future' (*ibid.*, p. 147).

A useful example lies in the project reported by Cohen (1990) which developed a course in photography as a form of social and personal education for students in a school-work transition program. Seeking a form of 'really useful knowledge', Cohen and his colleagues chose an apprenticeship model of pedagogy, combining learning on the job from skilled practitioners with the social relationships of co-worker which such a paradigm makes possible, but also including 'a wider process of social and cultural mastery over the process of representation' (*ibid.*, p. 3). Cohen chose a cultural studies perspective for the educational connections it provided between cultural theory and political consciousness, and between technical and political education.

By producing photographic exhibitions of the nature of work, the transition process and their personal biographies, students explored the tensions between the official and unofficial versions of transition, and the 'autobiographical grammars through which these positions are lived and given meaning' (*ibid.*, p. 7). One project involved a group of mostly black girls in a community care course which explored the pressures from family, school and work which were channelling these girls into a traditional servicing role. In other work the issue of gendered transitions was developed in a project on the position of women in popular music. Working with a girls band trying to make the transition from amateur to semi-professional status, students explored the links between cultural practice and political and economic structure.

> The practical difficulties of combining their musical interests with having to earn a living by other means, the desire to 'make it' on the music scene without exploiting their femininity either ideologically or commercially, the excitements and anxieties of 'doing a gig', the construction of a group image, the pain and sweat of getting it all together, these were some of the themes which the girls addressed in their collective self portrait. (*ibid.*, p. 9)

The project sought to focus on the cultural practices which 'positioned boys and girls subliminally (and asymmetrically) within various fields of "personal" discourse centred on the youth question' (*ibid.*). Cohen notes that the popular cultures formed around computers, video, photography, and HiFi, illustrate how technologies can be transformed by the social relations of their use. Private home consumption combines with the public discourse of the forms, styles and practices of the media, but it is also true that 'the enlarged reproduction of dominant imagery is potentially interrupted by new facilities for do-it-yourself culture' (*ibid.*, p. 17). In all of this there is the development of the ability to decode the ideological messages of the culture industries, major potential sites of employment of the 'new' working class.

The important features of the project are its concern that students were able to critically analyze the ideological messages in the way transition to work is constructed in official policy, institutional practices and the common sense assumptions of their own milieu; the opportunity to represent the process of transition from their point of view, and to relate it to an exploration of their own personal biographies; the recognition that cultural practices are sites of economic and other forms of power, linking with gender, race and class concerns; and that the practice of representing these insights itself involves mastering the technology of cultural forms as well as their political and economic significance. The project shows how cultural politics can link to civil, political and social forms of citizenship, where students consider their entitlements and how they can maximize their access to them.

Another example is Connell's suggestions for a working class curriculum (Connell, 1989, p. 8), comprising survival learnings relevant to the needs of wage labour and household management, and transformative learnings aimed at collective action to transform current situations and experiences. The latter would include:

- new forms of expression, such as jointly-written and performed drama;
- skills of political participation and action, through democratically managed classes, courses and schools;
- knowledge that allows strategic choice, an understanding of the way our social system (global and local) works — an understanding that immediately connects to some of the 'survival skills';
- knowledge (for example, of other cultures) and imagination (for example, through literature and film) that allows groups to conceive of better ways of life and plan towards them;
- practical experience in how to change oppressive social practices, for example, working to eliminate sexual harassment and race prejudice in school life; and
- the personal confidence and maturity that will enable people to resist intimidation and tackle alienation.

These examples illustrate the kind of concrete and local knowledge that is both part of the everyday cultural experience of young people, and yet also in need of development if they are to be able to remake that experience in ways that are satisfying to them. They combine the practical understanding of the way their society works with the symbolic means for interpreting, commenting on and working to change it. As a result they provide the opportunity for young people to participate in a variety of ways and contexts which relate directly to their needs. The cultural emphasis is very relevant to the forms in which young people experience the social world and in which they are likely to feel most empowered. Compared with the processes of formal government, there is much greater scope for effective participation in a wider range of spheres.

Education for active citizenship must address the problems of political participation in ways that acknowledge the characteristics of contemporary political culture. By focusing primarily on abstract rational thought and ideas of a unified community as the embodiment of the citizenship ideal, and the processes of formal government as the major vehicle for practising it, the conventional approach cannot connect with the chief concerns or experiences of young people in an increasingly diverse and changing society.

Education for Citizenship and the National Curriculum

The discussion so far has identified a range of positions in which education for citizenship can be based. The range can be summarized in terms of the various approaches' key concerns for:

- equitable distribution of entitlements
- virtues and moral values
- politico-legal rules
- participatory decision-making in the broader public sphere
- the politics of everyday life
- cultural and economic practices
- the collaborative strengthening of identity

This range offers a template with which we can analyze the *Curriculum Guidance 8: Education for Citizenship* (NCC, 1990f), and it is useful to see how a number of these concerns have been combined in that document.

The introduction to the *Curriculum Guidance* sets some interesting parameters to the discussion. The first point of interest is the comment that the five cross-curricular themes will 'strengthen the bond between the individual and the community' (*ibid.*, p. 1). This dichotomy is a common rhetorical device, but its effect is to exclude the concrete contexts, practices and groups within which everyday life is carried out. Citizenship becomes a relation between the individual citizen and some amorphous abstraction called 'community'.

The second point is more important: schools are exhorted to 'lay the foundations for positive, participative citizenship' in two ways: 'by helping pupils to acquire and understand useful information', and to provide 'opportunities and incentives to participate in all aspects of school life' (*ibid.*). This signals a priority to the participative concern in political and civil spheres (the document eschews a focus restricted to government), but a significant omission here is any reference to participation or even observation of life outside school. If the development of identity for active citizenship requires a connection between ideas of citizenship and everyday life, particularly in terms of cultural meanings, this formulation is likely to mean that the connection will remain an abstract hypothetical one.

This difficulty is repeated in the outline of 'A framework for education for citizenship', where the aims are to 'establish the importance of' and to 'provide the motivation to join in' participative citizenship, and to help students acquire the information 'on which to base the development of their skills, values and attitudes towards citizenship' (*ibid.*, p. 2). This emphasis on motivation and information is of course important, but again the priority given to information is problematic.

The objectives of the document are more wide ranging, including knowledge, skills, attitudes and moral codes and values. Knowledge objectives list three elements: the nature of community (where, distinct from the earlier use, the term includes valuably diverse components from family and school to worldwide); roles and relationships in a democratic society (including cooperation and competition, and the diversity and interdependence of individuals, groups and communities); and the nature and basis of duties, responsibilities and rights (including the role of custom and law in prescribing duties, responsibilities and rights, and fairness, justice and moral responsibility) (*ibid.*, p. 3). The form of these objectives is typically abstract and general, and it remains to be seen whether this abstractness is rendered concrete and specific to particular contexts in later sections of the document. Without this, the emphasis on abstract virtues may become empty and unrelated to the experience of everyday life.

Skills listed are those of communication (arguing a case and evaluating evidence), numeracy, study skills (including arranging a visit to an outside organization), problem-solving (defining problems and making choices on evidence), personal and social skills (working with others and making decisions in school), and information technology skills (processing data and preparing a case, and, significantly, 'taking action to retrieve, or test the accuracy or use of, personal information stored by electronic means' (*ibid.*, p. 4)). With few exceptions, these skills do not seem to address the critical approach to issues or the skills of analyzing or using the media which would be needed to participate in a political economy of the cultural in everyday life. The skills of information technology, on the other hand, do illustrate a potentially critical action orientation to citizenship compatible with the arguments mounted in this discussion.

The range of attitudes listed as objectives are diverse and appropriate to a concern for the virtues and morals approach to citizenship. In a long list of individual virtues of independence of thought, enterprise, respect for others, for rational argument and for non-violent conflict resolution, and 'appreciation of the paramount importance of democratic decision-making' — the list endorses the classic liberal emphasis on the negative liberty (that is, freedom from injury, insult or imposition by others) of rational autonomous beings. The educational problem here is that such virtues, tied as they are to abstract and universal notions of rational persons, seldom touch the real contexts and issues of people's experience, so that discussions become hypothetical and distanced from everyday life. Nor do they address important elements of face-to-face relationships; the term 'respect', with its implied distance and reserve, is the norm, 'care' or 'concern' the rare exception. Similarly, the emphasis on tolerance and understanding, and the way the 'sense of fair play' is translated into the processes of law, shuts out any notion of personal indignation or action at injustice or discrimination, not only for others but also for oneself.

Only in the references to 'a constructive interest in community affairs' and 'an active concern for human rights' do we see a commitment to positive freedoms, but these are weak and undefined. The list excludes entirely any reference to group commitments or collaborative action such as would be involved in the identity politics of social movements. As a list of attitudes which are necessary in certain circumstances, the list is useful, but as a core of virtues and morals for democratic citizenship it is highly selective, and inadequate to dealing with the experience of power relations in everyday life.

It would be possible for the deficiencies of the approach to attitudes to be resolved in the treatment of 'moral codes and values', but the approach here is similarly partial (in both senses of the word). While the list is not exhaustive, under shared values are mentioned only concern for others, industry and effort, self-respect and self-discipline. Moral qualities mentioned are limited to honesty and truthfulness. This is exactly the kind of overbearing moralism that has made citizenship an austere imposition rather than a welcome protection and resource for action. It is far from clear how developing citizens are to find in such prescriptions a cause to be motivated to citizenship. Such statements give no indication of how citizenship can be of value to people in their everyday lives.

The same could be said of the 'essential components' of content, which are listed as the nature of community, a pluralist society, being a citizen, the family, democracy in action, the citizen and the law, work, employment and leisure, and public services. This is a comprehensive list of topics and contexts, and suggests a broader focus than earlier sections. It does not change the emphasis however, since the abstractness and moralism remain, with few points of contact with everyday experience. The outline of community focuses on 'duties, responsibilities and rights', 'how order and stability are maintained', and a generally functionalist sociology of individuals, groups and society, with all the pitfalls that implies (Skidmore, 1975; Wrong, 1964).

The study of a pluralist society is a good example of the detached and rather lifeless character of the specification of content. Beginning with the observation that a democratic society is based on shared values and a framework of laws which allows for a variety of cultures and lifestyles, it follows with the unqualified and therefore curious statement that 'all citizens can and must be equal' (NCC, 1990f, p. 6). The substance of the component is then listed as a series of abstract characteristics such as interdependence, similarities and differences, and different perspectives on history and culture. Again the content is not connected to the daily experiences of students beyond school.

These elements illustrate the formal concepts of citizenship identified earlier, where the emphases are on rules and procedures, and the abstract approach to the content limits any direct connection with the kind of experiences students have in families, workplaces, and elsewhere. Even the element on work, employment and leisure, which contains a long list of useful information such as the legal responsibilities and rights of employers and employees, unemployment support and leisure time, nonetheless couches these items in the language of school learning — generalized, formal and detached.

The final aspect of *Education for Citizenship* of interest here is the lists of activities suggested for the content components at each of the four key stages. If the content is to be taught in such a way as to promote the personal experience and identity politics of students, this should be evident in the illustrative teaching activities. There is an encouraging range of activities in the lists provided, grouped here by type of activity in table 1.1. Examples are provided of information topics, issues to be discussed, in-class experiential activities, and out-of-school activities. The range is not quite as comprehensive as this might appear, as the out-of-school

Table 1.1   Activities for education for citizenship (National Curriculum Guidance 8)

	Learning information	Discussing issues/values	In-school experience	Out of school experience
Key Stage 1	Types of groups and roles; family roles across cultures; students' needs and how they are met.	Harmful behaviour.	Role play bullying, cooperating; allocate class jobs.	Work roles at local swimming pool; survey local library.
Key Stage 2	Law and conflict in early civilizations; case study of a leisure activity; history of public services.		Languages survey among classmates; plan a residential experience.	Investigate local links with Europe; discuss changing family with relatives; field study of anti-social behaviour.
Key Stage 3	Media images of family life.	Human rights issues from media; impact of planning proposals on environment and quality of life.	Role play effects of actions on others; simulate employment prospects of various community groups; mock trial to practice use of evidence; role play tribunal on workplace accident.	Develop and evaluate a community or business enterprise.
Key Stage 4	Links with other world communities; history of migration.	Pros and cons of leaving home.		Participate in community service program.

activities in the first two Key Stages seem to be for the purpose of obtaining information. Notwithstanding this, they do deal directly with local sites with which students' are likely to be familiar.

The interesting point about the activities is the relative lack of explicit reference to what have previously been argued to be the main objectives and elements of the cross-curricular theme. Responsibilities are mentioned in only three of the activities, and rights in only two. Shared values and attitudes are implicit if present at all, and yet a number of the activities seem to be very pertinent to the attitudes and values being promoted. For instance, the study of employment prospects seems clearly intended to raise the issue of discrimination, but neither this nor any other value is referred to. Rather, students role play the potentially discriminating situations and 'share their findings' (*ibid.*, p. 24). There is no reference to anti-discrimination law, possible actions that might be taken in the school context or beyond, or local groups who might support such action.

The activities, like the rest of the document, assume the ideal of the universal citizen, unaffected by the specifics of race, class or gender. The consequence is a focus on an abstract role which fails to connect with the experiences of people in particular contexts.

Conclusion

Education for Citizenship provides an open framework from which a range of diverse and contradictory approaches can be drawn. It is dominated, however, by signs of the grand narratives which Heater admires and Lyotard rejects. The central idea is of the citizen as anonymous, universal and rational, a person for whom the key relation is between individual and community. While community exists on a range of scales from local to global, it is amorphous and indistinct, lacking the specificity of culture, class, gender or place. Rationality dictates a distance based on tolerance and respect, rather than the commitment of care or solidarity. Rules rather than shared values or experience become the cement which connects citizens.

It is this very abstractness and formality on which the terms of the *Education for Citizenship* fail on the issue of the approach to identity. If citizenship is a status endowed with entitlements which people can legitimately claim, then to be a citizen is to regard these entitlements as one's own, part of one's personhood, one's identity. If it is a set of values and moral virtues to which people are to be committed, their involvement in the discourses of people's everyday lives needs to be shown. If citizenship is a set of rules, to be agreed on and followed, then the value of these rules in everyday experience needs to become a matter of practice and debate. No concept of citizenship can succeed if it does not connect with the way in which people see themselves and their positions in the discourses of everyday life, that is, with the subjectivity in which they recognize their identity as persons and as members of a variety of shifting group memberships.

Traditional approaches to education for citizenship have not adequately considered the nature of political identity in the contemporary world. Having inherited the idea that political identity consists of a sense of nationality (Mackenzie, 1978), writers have grappled with the problem of translating this abstraction into terms which have meaning in and for the lives of citizens. Those who found the problem insoluble sought some other way of defining the essence of citizenship — entitlements, virtues, rules — but in dispensing with a concept of identity, they lost the means of connecting with the experiences of people, and of engaging them in an active commitment to a citizenship ideal. These problems are even more significant for the young, where even the minimal experience of traditional notions of citizenship as formal government is for them a thing of the future.

A better course would recognize the importance of modern cultural forms and discourses, how these shape people's understanding and actions in the world, and how they can be used to make sense of experience and explore alternatives. This opens up for development and productive work the very forms of reflection and judgment with which young people are most familiar. When applied to issues of direct importance in everyday life, such as just relationships and practices in family, work, and elsewhere, these forms are useful tools for thought and action. Through exploring the rights and duties of citizenship in students' cultural spheres, as well as the civil, political and social spheres, education for active citizenship is connected with their everyday milieu. In such a context, the development of citizenship and identity becomes one process.

Chapter 2

Narrations of 'Self' and 'World' Through the Economic and Industrial Understanding Curriculum

Jeff Vass

Introduction

Understanding the social and economic institutions and practices in which we live out our day-to-day lives appears to be something that we can shape into a curricular form. On the one hand, we feel we have access to socioeconomic knowledge, from experiences we have in our daily social and economic exchange. On the other, we also recognize that contemporary socioeconomic forms and relations are diverse and are organized in complex ways. Indeed, such is their complexity that we employ social scientists and economists who interpret myriad events, tables and charts for us about complex and mysterious forces of which we have only a shadowy grasp, and whom we allow to invent and use special languages and metaphors. This special 'discourse' firstly, constitutes their expertise; secondly, organizes their working lives; and thirdly, socially constructs socioeconomic fictions — whose interpretation and manipulation affect the contents and boundaries of the mundane forms of exchange and transaction that affect us all. Let us examine one word and take it through some of the different social domains where it might be used. 'Inflation' is a theoretical term, which attempts to grasp and conceptualize the behaviour of occult 'forces' in something called 'the market' (itself now a quaint metaphor, recalling medieval towns, oriental trade routes and Eastern bazaars rather than electronic money passing as data around the world faster than it takes to turn on a light). These occult forces cannot be grasped in their entirety; if we were able to do so, then social and economic policies would have predictable outcomes and Chancellors of the Exchequer would, on the whole, last longer in office. The term inflation, depending on the domain in which it is used, has implications:

- as a theoretical term;
- as a practical device, by which real transactions can be effected and routinely organized (such as banks' base rates, the setting of APRs on personal finance etc.);
- as part of the rational accounting procedures, by which people make

decisions about buying cars (for example, depreciation values), houses (secured loans), pensions or investments; and
• at street-level and gossip use, by which people can access economic fictions, taking them for almost occult realities (like our forebears blaming elves and witches for misfortune, we can point to the phantoms of socioeconomic theory for ours).

The movement of a word like inflation between the various discourses in which it appears does not usually reveal its fictional character, nor the heterogeneity of its derivation, usages, and powers to organize ideas, rationalise or invoke. On the contrary, the way it moves between these usages tends to reinforce our belief in an unseen reality looming 'out there', whose presence is felt in the myriad traces of countless transactions. Consideration of this one word alerts us to the operation of whole *narratives* which traverse our culture, construct our realities, and with which we socially position each other, and make contracts with and identify others. However, we are ordinarily unaware of these movements between domains, even though we know how to change our behaviour and usages to fit in with their special requirements when making meanings.

It may seem, in an everyday sense, to be quite a solvable matter to put together a curriculum that is rooted in the mundane and routine experiences children have of economic life, and to plot a course (through the statutory subjects) towards a more sophisticated grasp of those 'forces' that surround and embed us. The only difficulty that may appear to us as educators is that no specific place has been given to social and economic understanding in the National Curriculum: but we assume some practical ingenuity in the construction of the cross-curricular themes should deal with this (see Introduction in this volume). It would seem that, by making tactical, strategic and imaginative links between specific topics across the curriculum, such courses can be plotted through these themes, and socioeconomic understanding can thus be achieved. The question that needs to be asked in this chapter is to what extent this practical ingenuity generally manages to ignore or suppress awareness of the different usages across the boundaries of domains. We may be subjecting ourselves to using meanings which construct our social being, but over which we do not exercise control.

As already implied, plotting such curricular courses or creating such 'narrative enterprises' may have some surprising implications. (By narrative is meant a special mode of constructing an account or story, so that we can create legitimate narrations in each domain, such as in science, history, casual conversation etc.). Just as innocent words cross discursive boundaries, the creation of narratives which cross domains may produce unexpected concealed effects. Such a move may construct realities that we had not intended, can produce identities for the user in ways not imagined, and can position other narratives and their contents in ways which are undesirable. I want to explore what is involved in this as we construct cross-curricular themes, and to suggest that such linking practices will involve us in ideological work. As we manipulate topics and make links, we reproduce hegemonic social conventions, which structure curriculum subjects and promote some narrative orders while suppressing others. In making these links we employ our own mundane experiences, thus subjecting our own rationalities, memories, forms of speech, mundane and private metaphors, figures that give us a grasp on the world — in short, our 'selves' — to these hegemonic narrative orders. Such practices construct selves, in ways which we may not have intended. I am writing this, then, as a cautionary tale within the sociology of the curriculum.

To discuss these issues I will be drawing on theoretical approaches in the analysis of curricula (for example, Walkerdine, 1988; Wexler, 1987). There is already a strong and growing tradition in curriculum studies that views the curriculum as a 'textual practice' (for example, Vass, 1993a and in press; Dowling, in press). Briefly, using the metaphor of 'text' in the social sciences allows a discussion which relates real life communication between people (in the special and historically contingent situations in which they find themselves) to the traditional questions of social power, class, legitimation, authority and so on. It emphasizes practices of communication, and all the mechanisms and processes (stored in our own routines, habits and institutions) that we use to structure those practices. The textual metaphor permits us to say more about the production of meaning than does linguistic analysis. For example, the latter tells us that syntax is a structural process that determines the organization of sentences; but what sociology needs is a way of describing how social forms act to select and shape communicational encounters, and the 'tellings', 'stories', 'accountings' or, as I shall call them, 'narrations' in which they are situated. Such communication encounters are the sites where we position and define each other, because the multitude of communicational genres that there are in our culture determine the ways in which narrations are selected.

I will argue that in the cases of those cross-curricular themes that include social and economic understanding, a dominant narrative form is reproduced, and that this puts teachers, children and their experiences in a particular position, locating them in a culture that is structured by discourses of class, gender and ethnicity. But first I will suggest how a dominant narrative form able to do all this is interwoven with our experiences of ourselves, as being 'in' a social 'order' which 'contains' all kinds of mappable and understandable social and economic processes. In constructing cross-curricular themes we are *signifying*, and this is structured (in ways concealed from us) by practices of domination and legitimation (Giddens, 1981). It is important to realize that the construction of any meaningful activity (in this case, following learning objectives) must be carried out using 'authorized' and 'legitimated' pedagogical resources. Anything we want to construct will take elements that are already within authorised narrations (for example, from the core and foundation subject curricula, which come with all their internal discourses that justify and legitimate them). In our culture some narrations, some voices, are in a position where they dominate over others. How does the structuring of narrations take their current form? Two things are important: firstly, that since the late eighteenth century we have come to see ourselves as being located within a particular social and economic 'order' (Foucault, 1970); and secondly, that we have constructed ways-of-speaking about that order which in effect lay the foundations and rules about what may be legitimately said about anything at all — that is, limiting our powers to narrate and to create links between one area of experience and another. An example of such limits is given later in this chapter, drawn from the Renaissance period. This is the crucial point with the social and economic understanding cross-curricular themes: we are trying to make links — producing 'new stories' in pedagogical discourse about life experiences — but trying to do this with reference to a fictitious order, that has, since the eighteenth century, been increasingly concerned to construct and locate us as subjects, in specific ways as selves (Foucault, 1980).

Reflecting on Socioeconomic 'Order'

It is probably because we are in fairly continuous contact with other cultures (or other 'orders' in social life) that we feel that our own way of doing things, our own society, is an 'order' or 'system' that can be described, its elements fixed and their relationships mapped. The social subjects curricula are full of pedagogical means to indicate and produce discourse about relationships such as these. The 'otherness' of other cultures, where we perceive a system and an entirety, comes to us through the discourses of (for example) anthropology, history and tourism. When we take part in these particular discourses we find an image of these cultures, as a seamless web of social and economic relations, customs, mores, methods of work and trade, and so on. To give an example, looking at the chapter headings of books such as *Life in Norman England* or *Everyday Life in Ancient Rome* we find that they are constructed within and reflect a peculiarly modern narrative tradition, and one that has recently been attacked in post-modernist critical work (White, 1978). The descriptive chapter headings used to describe a culture — such as 'towns', 'trade', 'domestic arrangements' — narrates these relationships into an immediately recognisable pattern. This effectively disguises social changes or developments, so that *Everyday Life in Ancient Rome* draws in this way on the (unquestioned) categories of 'family' and 'science and medicine', but with examples drawn from over 700 years of the Roman Republic and Empire, treating them as stable elements in stable relationships. Similarly, the description of Norman England includes an independent 'Norman identity', distinct from other European peoples: again, this is used to convey a structure that seems already stable. This modern narrative tradition emphasizes a form of description that seeks to be complete. While it may recognize that no description possibly *can* be complete, it will leave potential spaces into which new evidence can be absorbed, or fresh pieces of the social puzzle be placed. If it turns out that the weight of the new evidence distorts the complete image, we will construct new images of completeness or 'paradigms', rather than live with this fragmentation (Kuhn, 1962).

The same modernity that gave us the narrative traditions of history and anthropology has the contemporary curriculum as one of its products. Because we can describe the way in which these other social orders fit together, we should be able to do the same for our own culture; and one of the places where we could present this description of our own society would be in the particular and special narrative context of the school curriculum. At the latter end of the eighteenth century the writing of history and anthropology changed dramatically (White, 1978; Foucault, 1970). This meant that the way other cultures, distant from us in space and time, were narrated to us changed at this time. These narrations became descriptive, displacing their earlier rhetorical style.[1] In the same period curricula underwent a similar change, and they were produced with an emphasis on propositional-descriptive signification, rather than in forms that were primarily rhetorical (Vass, 1985 and 1993b). It is because of this change that we now see the understanding of social and economic relations, the functions of trade, the cultural and financial implications of commerce and industry, and so on, as basically a matter of describing processes and defining institutions, persons and agencies. It is possible — indeed, it is necessary — that we fix, describe, diagram and depict all of their complex relationships with each other, and they are transmitted in this form across different representational media — and the curriculum is one such medium.

The school curriculum is designed so that the ideological struggle over the narrative *basis* of these descriptions is always a secondary or deferred consideration. Our learning is constructed in such a way that any possible ideological disputes over descriptions are always deferred until we reach advanced levels of study; and by this time the basic narration is well-established, and the disputants are divided into legitimated interest groups (sociologists, economists, consumers, sport commentators etc.), each of whom respects the narrative conventions of their own fields. We anticipate and expect rhetorical disputes over descriptions of social and economic events, but these disputes are about interpretations of describable situations. In the course of such dispute, it is permissible to offer multiple re-describings ('let's look at this another way . . .'), but we cannot move outside of what counts as a legitimate account. I shall return to this question later.

Socioeconomic history narration in part defines epochs and eras, so that patterns of relatively complete relationships can be seen and described. It is ironic that we have now developed the art of such narration to the point of meaninglessness. We have never been more articulate in our definitions, more painstaking in our descriptions, and never have pictures of social orders had such a high degree of resolution. Yet, as we gaze into this pageant of cultural 'orders', spread out in space and time, we can no longer sense ourselves as belonging to anything whole or complete. Because of this we refer, by default, to our times as a 'post-modern' period, to our industry as 'post-industrial', and to grasp our order we need 'post-structuralism'. We live in a kind of afterlife, with civilization dimly glowing behind us. The sense of chaos and fragmentation that is typical of the post-modern experience is related to our inescapable and rational proclivity to identify order as being *not here* and *not now*, but always elsewhere — in our own past, in other cultures. The rational discourse of our narrative activities used to give us an image of ourselves as whole, and a position from which we could look out on stable patterns of social relationships. This was the case in early modernity. Now the same mirror gives us an experience, as Gilbert (chapter 1) recounts more fully, of ourselves in dissolution and fragmentation, jostling about in a multiplicity of heterogeneous discourses, with multiple styles and genres of narration, that continuously startle us with the contrast of the realities which they socially construct.

These issues are significant when we consider economic and industrial understanding. I want to show this as a problem, in that the whole and ideal descriptions of the economic and the social that were given in the discourses of the Enlightenment and post-Enlightenment have now, through their very rationality, apparently failed us in the context of our modern experiences of social and economic life. The curriculum guidance document *Education for Economic and Industrial Understanding* (NCC, 1990b) narrates an account of social and economic life that suppresses our local, fragmented, contingent and rhetorical 'feel' for the events that characterize our (post-)modern socioeconomic experiences. This suppression is a side-effect of our current economic narrative habits. The narrative tendency of the NCC's document seeks to orientate first us, and then children, to a high resolution view of a social order that is made up from a rational pattern of tangible processes, mechanisms and activities. The vision of this order guides the construction of learning objectives. I maintain that this order is fictitious; it demonstrates how far this Enlightenment discourse on the economy can construct a form of pedagogy and make it appear rational (see further below). The same document also translates a socioeconomic narration into the realm of school discourse (Vass, 1993c), where this particular narrative idiom is resignified and transformed by its juxtaposition with other, heterogeneous, narrative styles (for example, related to orthodox teaching practices, or to the narrative styles of subjects such as science, history or technology).

For example, given the task of explaining international trade by the NCC document, a teacher might at first sight think to attempt this by attaching it, in cross-curricular style, to a historical narrative that included Roman frontier trading relationships. But what is ignored in this is the responsibility of the teacher and pupils to also produce accountable and intelligible responses to this material *within the orthodoxies of the dominant discourse* in which they are currently situated. If we attempt to 'illustrate' what a trading relationship looks like, we could choose any example from history or geography. Roman frontier trading (as in Roman Britain) was part of a system of colonial expansion, of exploitation of resources, of military recruitment and of imperial communications. We must ask which of these meanings are deleted when we use *Roman* trading as a general example to illustrate trading as conceived *generally*. Does the teacher, in justifying his/her practice within the orthodoxies of teaching, attempt to be more accountable to the history curriculum requirements or to those of 'trading' as defined in *Education for Economic and Industrial Understanding* (NCC, 1990b)? How and when are such judgments made? Do such judgments change in response to classroom contingencies or to personal knowledge and understanding? Innovators in teaching practices often see with horror the way in which their ideas are handled by classroom teachers. The innovator's 'good idea' never gets the 'right treatment', and is in some way bastardized in practice. But what the innovator rarely sees is that the teacher has to carry out a process of translation, in managing to incorporate and deliver the innovator's new narrative into other heterogeneous narrative forms. Both innovator and teacher *appear* to be using a single and common language, that refers to a single world 'order', and neither can understand why things go wrong. The heterogeneity of the narrative forms we manage is disguised by our experience of a common language, because this allows us, through its seeming transparency, to see a world of common reference.

The fictitious economic order presented in *Education for Economic and Industrial Understanding* gives us a mirage that stabilises us as coherent economic selves. We can simultaneously manage a number of narrations, but we must be able to choose between them in some way, because the heterogeneity of discourses found in contemporary life has the potential to destabilize our sense of self. For example, our civic identities are often narrated in the media through dominant socioeconomic ideologies (even though there are competing ideologies in the current public domain, the 'reality' about which they struggle is not up for dispute: policies and propaganda are constructed around commonly identifiable problems).

This discursive mirage about the economic order, given here in the form of a curriculum, narrates a form of self for us, portraying this as a stable feature within a pattern of economic relationships. We are encouraged to read ourselves into the description of the great chain of economic order, with its firms, banks, institutions and trade routes (many of which were established in vintage years), and in doing this we stabilise the potential economic incoherence (our lived experience, for example, might instead be of an area in which many businesses and shops, which provided mental landmarks or a cognitive geography since we were children, have disappeared). The mirage created is at odds with the disoriented self, insecure in a post-modernity, where we take (at best) calculative stances on our social place within the seductive and enticing pictures of socioeconomic order and stability (Giddens, 1981 and 1990). The mirage of the curriculum guidance document is pretty, and satisfies intellectual and rational enquiries into our current circumstances. We can use it to account for the myriad economic events and activities in which we engage: it gives us a sense of 'place' and an image of what we 'belong' to. But our sense of belonging is not such a straightforward matter. As Shotter ably argues (1993a and 1993b), images like this are 'monologic' in character; in our uncertainty they offer us constructions of the world around us, with our selves as centres of mastery and control. Monologic talk suppresses the contingent and 'dialogic' character of socioeconomic life. As we engage in transactions we do not experience ourselves as dialogically creating the economy, rather we feel ourselves to be filling 'gaps' in an established picture, a picture which we do not feel our 'selves' had any part in the making.

Self, Narrative and Curriculum Discourse

Analyzing educational practices and forms of communication as 'discourses' has become a new orthodoxy. By discourse, as used below, is meant all the means we have to signify, that is to make new meanings. This grew from the tensions inherent in our culture, discussed above and in Gilbert (chapter 1). As a post-modernist and post-structuralist critical strategy, discourse studies was a response to the inadequacies of theoretical critical schools such as Marxism in the 1970s. Such critical theories had a globalizing tendency to produce pictures of complete social and economic 'orders' in historical evolution. Coupled to this was the debate on subjectivity and on how selves are constructed through social practices.

To look at social practices as 'textual' means examining the ways in which discourse employs themes, social structures, habits, routines, rituals and conventions to weave together the basic material that makes up the 'fabric of meanings' available in our culture. As we act we weave and reproduce the basic patterns in the fabric: but we also produce ourselves since 'we' are nothing apart from the fabric. For example, the social structural determinants that run through the fabric become part of our routine activities, in a similar way to how grammatical structures become part of our speaking. Thus, to act at all implies complicity with the hegemony of these determinants of social structure, in much the same way that to speak at all implies that we subordinate ourselves to grammatical structures. The patterns contained in the fabric mean that we will produce our 'selves' so that we particularly 'fit' that fabric. In other words, there are 'representations' of what it is to be a self in any particular culture, contained in the 'texts' which that culture produces.

When we examine the texts of curriculum discourse, we may therefore find representations of teachers, children and parents. The curriculum content consists of narrations, or stories told about the world. These refer to a world of order, explicitly or tacitly: and this order is part of the background expectancies which all stories require of their readers/viewers/listeners. For example, to understand the simple narration {John went to the sweetshop} we engage in expectancies and assumptions, which we have selected from among alternatives provided by discursive constraints and possibilities. These discursive constraints operate in everyday life contextually, historically, locally, contingently and dialogically. In this particular example, John and the sweetshop are brought together through grasping of much which is absent in the narration. Together with our children, we are embedded in forms of everyday life which use these narrations in dialogic ways: we can choose to ask further questions about them. Expanding a narration in this way involves further story-telling in response to these questions. The formal curriculum, on the other hand (structured as it is by post-Enlightenment discourses) may view the contingent and local understanding of the narration as incomplete and deficient. Children may deduce the motives that take John into a relation with the sweetshop (because knowledge of these motives form part of their background expectancies), but if they do not know about the sweetshop owner's motives in relation to any potential transactions (profits, etc.) then they are said to be lacking in socioeconomic knowledge.

This may well be the case, and we will look at this economic detail shortly. The curriculum attempts to situate the local and contingent knowledge the child possesses (seen as incomplete) into narrations that are striving to be complete. These narrations tend to be monologic in character: they seek abstract, relational and reciprocal descriptions of persons and situations in their story-telling. Their story-lines are legitimated by reflecting a view of a true and complete order 'out there', in which we may construct our 'selves' in the spaces the view makes available to us.

Much of schooling is about constructing the self, in relation to a set of these monologic narrations which describe the world and locate the self as a subject in its discourses. So, I turn briefly once more to the idea of discourse. The human subject is neither the coherent self nor the social person which we recognize as the private individual (see Ross, chapter 4). The private individual is a constructed character in dominant and hegemonic narrations since the seventeenth century: the individual is a key theme in the discourses of Western capitalism. It is impossible to be a reader/viewer of any modern narration without implicitly identifying oneself with narrations in which characters are individuals, who possess both psychological faculties and a place in the 'order', located by property and status. This idea of 'possessive individualism' even applies to the ways we tell stories about ourselves. If I narrate an event in my life, you would understand it as coming from my stored, 'possessed' experience, and as subject to any incompletenesses from my deficiencies in remembering. Memories were not always thought of as either the properties or the responsibilities of individuals. To take an example from antiquity, in the opening lines of Homer's *Illiad* the poet calls on the Muses to 'sing in' him the story of Achilles. Here the 'self' is constructed as a vessel for events going on elsewhere, and is a very different conception of what it is to be a human being.

In contemporary life there appear to be many discourses, and our dynamic involvements with their texts give us many subject 'positions' within them. Each of these positions legitimates the selection and deletion from among the range of available meanings. Each 'discursive formation' (for example, medical, legal, financial, and so on) provides textual resources to locate the subjects and their relationships within its particular discourse. As a patient or as a customer I enter a surgery or a shop and become a specific kind of subject, and must respect the narrative forms available within that discursive formation.

In this context, current policy making in the UK is using a rhetorical narrative that situates the 'citizen' as a consumer in *all* situations, irrespective of the practices and texts involved in those situations. We might view this as an attempt to impose a monologic description of the world drawn from an economic viewpoint. Such a viewpoint will narrate events in the world according to its own particular 'regime of truth' (Foucault, 1980). The moment that I am constructed as a consumer in medical discourse, medicine is immediately constructed as a product. But in the context of 'the consumer', these relationships should then be narrated according to the rules of economic discourse. The contingencies of medical situations will resist such monologic descriptions. Because economic discourse is hegemonic, the result is likely to be an impoverishment of the language available to deal appropriately with medical issues in the public domain (Vass, 1993b). At an ideological level, it may appear that rationalizing us to become individual consumers is helpful and simplifying, and will empower us. But such an imposition of one dominant hegemonic (economic) discourse, not geared to deal with the contingencies of heterogeneous and multiple circumstances, will lead to further alienation.

Discourses establish us with *provisional* identities (see Wexler, 1987; Dowling, in press; Vass, in press; Brown and Dowling, 1993; Walkerdine, 1988 for some examples relating to education). Management of an identity constructs the human subject in relation to a regime of truth. Within most discourses there are significant textual resources that establish subjects according to differences in gender, class and ethnicity. For example, the discourses of 'equal opportunities' and 'perfume advertising' narrate gender differences in different ways: both exploit and construct that difference through narratives that locate subjects as characters within stories. Barthes (1973) analyzed narrations of French food semiotically, and discussed the ethnic and gendered messages available in the consumption of steak and chips. Implicit in this consumption Barthes finds meanings that differentiate Frenchness from foreignness, and men from women. Dowling (1991a and 1991b) similarly analyzes school mathematics texts and shows that gender and class differences are implied and form part of a 'message structure'. This structure regulates the texts, in which subjects read in pupil identities. In this way, long-standing features of our class-based social structure become part of the textual resources available in schools. Elsewhere (Vass, 1993a) I have looked at the production of social identities within 'pedagogical apprenticeships', emphasizing the local and contingent features of the relations involved.

Following Foucault, I have suggested that subjectivity is constructed through those textual media that are part of the social structure in our culture. Discourses often have extreme stylistic differences from one another (mathematics education and pornography for example), yet both are governed by the same regime of truth. In disputes over 'what is', regimes of truth govern the form of dispute, so that people with opposing viewpoints can make judgments about each other's arguments, in terms of their appropriateness or reasonableness. Since the Enlightenment, we have been subject to particular regimes of truth which contrast with those that came before. Foucault suggests (1970) that patterns of constructing knowledge underwent a fundamental change in the late eighteenth century.[2] During the period of collapse of the old regime of truth the experience of 'selfhood' underwent a period of unsettlement. Barker (1984) examines a number of texts from the period including Pepys' Diary. Barker claims that this is one of the first autobiographies in the tradition of a 'subject-centred discourse'. The diary reflects how an identity is established and maintained when there is no longer a regime of truth that will, unproblematically, underwrite the discourses. It is within discourses that the self is now active in making judgments, reflecting on the form of links made in the production of knowledge and so on.

> The political upheaval of the mid-century established . . . a new set of connections between subject and discourse, subject and polity, and in doing so altered fundamentally the terms between which these mutually constitutive relations held. In the space of a relatively few years a new set of relations between state and citizen, body and soul, language and meaning, was fashioned. The older sovereignty of the Elizabethan period was disassembled, and in its place was established a conjunction of novel social spaces and activities, bound together by transformed lines of ideological and physical force, among which new images of the body and its passions were a crucial, if increasingly occluded, element. (p. 10)

The construction of our selves in discourse is not simply a matter of applying different descriptions to the same basic substance. Such a conception of social constructionism is itself a very modern style of talking. Barker and Foucault present readings of texts in which fundamental alterations to 'being' are implied, as there is a move from one regime of truth and its discourses to another. It may be that we have now come to live in another period of unsettlement and call it 'post-modernity'. Foucault characterises the new practices of the eighteenth century as establishing the 'new social spaces' about which Barker writes. In these we appear as economic subjects, medical subjects, legal subjects, political subjects, subjects of leisure etc. The pre-existing sense of social life was shot through with a new sense of 'order', no longer dependent on practices of truth giving rise to resemblances, continuities and analogies which had characterized previous narrative styles. The new 'order' was based on practices relating to analysis, establishing functional relationships between isolatable elements, and breaking the world into components and describing their relations and interactions. Narrative styles based on these practices have allowed me to write this chapter, and to make some appeal to your sense of judgment in the context of the realm of truth in which we are both implicated. The practices of truth established during the Enlightenment have been some of the most successful the world has seen. Their sense of order showed them to be all-embracing, and promised to situate all competing viewpoints eventually in a vast, clear scheme: the local and contingent is shifted to the periphery, while an 'absolute' truth rules at the centre (and the tenor of the central absolute truth is increasingly economic). Some peoples' sense of judgment was disturbed by the fact that 'man' as a rational individual had been discovered at the turn of the eighteenth century, that new discourses were produced to narrate 'him' (sociology, anthropology, psychology, economics), and the that he now appeared to come in analysable components. The abstract physics-as-truth horrified Mary Shelley, who dramatized her response to man-coming-in-bits in her novel *Frankenstein*. This was the response of the romantic imagination to a new dominant, and increasingly orthodox narrative style.

Words and concepts about the socioeconomic order that had served since Aristotle were no longer viable. As sociology was founded, the world of late eighteenth century Europe rendered terms like 'community', 'authority', and 'status' inadequate. In the same way today, the words 'market' and 'society' now seem inadequate to grasp electronic global capitalism, or to embrace the extreme conditions of the dazzlingly rich and those living in cardboard cities. King and peasant in feudal society were related through mechanisms of service and reciprocal obligations. International financial speculators are related to the very poor through distant choices based on the mathematics of risk, in which 'person' and 'commodity' are symbolically interchangeable. This is stretching the idea of a 'social relation' somewhat, and new Mary Shelleys are reacting in horror to it.

I will now return to the curriculum as a textual medium. While this offers ways of producing knowledge between topics, through narrating links in a creative fashion, there are other processes involved. The creative act of producing such links is itself a hegemonic regime of truth, one which prefers analytical description, and makes all local and contingent viewpoints peripheral while putting its own rationality at the centre. Furthermore, as it is narrated the curriculum constructs the subject, the self, and places it in the order 'out there' which it constructs.

Contemporary Curriculum Practice

Given all this, it would seem foolhardy to try to put together a curriculum about a social economic order. Any such order might be a mirage-like effect, emerging from a now collapsing regime of truth. The heterogeneity of the discourses which make up the post-modern, as Gilbert (chapter 1) describes it, conspires against the easy transparency which characterizes the task. The 'National' Curriculum in the UK may appear as a monolithic attempt to deny and suppress the very heterogeneity over which it attempts to preside. The topic-based celebration of heterogeneity of the primary curriculum was anathema to the designers of the National Curriculum. The touching faith of the National Curriculum writers in the economic order of the nineteenth century led them to strive to reestablish a curriculum of something like the same vintage. The reintroduction of strong subject divisions in the primary curriculum altered the shape of possible narrations of texts in the classroom. The previous orthodoxy governing the primary curriculum fostered a relaxed sense of judgment, combined with respect for Enlightenment styles of narrating knowledge. The modern regime of truth is found in pedagogy itself. Walkerdine (1984) argues that modern discourses of child development focus on the truth of the child, who is monitored according to the analytic conventions of modern psychology. Whatever the implications for the production of knowledge, the primary curriculum orthodoxy will have different social effects when it works under the conditions contrived by the National Curriculum. I raise this since I want to link the cross-curricular theme of economic and industrial understanding to the ideological origins of the integrated curriculum. As indicated, the politics of curriculum change in the 1970s found much of their legitimacy in what can be said about the psychology of children and 'how they learn', a discourse that began with the founding of modernity and the narrative practices of the Enlightenment. Sociological corroboration of this came in the 1970s, with Bernstein's work on the curriculum (Bernstein, 1971). His compelling account contrasts the social structural implications of integrated and non-integrated curricula. In the latter he found that subject 'insularity' reproduces vertical commitments and loyalties within subject departments in schools, and that this fosters deference to institutional expertise and to the academic production of knowledge. This resulted in particularly narrow access to the mysteries of knowledge; authority in a discipline is gained through organized rites of passage that set limits to the degree of connection and linkage to be found in curriculum content in the classroom. Bernstein expressed this in his discussion of classification and framing:

> Classification thus refers to the degree of boundary maintenance between contents . . . frame refers to the degree of control teacher and pupil possess over the selection, organisation, timing and pacing of the knowledge transmitted and received in the pedagogical relationship.

Though he does not question at this point the nature of the knowledge that is 'transmitted' in respect of its reproduction of a regime of truth, his vocabulary implies that he has a stance of anthropological relativism, in which he treats knowledge as an intraculturally valued resource, over which one can have more and less power and access. He does raise concerns about the degree of authority, autonomy and power that participants to curriculum practices can exercise under various curriculum styles. It is in this sense that he promotes the idea of the integrated curriculum, and refers to the 'subordination of previously insulated subjects or courses to some relational idea'. 'Relationality' in the curriculum is the key unlocking the possibilities of control over the knowledge base and moving the authority to teachers and children to play with the form of the curriculum subjects, instead of reserving this authority to ratified experts. Bernstein, somewhat cheekily, relishes the idea of children and teachers making intellectual and playful connections and links in their narrative practices with the curriculum texts since hitherto this had been the special preserve of subject experts who had been initiated into the relevant mysteries.

One suspects ideological disquiet over the code for integration was in many ways greater than the disquiet over critical, but strongly classified, subjects like peace studies. Under central government control, Statutory Orders confer on the Secretary of State the power to delete undesirable subjects. But to control curriculum integration or 'relational ideas' and the production of linkages requires a different strategy. The National Curriculum exerts control over these by ensuring that curriculum practice is based on a system of surveillance of child development, known as assessment and testing. This has become the basic mode of organization of knowledge in the curriculum, *irrespective* of the amount or style of assessment that is practised (Merttens and Vass, 1989). The curriculum has been turned into an elaborate device for monitoring the development of children, the practices of teachers, the performance of schools and the politics of parents as education consumers. What is the fate of relational ideas in the context of the National Curriculum and economic and industrial understanding in particular? In the last part of this chapter I want to look at the strategy of integration and the production of narrative links that has been suggested by the National Curriculum Council (NCC) for economic and industrial understanding. I feel that the conditions for Bernstein's optimism in the educational politics of subject integration are no longer applicable or relevant. Indeed, I would say that the question to be faced now is that of the struggle between centralizing/totalizing discourses that describe the world and its order from a positional 'centre', and the peripheral discourses where we strive to maintain our selves in everyday life. The former tends to absorb the latter. One of the mechanisms of this absorption in education is the curriculum, which as we have seen, determines what can be legitimately narrated in the classroom.

Cross-Curricular Guidance: A Tour Round the Truth

The NCC curriculum guidance document *Education for Economic and Industrial Understanding* (NCC, 1990b) sets out a cross-curricular agenda for socioeconomic knowledge that has no other place within the National Curriculum foundation sub-jects. Some of the links which it makes as it pursues this knowledge through the nooks and crannies of these established and statutory subjects deserve comment. Through its orthodox description of what constitutes 'good' curriculum practice, the document attempts to relate children's experiences of socioeconomic order to a disciplinary knowledge base. The booklet is full of engaging photographs of children playing shops, visiting bakeries and dairies (the younger pupils), looking at retailing and pharmaceuticals (the older ones). The assumption is that, under pedagogical guidance, 'being' in a supermarket can be directly connected to under-standing retailing. In part, this assumption is that experiences can be narrated anew for children, resituated within a centralized vision of (economic) order, instead of extrapolating former narrations in the peripheral zones of children's everyday experience. Contingency, incompleteness and 'localness' (the view of the periphery seen from the centre) become the property of the pupil, who is assessed in relation to his/her grasp of this vision. This curriculum 'prepares' the pupil for their con-structed place in this vision:

> It prepares them for future economic roles: as producers, consumers and citizens in a democracy. (NCC, 1990a, p. 1)

The document sets out the shape of this centralized vision and places the pupil in the smallest of a set of nested boxes:

> Pupils need education for economic and industrial understanding to help them contribute to an industrialised, highly technological society. With increasing economic competitiveness, both the European Community and world-wide, the nation's prosperity depends more than ever on the knowledge, understanding and skills of young people. To meet this challenge pupils need to understand enterprise and wealth creation and develop entrepreneurial skills. (*ibid.*, p. 1)

These 'needs' are defined in the political realm, and are then translated into education discourse — this tells teachers to become concerned that pupils know their places in the world order, and that they understand this. This 'understanding' develops through the mechanism of the cross-curricular links between the more strongly defined foundation subjects. This pattern of links should 'enrich a pupil's curricu-lum' (*ibid.*). The payoff for the insulated statutory subjects is that this enriching web will provide 'a context relevant to pupils' lives through which subject know-ledge and skills can be developed' (*ibid.*).

Examples in *Education for Economic and Industrial Understanding* of such enriching webs are provided 'ready made' by the ingenious curriculum technicians who compiled the document, and, from within the discourse of what counts as good curriculum practice, the results are compelling. As suggested earlier, however, such praiseworthy attempts involve concealed practices of domination and legitimation (Giddens, 1981). These practices are carried out through the competitive interplay of the various modes of narration within the subject areas. We may consider each mode as a voice, telling a story in a particular way. For example, the economic narrative voice may speak about 'poverty', but will situate it and its implications differently, and on different grounds of legitimacy and authority, than, the way in which poverty might be discussed in the English curriculum in relation to a nineteenth century novel. Currently these different voices are in open competition. The guidance document proposes a merger. Open competition implies *alternative* descriptions of the world about which one makes judgments. This document suggests very strongly that narratives that link English and economics can 'enrich' understanding, by showing *the same reality* from different curriculum standpoints. To what extent is English still a potential critical domain in relation to economics? What is lost sight of, as the curriculum designers construct these linkages, is both how their own ingenuity is hidden, and how their links are not really about knowledge but are about local, contingent and rhetorical attempts to make us see the world from a certain viewpoint. On page 45 of the Curriculum Guidance Document is a photograph of two pupils apparently measuring the rear end of a cow. The legend beneath says 'Business enterprise: pupils rear and assess cattle for market'. This is at once semiotic and rhetorical — it might have said 'Data handling: pupils apply mathematical skills to the real world'. In either caption, the 'real world' experience of cow-measurement is justified in relation to school knowledge, and both imply cross-curricular enrichment. But this enrichment can only take place by reference to a 'real world' established and ordered according to a regime of truth. The pupil is the site where the making of this enriching connection succeeds or fails. While the pupil's experience is centred around a task which is local and contingent, the curriculum designers want to locate the experience in a discourse called 'business enterprise'. To make this enriching, the designers must draw the pupil into an order that can be reflected in another subject area that has its own discourse (say mathematics). The designers do not see the rhetorical nature of the caption that they write in *its own* localness and contingency. The description of the activity as 'business enterprise' is legitimated by reference to an Enlightenment vision of the world order.

The power to invent such links depends on both the legitimation and the authority connected with this. The order 'out there', which underwrites this invention, assumes that its essential concerns are unchangeable in meaning and value, across all the narrations in which they may be discussed and represented. It is assumed that continued exposure to the links will lead to pupils making more connections across the curriculum landscape, towards a centrifugal, monologic, fully enriched description that displaces their local/peripheral experience. It is assumed that the voices of the statutory curriculum speak with the same degree of power. This suggests further points. The organization of the curriculum contents into assessable statements of attainment means that any lack in understanding is located with, and is the responsibility of teachers and pupils (see Brown, 1990). It also means that in the same act of organization the legitimacy of the regime of truth of the socio-economic order is reestablished.

For the purpose of constructing these links, *Education for Economic and*

Industrial Understanding divides socioeconomic knowledge into the following areas (NCC, 1990b, pp. 31–4):

- Economic concepts (for example, resources, competition, trade);
- Business enterprise (for example, costs, management);
- Industry and work (for example, jobs, design, technology, production);
- Consumer affairs (for example, money, prices, advertising, rights); and
- Government, economy and society (for example, economies in Europe, conservation).

Within each of these areas examples are given in how to adapt and relate established subjects to the themes of the document. For example, when approaching the economic concept of the scarcity of resources, it is suggested that this might be investigated across a range of subjects which includes English, technology, geography and history (p. 31):

> Under technology it suggests 'recognize potential conflicts between the needs of individuals and society'
> Under history: 'investigate the poor law in early nineteenth century England'
> Under geography: 'analyze costs and benefits of road and rail transport'

In other places, cross-referenced maps are given to facilitate the making of links. The vision of order uniting these diverse statements transcends the subject areas' internal struggles to establish viewpoints and styles of argumentation. The structuring of these ideas makes transcendent and transparent links between areas, and creates a master viewpoint, in which the subjects appear on a horizon. The varied and heterogeneous narrations *within* the different subjects become homogenized, and is put in relation to something called Economic Concepts.

Consider how some of the constructs of the subject of history appear from this master viewpoint. The five divisions in socioeconomic knowledge offered by the document (noted above) are each pursuing their own curricular agendas, but what they cannot preserve are the modes of narration and the agendas of the particular subjects. For example, studies in both history and sociology established the importance of slavery to ancient economies, and drew the issue of slavery into analyses of cultural resources linking them to practices of social domination. How is the slave or feudal peasant to be situated in a narration based on these socioeconomic divisions? The authorized link between an appropriate history attainment target and one of the document's sub-divisions must involve a selection of material appropriate to both. If the slave cannot appear under Consumer Affairs, can s/he appear under Economic Concepts or Business Enterprise — and if so, how? In older schoolbooks the slave is often narrated under descriptions of domestic life, while economics is related to land and military conquest, and all this was realised in a discourse of intellectual achievement (the Greeks) or political achievement (the Romans). It is clear in *Education for Economic and Industrial Awareness* that principles of selection are at work. History appears only once, as a linking example under Consumer Affairs, where it is suggested that pupils 'investigate the development of tourism in the twentieth century British economy'. Consumer Affairs and Business Enterprise are constructed as 'doing areas' of the curriculum. Given that what is counted as legitimate in any area will be selected from foundation subjects, the principle of selection is not likely to be based on the more esoteric agenda of a subject such as history. It is more likely to be based on accounts of the economic order that are *recognizable* as an economic order, and these in turn are more likely to follow the older textbook divisions in which slavery, say, appears in a narrative on domestic life. Now consider the task of the teacher in managing this multifaceted curriculum issue, and the kinds of resources at her disposal. To entertain both the issue of slavery and the issues of business culture is to create two problem areas. Teaching requires that one area appears relatively stable so that one may look at something more problematic in the light of what has been already established. In any case, the selection-making involved has the effect of making our own economic discourse stand for that of any other period or place.

The same principle occurs in an example linking Consumer Affairs to Geography, which suggests that pupils might 'analyze consumer patterns for goods and services'. Why was tourism not the example here? Under Consumer Affairs, tourism becomes the object of an historical investigation, where pupils will look at the background to what is a modern feature of our economy, narrated in a story about *our* consumption. Yet tourism is one of the key critical issues in modern geography. But it is more difficult to narrate, because it is a controversial issue and calls on pupils to use skills and textual resources. Tourism, as a modern form of colonialism, refers to our consumption *of them*, that is, of 'other cultures', which has far-reaching effects on *their* ways of life. Again the Eurocentric sense of order, while it does not altogether rule out critical geography from economic and industrial understanding, imposes a problem for including it in the classroom. This problem arises from the solution to the question of 'What makes a good link between geography and one of the five economic/industrial divisions?' The answer appears to be those bits of geography which can plug any available gaps in a world order that is narrated by an uncritical economic discourse. The sense of economic order that teachers will be able to provide starts in local experience, so a view of the economic must start from what can be recognized and described in the vernacular. The links made must be accountable in terms of both everyday experience and pedagogical discourse.

History and geography compete with core subjects, such as mathematics and English, in terms of the time that they can occupy. However, other competitions take place. In examining this hierarchy of subject narrations, we might look at how topics have been organized for the Industry and the World of Work Division, comparing core and other foundation subjects (*ibid.*, pp. 41–2). In considering the 'effective management of people and other resources' pupils can look at ways of 'maximizing efficiency, output and job satisfaction'. The curriculum designers feel that these issues can be treated under the narrative conventions offered by technology, work experience and an enterprise activity. However, 'important issues and concerns for people at work' might be dealt with in the narrative conventions offered by English ('express and justify feelings'); history ('examine the way in which the roles of women at work have changed'); and PSE ('issues that arise from women going out to work').

From the viewpoint of the economic 'order' what is essential can be discussed under technology, work experience and enterprise activity. There must be discussion about the effective management of people and resources. But given the arrangement described, technology carries the essential messages, while English, history and PSE carry what everyone will recognize as the non-essential issues. While it is laudable that the critical narrative voice is included, it is within the document in particular narrations which are not able to compete on the same basis as others. Why is job satisfaction narrated in technology, while issues related to feelings are in the domain of English? A businessman or woman looking at this document might want to ask why English (with its attainment target in speaking) does not have an example of pupils persuading someone to buy a second-hand car or cow, where such activities are give as examples under PSE. Our feelings about our economic reality compete with how we socially construct English as a curriculum subject, and what we are prepared to let English be about. Somehow poetry and selling do not seem to belong to the same narrative voice. Indeed, the idea of persuading others in a business context appears almost anathema to the writers of this document. They want to show us and describe to us the world of work within the good primary teaching tradition. Although we could practise our selling skills in English the document would rather have us as part of art 'design and produce a poster to persuade consumers to eat healthy foods' (*ibid.*, p. 33).

These ingenious examples of links given in the document in many ways reflect existing patterns of curriculum interpretation by teachers. Teachers need some identifiable and common vision to work from, and *Education for Economic and Industrial Understanding* must to some extent reflect and use that common vision. And English, science, history, geography are presented in this as being part of the world constructed in that vision. Pupils are invited to analyze and investigate the vision presented in the document of a text to discover its order. The mechanisms by which they do so is presented, in Enlightenment tradition, as transparent and equally-valued instruments. A process-based narrative (as in technology) is seen as complementary to narratives where feelings can be described (as in English). The assumption is that while these narrative styles on offer are very different, they each *add a dimension* to a cumulative process that ends in a single vision. I argue that these are different, heterogeneous narratives that have different, necessarily competing interests in rhetorically organizing the world and constructing it for us. The organization of economic and industrial understanding in this document unwittingly prioritises and relegates the messages and interests of various groups, simply by drawing on the structure of the curriculum and attempting to make *rational and obvious* links between areas. Facts appear in technology as it narrates Business Enterprise; opinions appear in English where responses to facts are expressed as feelings about industry and the world of work. This amounts to a concealed division, hegemonically structured into our curriculum practices. Narrative voices are related to one another through acts of selection and deletion — not by individual designers, but by the organisation of meanings in our culture realised in our practices and discourses (see Vass, 1993b).

The document looks as if it is striking a good balance, if judged in terms of orthodox curriculum discourse. It has attempted to strike a balance (though from what perspective do we see 'balance'?) between national, cultural, political and economic objectives and what amount to critical accounts of some of those objectives. But to carry out this task it starts out from an unquestioned regime of truth which invisibly regulates what may be said, and who may say it. It is a document of translation. It attempts to reconcile the world of business and industry to curriculum discourse, and this translation has some difficulties. Its strategy is to 'domesticate' this economic world for the consumption of teachers and pupils, and in so doing it reproduces a standard vision of the common-sense world. This economic vision could stand naked before us, but we are required by *Education for Economic and Industrial Understanding* to view the economic body through established subject peep-holes. The cross-curricular theme guides us through which peep-holes to look. The more we look, the better we see what is 'out there'. I have indicated that the game played by the document is a loaded one.

Finally, I want to return to where this connects with the issue of selfhood and subjectivity. The critics of post-modernity see the self, the subject, as divided. In order to keep qualifying for acceptance in a multitude of social locations and spaces the subject has to switch into a schizophrenic multiplicity of narrative voices. We must know how to be intelligible, and accountable, and know how to narrate in all these spaces. This confusing plethora is reflected in our attempts to construct a 'whole' ('healthy', 'holy'?) curriculum. The struggle to impose coherence, by finding appropriate places for narrating voices, is part of a struggle to make our 'selves' cohere in everyday life, despite the heterogeneity of divisions that traverse us and pull us into the spaces they provide. Our strategy of coherence is associative: we produce links between one area of experience and another. What concerns me is how we reflect on those links. Do we leave it to fortuitous associationism ('we're doing cats, that's animals, that's biology; we'll count their toes, that's maths') without any attention to the foundation discourses that structure the production of those links and make them feel legitimate? Because the monolithic and monologic 'centre' structures and regulates the social fabric, we lack subjective coherence on the periphery of discourse (see especially Shotter, 1993a and 1993b). In reviewing the *Education for Economic and Industrial Understanding* document I have chosen to read it as a monolithic response to an already monolithic attempt to control the curriculum from the political centre. This characteristic stems from its dependence on the Enlightenment discourses which structure narrative voices. It also suggests that the discourses narrate the same stories, about the same thing. We are led through chains of association around an apparently real, stable and neutral knowledge landscape, and invited to enrich ourselves through exposure to its diverse features. I acknowledge that the document is providing only suggestions; nevertheless, it reflects constructive textual tendencies which make these suggestions appear rational to schools, through the truths in which the world 'out there' seems to consist. And it is these truths that I feel are worthy of our closest attention.

Notes

1 Quite literally, the curriculum ceased to be about the art of speaking, persuading, and relating words to a sense of judgment about the form of discourse. Instead it became concerned with the referential quality of words, and the ability to gesture to an 'out there' by use of them.

2 During the Renaissance styles of narration had been based on the perceived patterns of resemblance and the correspondence between things. Examining the texts of that period reveals, in the construction of argument and discourse, an attention to form which has an alternative mode of judgment to that which we would now be used to. This mode suggests a different regime of truth, governing styles of narration, what may be said and judged appropriate, and the practical ingenuity involved in producing knowledge. In looking at treatises on various topics from the period, it appears to be indicated that, in drawing together and juxtaposing ideas and creating narrative links between them, writers would respect (for example) analogical relations between natural and cultural facts. Thus social and theological truths were found to be 'reflected' in relationships in nature. The great Renaissance chain of being rattled with 'sympathy' throughout its harmonic spheres. Hence the production of medical knowledge might involve narrating a disease as a disturbance in the proper operation of harmonies between person and cosmos. The ingenuity that discovered resemblance, continuity and analogy everywhere was realised in a number of discourses. Foucault finds the same style in period texts covering topics as diverse as a History of Monsters to a Treatise on Ciphers. The conduct and practice of this style depended on a particular regime of truth, which underwrote all contemporary discourses. It began to be shaken in the seventeenth century, and the eighteenth century saw the establishment of new styles of truth that could be rehearsed, produced and appealed to.

Part 2

The Construction of Social Curricula

Chapter 3

The Rise and Fall of the Social Subjects in the Curriculum

Alistair Ross

A man who is ignorant of the society in which he lives, who knows nothing of its place in the world and who has not thought about his place in it, is not a free man even though he has a vote. (*Half Our Future* (Chair: Sir John Newsom) (CACE, 1963, para 99))

There is no such thing as society: there are individual men and women, and there are families. (Margaret Thatcher (reported in *The Guardian*, 6 September 1989))

The purpose of this chapter is to examine how the social subjects have been organized within the school curriculum, and in particular the way in which they began, in some places, to come together in the 1960s and 1970s, and then disappeared in the curriculum reorganization of the 1988 Education Reform Act. This analysis of the evolution of the subject area within its political, social and economic context will necessarily include a diachronic dimension: as Ivor Goodson (1989) suggested in his studies in curriculum history, the curriculum itself 'is a social artefact, conceived of and made for deliberate human purposes' (p. 131). The two quotations above point to the social curriculum itself being a socially constructed product of its setting. A further dimension is necessarily provided by cross-national comparisons: in the period spanned by the same two quotations, there was a most distinctive increase in the provision of social studies education in nearly all countries. Suk-Ying Wong (1991), analyzing 110 national primary school curricula, has characterized this change as a revolution: 'the emphasis placed on social studies has increased dramatically . . . [it has] expanded almost everywhere, with the exception of Eastern Europe'. And in the United Kingdom, where there has been an unparalleled decline, to the extent that it has been possible to refer to the social subjects as 'the subjects that dare not speak their name' (Ross, 1993). What is there in the British definitions and conceptions of the curriculum that make the position of social subjects so tenuous? What kinds of knowledge, skills and understanding are implicit in the area, and do they explain the perceived threat social studies offers? Or is the alternative and peculiarly British organization of the curriculum so much more robust that social studies must inevitably wither? In the chapter that follows this, I will examine some of the ways in which aspects of social studies have seemingly been revived (albeit with new names) in the Whole Curriculum that derived from the 1988 Act, but will also draw attention to the rather invidious redefinitions in the purposes of social studies education, and in the underlying conceptions of the nature of, and relationship between, the individual and society. The roots of these reformulations lie in the reasons for the decline of the social subjects.

The Development of the Social Curriculum in the Primary and Middle Years of Schooling

In a celebrated and much-quoted essay written in 1971, Bernstein observed that 'how a society selects, classifies, distributes, transmits and evaluates the educational knowledge it considers to be public reflects both the distribution of power and the principles of social control' (p. 47). This chapter considers the ways in which an aspect of educational knowledge has been selected, described, disseminated, and taught (and at times tested) to primary and middle school aged children, over the past twenty-five years. Such a curriculum history will enable us to examine the role that professionals have played in the social construction of social knowledge. In the context of secondary education, Goodson and Dowbiggin (1990) have suggested that 'teachers have been encouraged to define their curricular knowledge in abstract, formal and scholarly terms in return for status, resources, territoriality and accreditation. . . . to surrender solicitously to the definitions of 'valuable knowledge' as formulated by University scholars'. Is this pattern also true in the case of primary school teachers? Or have their rather different curricular traditions and perceptions of their professionalism (Alexander, 1984) led curriculum development and change in this area along a rather different path?

There are competing models for the description of any curriculum. Goodson (1987) identifies three: the academic, the utilitarian and the pedagogic. The 'academic' curriculum comprises subjects that are content-focused, stressing levels of abstraction and theory, and have as 'a central criterion . . . whether the subjects' content could be tested by written examinations for an "able" clientele' (p. 25). The utilitarian curriculum is in some senses the mirror image of the academic: it centres on practical knowledge, not easily assessed by way of traditional written examinations: low status knowledge, related to everyday personal and social life and, in working life, to the non-professional vocations. The pedagogic tradition is less concerned with knowledge in either of these forms, but with the way the child learns, and makes this central to the devising of the curriculum. (Alan Blyth, an important innovator and analyst of the primary school social studies curriculum, made a rather similar distinction within the primary curricular traditions, into preparatory, elementary and developmental (1969).)

The competition between these traditions has always been acute: it was portrayed most publicly in James Callaghan's Ruskin Speech, that opened the self-styled

Great Debate of the late 1970s, when the Prime Minister combined personal development within a social context and utilitarianism: 'The goals of our education, from nursery school through to adult education, are clear enough. They are to equip children to the best of their ability for a lively, constructive place in society and also to fit them to do a job of work. Not one or the other, but both' (Callaghan, 1976).

The contrast was repeated the following year, when the Warnock Report on special educational needs contrasted the same ideas of a pedagogic curriculum leading to personal self-fulfilment with a curriculum aimed at the broader needs of society, through a utilitarian curriculum that was paralleled, for the more able child, by an academic curriculum, asserting that all three traditions must be represented. The aims of any educational system, wrote Warnock, were 'first, to enlarge a child's knowledge, experience and imaginative understanding, and thus his awareness of moral values and capacity for enjoyment; and secondly, to enable him to enter the world after formal education is over as an active participant in society and a responsible contributor to it, capable of achieving as much independence as possible' (DES, 1978, p. 5). The Schools Council for the Curriculum and Examination, pressed later to concisely define the purposes of the curriculum, claimed of this statement that 'there is no better general statement of the aims of education' (Schools Council, 1981, p. 14).

Such analyses can be used in tracing, within secondary school education, the cycles of development and decline shown by the 'social subjects' over the past half-century. Cannon (1964) so dissected the social studies movement of the 1940s and 1950s, and Whitty (1985) has analyzed the 'new social studies' innovations of the 1960s and 1970s. In the first of these two phases, those teachers involved rejected attempts to academicize the subject and invest it with the status of an examination subject, insisting instead that it was both a utilitarian practical subject, close to the everyday 'commonsense' experiences of pupils, and delivered in a pedagogically sound manner. It was for these very reasons, Whitty concludes, that it was 'doomed to marginalization in a situation where the academic tradition was reasserting its dominance even in schools supposedly intended to foster the alternatives' (*ibid.*, p. 152). On the other hand, the new social studies movement that followed this, promoted for example by Lawton and Dufour (1973), was to establish sociology as the basis for a social studies curriculum subject that would emphasize abstraction, conceptualization and structures, to be examined in traditional forms. While the movement 'paid some lip service to the alternative utilitarian and pedagogic traditions in English education, its central thrust involved the acceptance of the values of the dominant academic tradition' (Whitty, 1985, p. 156). Despite the threats posed by (and partly carried out through) the imposition of the National Curriculum (described, for example, in the special issue of the professional journal *The Social Science Teacher*, 1988), secondary school sociology has since grown further in strength, particularly at the post-16 stage.

In this development towards the status of an accepted subject, secondary school social studies has followed a very similar path to that charted by Layton in his analysis of the subject of science in secondary education from the nineteenth century:

a first stage in which the subject is 'justifying its presence on grounds such as pertinence and utility . . . Learners are attracted to the subjects because of its bearing on matters of concern to them . . . The dominant criterion is relevance to the needs and interests of the learners' (Layton, 1973). This is followed by a period in which 'students are attracted to the study, but as much by its reputation and growing academic status as by its relevance to their own problems and concerns'. At this stage, the subject matter begins to be selected and organized from the logic and discipline of the subject, rather than from any consideration of usefulness. In the final stage, specialist teachers 'constitute a professional body . . . subject matter is determined . . . by the judgment and practices of specialist scholars . . . [and] students are initiated into a tradition' (*ibid.*). This pattern of evolution seems common to many secondary school subjects that aspire to the academic tradition (Goodson, 1994).

Does the same pattern hold true of the social subjects in the primary and middle school curriculum? It may first be useful to consider some of the very varied ways in which these elements have been described in the primary school curriculum over the past quarter century. The curriculum has been described and prescribed in a remarkable series of official and semi-official documents over this period. In each, the 'social areas' of the curriculum has been described in differing terms. Table 3.1 shows the changes used in the terminology of the areas that consider (in whole or in part) aspects of human social behaviour.

The table is arranged vertically to show the development over time, and the three columns are used to indicate the rather different terminology of Her Majesty's Inspectorate from 1976, the Department of Education and Science in the 1980s, and the various official curriculum groups that have existed over the period.

This tracking of the descriptions of the curriculum is not intended to suggest that it represents an accurate view of what was necessarily happening in schools. Rather, it shows how the authors of various official documents elected to either categorize their observations, or to organize their prescriptions. Classroom practice in the period will certainly have shown wide variations in curriculum organization (as the HMI surveys point out), and it would be difficult to determine in any quantitative way how these variations changed over time. Techniques such as the analysis of how textbooks in the areas construct children's identities (Ahier, 1988), or the investigation of individual school timetables will not show the range of practices in curriculum organization; while analyses of classroom practice (for example, the ORACLE project; Galton *et al.*, 1980; and Galton and Simon 1980; Mortimore *et al.*, 1988) focus on the nature of the teacher-learner interaction, rather than the subject matter of what is being learnt.

The Plowden Report *Children and their Primary Schools* (CACE, 1967) echoed the earlier Hadow Report in decrying the notion of 'subjects' as an adequate description for the primary school curriculum. Nevertheless, in its chapter describing what it saw as good practice in primary schools, it used only the very traditional subject labels of history and geography (and covered certain other social aspects under religious education and sex education). This highly conservative set of descriptors were not used again in the following twenty years: they were not to be

Table 3.1: *Changes in the descriptions of the social subjects in the primary and middle school curriculum in England and Wales, 1967–91*

	HM INSPECTORATE	DEPT OF EDUCATION & SCIENCE	SCHOOLS COUNCIL	CENTRAL ADVISORY COMMITTEE ON EDUCATION
1967 (CACE)				**The 'Plowden' Report:** History Geography Religious education Sex education
1977 (HMI)	**Curriculum 11–16:** areas of experience, to include 'the social and political'			
1978 (HMI)	**Primary Education in England:** Social studies (history, geography, religious education)			
1980 (HMI)	**A View of the Curriculum:** History and social studies Geography Religious education			
1981 (DES)		**The School Curriculum:** Topic work (history and geography) Religious education	**The Practical Curriculum:** *Infants* Environmental studies Religious education *Juniors* From social studies, history and geography Religious education	
1981 (SC)				
1982 (HMI)	**Education 5 to 9:** Learning about people Religious and moral education			
1983 (HMI)	**9–13 Middle Schools:** History, geography and religious education			
1985a (HMI) 1985 (DES)	**Curriculum Matters 2:** Spiritual Human and social Health education Moral Economic understanding Political education Environmental education	**Better Schools:** Religious education, history and geography, and the nature and values of British society Health education Moral education How people earn their living		
1986–89 (HMI)	**Curriculum Matters:** Geography (1986) Health education (1986) History (1988) Careers education and guidance (1988) Environmental education (1989)			

Table 3.1: (Cont)

1987 (DES/WO)	**National Curriculum:** History Geography	
		NATIONAL CURRICULUM COUNCIL
1990a		Whole Curriculum
1990b		Economic and industrial understanding
1990c		Health education
1990d		Careers education and guidance
1990e		Environmental education
1990f		Citizenship
1989–91	**Aspects of Primary Education:** History and geography (1989)	

(Adapted from Ross, 1993)

resuscitated until the plans for the National Curriculum were published by the Department of Education and Science and the Welsh Office in 1987 (DES/WO, 1987). The intervening period saw the rise and fall of the social subjects in the primary curriculum, with the word 'social' being advanced by HMI, and being deliberately avoided by the DES. These developments over the period can be derived from the publication of the Plowden Report in three ways: two recommendations and an omission.

The first of the recommendations was that the progress of the primary phase of education be regularly monitored by HMI, at approximately ten-year intervals. This has broadly been achieved: *Primary Education in England* (HMI, 1978) surveyed primary schools, and the smaller numbers of differently arranged schools were similarly covered in *Education 5 to 9* (HMI, 1982) and *9–13 Middle Schools* (HMI, 1983). The second phase was achieved in the series of publications between 1989 and 1992 under the title *Aspects of Primary Education*, generally arranged under 'subject' headings. The significance of this implementation was two-fold: firstly, it required HMI to define a terminology with which to describe the curriculum — a process that, from the evidence of the sequences in table 3.1, they did not seem to find easy in the area of the social subjects. Secondly, HMI were able to use their surveys to counter what some of them, at least, saw as the attack on knowledge, and the discipline-approach basis of knowledge that Plowden represented. Geoffrey Elsmore, the Senior Primary HMI responsible for the 1978 survey, saw Plowden's attack on curriculum specialism in the primary school as insidious,[1] and the opportunity presented by the decenial survey allowed HMI to begin its discrete and persistent lobbying for the reintroduction of 'the subject' into the primary curriculum (see below; also Goodson, 1989, p. 137; DES, 1983, para 64).

The second recommendation of the Plowden Report that proved to be of relevance to the social subjects was that the primary-secondary school divide be bridged by the creation of middle schools, catering for the 8/9 to 12/13 age range. The suggestion was taken up in a number of local education authorities, and the

Schools Council (the semi-autonomous body established in 1964 to advise and innovate in curriculum and examinations) set about 'stimulat(ing) discussion about the kind of curriculum most suited to the needs of pupils between the ages of 8–13' (Lincoln Ralphs, 1969). As will be shown below, the activities arising from this discussion were one of the most significant reasons for the rise of the social subjects.

The final significance of the Plowden Report lies with what it omitted. The comments of an American visitor to Britain at the time express this most clearly. Vincent Rogers, Professor of Education at the University of Connecticut, spent 1967 on a field trip to England to report on the social subjects in English education. In considering primary education, he turned eagerly to the Plowden Report, anticipating it as representing 'the most recent thinking of large numbers of England's most influential and respected educators . . . their views will surely be of help as one attempts to look into the immediate curricular future'. He was incredulous at what he found.

> One might begin one's analysis by looking through the index and table of contents for references to 'Social Science', 'Anthropology', 'Economics', and 'Political Science'. I did; and despite the concern expressed (in the section on the 'Aims of primary education') for an education that would, among other things, help children cope with social and economic change, critically analyze their own society, understand the nature of a democratic society, etc., etc. — I could find *no* reference to *any* of these disciplines. This straightforward omission states the Committee's views far more eloquently, I think, than would an explanatory paragraph or two. Obviously, in Plowden's view, the insights of the social sciences are not perceived of as necessary, useful or appropriate segments of the primary school curriculum.

> I find it exceedingly difficult to imagine how one learns to either understand, predict, or cope with economic, social or political change without utilizing these disciplines. . . . the section devoted to geography . . . makes no mention of the ways in which geographers are utilizing concepts drawn from anthropology, economics and the other social sciences. (Rogers, 1968, pp. 49–50)

Rogers' critique of the place of the social subjects in British primary schools rests on eight points:

1   The 'undue influence' of Piaget in British education, 'often leading to overtly simplistic, intellectually undemanding studies emphasizing the "concrete" . . . [and] consistently putting off more challenging approaches that might begin to develop more complex thinking strategies and studies at much earlier age levels' (p. 40).
2   Ignoring the potential role of social studies in the development of attitudes, values, prejudices and stereotypes in younger children.

3   The focus of curriculum debate between an emphasis on basic or core facts
     or items of knowledge, and an unrestricted curriculum centred on the
     individual child's own perceptions of their needs: Rogers' alternative fol-
     lows Bruner, in focusing the social studies curriculum on the development
     of transferable and fundamental social science concepts and generalizations.
4   A lack of concern about sequence, progression and development in social
     studies teaching (in marked contrast to the emphasis on progression in, for
     example, the 'new mathematics').
5   An overemphasis on studies of the local and parochial as an end in them-
     selves, rather than as a known focal point for comparison with other areas.
6   An overemphasis on first-hand physical processes at the expense of intel-
     lectual analysis.
7   An overdeterministic approach to other societies, focusing on contrasting
     physical surroundings and patterns of life (ignoring cultural similarities, or
     different social adaptations to similar physical surroundings).
8   The tendency of primary education to cocoon children from the real, com-
     plex and controversial world, avoiding discussion of conflict.

The Rise of Social Studies

Roger's criticisms were not isolated. There were parallel concerns expressed, for
example, by Blyth, in his contemporary sociological analysis of English primary
education (1969). He observed that many local environmental studies 'can become
something rather Arcadian and bucolic . . . almost an opiate of the peasantry' (vol
2, p. 101), often with a rural bias that he traces back to Rousseau and to Pestalozzi's
Heimatkunde (p. 84). Ahier (1988) also points to this creation of a rural tradition,
particularly in history schoolbooks of the period. Blyth's contribution at this stage
was to make the crucial link between the different primary curricular traditions
which he identified and what he was at that time calling environmental education.
The elementary tradition he characterized as essentially utilitarian, quoting Robert
Lowe's introduction of the Revised Code in 1871 'We do not profess to give these
children an education that will raise them above their station and business in life
— that is not our object — but to give them an education that may fit them for
the business' (quoted in Birchenough, 1938, p. 99). It was here — particularly in
the country areas — that Blyth (1969) observed that the curriculum might use the
rural environment: 'fewer topics have proved such a fertile field for intelligent
speculation by people educated in the traditional urban manner . . . the picture of
little peasants at work, observing, measuring and cultivating their simple world
has exercised a steady fascination' (p. 84). The preparatory tradition, by contrast,
presented an academic curriculum designed to lead to further study of traditional
subjects. Tawney (1923), developing Labour Party policy on education, saw the
role of the primary school clearly in this tradition: 'secondary education being the
education of the adolescent and primary education being education preparatory
thereto' (p. 7). The curriculum subjects were determined by appeal to academic

respectability and status, and perhaps all by public examinability: Goodson (1987) examines the emergence of geography as such a subject in the first half of the twentieth century. The developmental tradition had its roots in both a psychological view of learning and in a belief in isolating children from the harshness of adult life: the consequences for the social studies curriculum can be seen in part, in some of the criticisms that Rogers raised above.

Plowden proposed a reorganization of primary education, suggesting that middle schools be created as a layer between first schools (essentially infant schools with an additional year) and high school education (starting at about the age of 13). This proposal led to the question of what might be a suitable curriculum for the years of around 8 to 13. The Schools Council, established in 1964 with a wide-ranging brief that included curriculum development, took this up. Steering Committee A (with responsibility for education from 2 to 13) organized a conference in September 1967 at Warwick, with the purposes both of stimulating a discussion on the most appropriate curriculum and to consult on how the Council might develop teaching materials for the age range (Lincoln Ralphs, 1969).

Three papers were invited on social studies, and these were given together in a session one morning. John Backhouse, a headteacher, described the development of social studies in primary education as moving from initially bringing geography and history closer to the classroom ('making them less abstract, more real') towards 'a less conscious injection of geography and history content into social studies') (1969, p. 45). John Hanson, from an Oxfordshire curriculum development centre, identified the area rather more in terms of the relationship between people and their environment (1969), but it was the paper from Denis Lawton, from the University of London Institute of Education, which initiated most discussion. Developing the theme from social science teaching with older children, he drew on the Newsom Report's (CACE, 1963) discussion on preparing children for the adult world to identify a set of aims for social studies education that he argued should be achieved by the end of full-time education — awareness of factual information about society; awareness of the complexity of contemporary society and their place within it; the ability to distinguish fact from opinion and develop hypotheses; the ability to distinguish and evaluate different kinds of evidence. Lawton argued that these were achievable after ten to eleven years of full-time education, but not if they were only taught in the final years. Social studies, he concluded, should be a 'properly planned integrated course, beginning in the primary school with simple social concepts, concrete descriptive materials and simple experiences' (Lawton, 1969, p. 56). The argument synthesized utilitarian needs for social studies education (from Newsom, CACE, 1963), academic and preparatory motivations (the development of abstract concepts for a later stage of education) and took note of the pedagogical/developmental traditions of primary education (with careful references to developmental needs, as well as to the work of Jerome Bruner). He suggested the Schools Council 'try and tidy up the teaching of social studies, which is so haphazard and patchy, and in some cases almost non-existent' (Lawton, 1969, p. 58), with research into children's social development, the identification and dissemination of existing good practice, and local cooperative curriculum development. Discussion groups after this 'questioned the place of traditional subjects in the middle school curriculum . . . subjects could often be grouped together as relationship studies or social studies'. If middle schools planned sequential learning, based on skills and concepts in social studies, this would be 'a valuable exercise which, unlike so many of the existing and more specialist projects, could have a unifying influence on the curriculum' (Schools Council, 1969, p. 85).

The Schools Council acted as Lawton had urged. He was invited to propose a project to survey existing practice in schools, and to recommend what additional materials and support might be needed: this was agreed by both Steering Group A (2 to 13 education) and the Social Science Subject Committee (Alan Blyth was a member of both groups), and the concurrence of Steering Group B (11 to 16 education) (Blyth *et al.*, 1978). Lawton's project, Social Studies 8–13, ran from September 1968 to April 1970, with two Research Officers and Lawton as part-time Director. They found the state of social studies all of the 'haphazard . . . patchy, and . . . almost non-existent' condition that Lawton had described in 1967. They described the situation as 'still far from satisfactory — based either on the complacent view that children will learn about their society incidentally from other subjects, or on the despondent view that this kind of abstract thinking is too difficult' (Lawton *et al.*, 1971, p. 9). The team asked LEAs for examples of good practice, offering a very broad definition of social studies teaching — 'any kind of learning which fosters the development of social concepts, general social awareness, and the understanding of modern industrial society . . . not . . . courses which were simply history or geography' (p. 13). Noting that many primary schools included some local environmental study (and welcoming this), they insisted that any social studies programme had also to get children to examine a wider view of their own society, to develop social science-based concepts, and to compare and contrast societies different from their own, both past and present. The teachers in the identified schools were surveyed to suggest the purposes of social studies teaching: they presented an extraordinarily wide range of ideas, and Lawton and his colleagues concluded that there was little consensus amongst the teachers — 'the purpose of teaching social studies differs greatly from school to school' (p. 149).

Eighteen schools were visited by the survey team. What is remarkable (though not identified by Lawton) from the detailed reports of the ten secondary schools and eight primary schools is the difference between the primary and secondary curriculum approaches. The secondary schools were each able to offer the team descriptions of regular programmes, ranging from one year to three years in length, in which there were identifiable sequences of learning with formal social science objectives. In contrast, the primary schools' work was eclectic, opportunistic and random. In seven of the schools a single project is identified, never more than of a term's length. In four of these, it is evident that the parallel class did not cover the same topic. The projects are not related to any earlier learning, or to work that might follow. In two cases, external organizations had triggered the particular project (a BBC educational broadcast series and an LEA cross-school project). In two other cases, the 'social' element of the learning had apparently emerged as an unexpected (albeit welcome) by-product of another discipline (mathematics and nature study).

Only in one school were two separate projects described, for a third year junior class and a fourth year junior class, but there was no apparently planned relationship between the two (based on Lawton *et al.*, 1971, pp. 32–92). But the team did conclude that little social science based work was going on in primary schools, and ascribed this not to lack of interest on the part of teachers, but 'more the result of uncertainty about what sort of social understandings should be encouraged, some underestimation of what children are capable of understanding about society, and a lack of knowledge about source materials and subject matter' (pp. 205–6).

Social Studies 8–13 offered two broad conclusions. Firstly, it provided a middle years framework for social studies, comprising a stage 1, with eleven non-sequential projects for the first three years (8–10 years of age), ranging from the study of groups of which the child is a member (friends, school), through local groups of which the child was not a member (the community, a local industry), to distant groups in time and space and imaginary and simulated groups. The 11–12-year-olds took a core course in evolution, animal societies and 'primitive' societies (a judicious admixture of the BBC *Man* series and Bruner's *Man: A Course of Study* (MACOS) project for the Massachusetts Education Development Centre. Stage 2, for the 12–14-year olds, had two sequential project-based studies, in community studies and ancient civilizations. The second major recommendation was more influential: that a development project be funded to derive materials from sociology, economics and anthropology, and to integrate history and geography with these; to provide in-service training for teachers about these; and to evaluate the whole.

Lawton's project had a Schools Council Consultative Committee to guide it, chaired by Blyth. As the draft report came to the various Schools Council committees (Steering Committee A and the Social Sciences Subject Committee) in early 1970, 'the other two subject committees, History and Geography, felt slightly suspicious that these two projects (Lawton, and the project he proposed) had pre-empted the major claims of their own disciplines' (Blyth *et al.*, 1978, p. 150), and an ad hoc working party between all three subjects was set up to bargain between the disciplines. At that time, 'a major project from the Schools Council required the allocation of over £100,000 for three years. The separate subject committees knew they had no chance of attracting such a resource allocation. In coalition, they could do so' (Derricott, 1993, p. 111). It was agreed that Blyth be invited to submit a proposal for a middle years project covering history, geography and the social sciences — in part, at least, because of the level of overheads that would be necessary for a London-based project were much more than would be needed by Blyth, based as he was at the University of Liverpool. The project was funded, with six full-time team members, to run from September 1971.

This was *the* major period of educator-led curriculum innovation in recent times in Britain. Goodson (1989) has retrospectively characterized the various projects of this time as constituting a 'tidal wave' — but also pointing out their long-term characteristics of only temporarily affecting some of the less substantial and prominent disciplines. Now, argues Goodson, 'standing out more clearly than ever on the new horizon is the school subject, the "basic" or "traditional" subject' (p. 132).

The problematic 'subject' nature of this project was evident from the first. Blyth's own project proposal noted

> two possible dangers — that of a centrifugal tripartite division into three subject areas, and that of a mixture, lacking in rigour or conviction . . . It should be emphasized that there is no justification for assuming that a new, cumbersome, tripartite 'subject' should necessarily be established, within which historical, geographical and social-science contents and techniques will always be equal, or that these three disciplines necessarily form a self-contained area of the curriculum. (1970 project proposal, quoted in Blyth *et al.,* 1978, pp. 150–1)

However, it was not directly the tension between the two established academic subjects and the newer subject of still dubious status that nearly led the project to grief in its first year, but the consequences of the critique of the curriculum *per se* that was developing at that time. The attempts to define and analyze the curriculum that had been explored by Lawton in 1971 (and which lay behind the Schools Councils tortuous deliberations on establishing the project (Plaskow, 1985)), were at that time being side-stepped. Some innovators saw 'critical studies of the curriculum as social construction [and] pointed to the school classroom as the site wherein the curriculum was negotiated and realized . . . the classroom *was* the curriculum. . . . The definition of the curriculum . . . was not just subject to redefinition at classroom level but quite simply irrelevant' (Goodson, 1989, p. 133). The processes of learning and teaching were those that defined the nature of knowledge, and it was argued that what was needed was not merely a reordering of the outmoded disciplines but "the analysis of the knowledge which constitutes the life world and knowledge of teachers and pupils . . . penetrating the symbolic drift of school knowledge, and the consequences for the individuals who are . . . attempting to construct their reality through it' (Esland, 1971, p. 11). The Blyth project members at first concentrated on developing the processes of teaching and learning as a form of curriculum development, rather than the more common materials-led curriculum development project. In this they were following the Lawton report's paragraphs on the need for in-service work with the teachers (Derricott, 1975 and 1984). They argued that each school was unique, and required its own unique development in these areas, based on the key variables of child, teacher, school and environment (Blyth *et al.*, 1976). Any curriculum development was therefore dependent on teacher development.

This was counter to the orthodoxy current at the Schools Council. A Project Officer had been appointed by the Council to liaise with the team, a senior civil servant seconded from the Department of Education and Science. Backed by the Council's Joint Secretary, he called a meeting with Professor Alec Ross, Chair of the Project's Consultative Committee, and the team in August 1972 and insisted that the brief was to produce materials that would increase teachers' possibilities of teaching in these areas (Derricott, 1993). The Council was not an in-service education provider. Blyth temporized: the team would produce materials that would act as exemplars for teachers, illustrating the processes of teacher-centred development: some materials might be used directly with children, but there would also be a substantial collection of material for teachers. Ivor Goodson (1994) has summarized the approach of many of the curriculum innovators of the period as wanting 'to be involved in action, not theory . . . Analysis of what was already in schools was therefore mere archaeology, and theorising if there was a need for it could come later: after the curriculum revolution' (p. 28). Blyth's position had a certain similarity with the social constructionism of Bernstein and Esland:

> Two values emerged as basic to the Project . . . The first of these was that each person and culture has its own claims to legitimate existence . . . Education should enable children to develop their own ways of looking at individuals and cultures and their own criteria for deciding which, if any, are preferable in their eyes. . . . The second basic value . . . that children should be actively initiated into the discussion of problems and issues in society, rather than being shielded . . . (Blyth *et al.*, 1976, p. 23)

The Project Team worked for four years, producing eventually a range of teacher materials (a planning handbook and a set of five supplementary booklets) and seven exemplar units of pupils' materials (for a summary description of them all, see Derricott, 1984). These pupil packs were not a great success. The only unit that had an entirely social science perspective was *Money*: in the words of one of its authors, 'it uses concepts from economics . . . and illustrative well-researched anthropological material to try and develop some social scientific understandings in 10–12-year-olds' (*ibid.*, p. 81). An analysis of the dissemination of this pack found that only two copies had been used with classes: the rest had been used in teacher's centres and initial teacher education libraries, and the like (Whitehead, 1980; see also Steadman, 1978 and 1980). The reason for this, it was claimed, was that while the teacher's guide laid out the conceptual framework, this was only really useful to the teacher confident with social science ideas: to 'the vast majority of primary, middle and secondary school users . . . with no background in the social sciences the unit can be daunting and have little appeal' (Derricott, 1984).

However, the project as a whole was by no means a failure. The curriculum planning guide was popular and was reprinted twice. It stimulated further developments. For example, in the Inner London Education Authority a social studies project for 8–11-year-olds, *People Around Us*, was a direct successor. One of the members of the Steering Committee for Lawton's project was the ILEA Inspector for Social Sciences, Howell Davies; he provided four schools (two primary, two secondary) for Blyth's project to develop ideas with. When Davies was able to fund a curriculum project in London, it was teachers from these two primary schools who joined the development team, and an adaptation of Blyth's list of concepts that formed the heart of the ILEA packages. *People Around Us* had three units, *Families* (ILEA, 1978), *Friends* (ILEA, 1979) and *Work* (ILEA, 1980a), and an accompanying set of curriculum guidelines (ILEA, 1980b). These packs were widely used by ILEA primary schools (Ross, 1982). There were similar innovations in other

LEAs: in Merton, for example, an imaginative project linked all levels of compulsory education in curriculum planning in social studies, producing *The New Approach to the Social Studies: Continuity and Development in Children's Learning through First, Middle and High Schools* (Harries *et al.*, 1983).

Perhaps even more significant was the beginning of the change in the vocabulary of curriculum description that became evident in the latter part of the 1970s, partly shown in the table earlier in this chapter. As part of the process of 'how subjects are made, how they are sources of status and identity for teachers, what processes . . . subject communities follow to raise their status over time, how school subjects are objects of political bargaining and conflict' (Hargreaves, 1994a, p. 5), the subject association for social science teaching in schools, the Association for the Teaching of the Social Sciences, had begun to identify and champion the cause of primary school social studies. In 1980 it devoted a special issue of its journal, *Social Science Teacher*, to primary school social studies, written largely by the ILEA group of primary teachers who were at the same-time developing *People Around Us*, and it followed this in 1984 with a primary and middle school social studies edition, which was more wide-ranging across England.

Social studies became a term that Her Majesty's Inspectors were prepared to use between 1978 and 1984: they had taken on the criticisms of the asocial nature of Plowden's terminology. In discussing the organization of the curriculum in the 1978 survey of primary education, the report observed that they would discuss it 'in terms of subjects such as English, mathematics or geography, or in relation to certain activities such as learning to read or to play team games. Many of the skills, ideas and attitudes referred to have applications that recur in various parts of school work. Because this kind of teaching is not wholly susceptible to fixed timetable periods many classes have broadly drawn timetables with times fixed only when resources or specialist teachers are shared' (HMI, 1978, para 5.1). They then use the term social studies to cover sub-headings in history, geography and religious education, noting that 'many schools used a thematic approach to the work in social studies' (*ibid.*, para 5.115). Five years later, the education provided in first schools was described. Again, they issue a warning about attempts to too firmly label the curriculum — 'a substantial part of the work could not be neatly categorized under discrete subject headings' (HMI, 1982, para 2.1), and then use the term 'learning about people', which they sub-divide into 'themselves', 'others', 'the locality', 'more distant places' and 'people in other times'. A year later, the report on middle schools noted

> on the timetables of some of the schools, history, geography, sometimes with religious education, environmental studies, integrated studies, project and topic work. In others, history, geography and were combined in broad areas of the curriculum described variously as humanities, social studies, religious education were timetabled as separate subjects for children in some or all year groups. (HMI, 1983, para 7.154)

HMI had long had a Social Science Committee, and while most of its work was concerned with the 14–19 age range, it had, since 1979, given some attention to social studies in teaching in primary schools. In 1982 and 1983, they conducted a small-scale survey of thirteen schools. They found three using *Place Time and Society 8–13* as a basis of planning, and three more using the ILEA *Social Studies in the Primary School* — 'none of these . . . was followed slavishly although their general structures were respected' (Anglesey and Hennessy, 1984, p. 83). They found that schools identifying the area as environmental studies tended to relate work to the natural sciences, while social studies programmes would tap individual social sciences from time to time — most often anthropology, least successfully economics. They suggested that there was 'considerable stock of expertise and goodwill, . . . most problems could have been met and solved by appropriate forward planning and most good work seen resulted from this. If there is one priority it is . . . a syllabus which sets out to answer the question: "What should infant and junior school pupils know about the size, shape and workings of their own and other societies, and of the economies on which they depend?" ' (*ibid.*).

It might have appeared that in the early 1980s social studies teaching in primary schools stood on the verge of acceptance as a legitimated subject within the curriculum in English schools. Given the perception of HMI and many other educational commentators of random, repetitive project work in the social subjects, with no continuity or progression, then the social studies movement was poised to offer conceptual and methodological frameworks that would bring some order and intellectual rigour to the area. There were some counter-indications, that had been developing since the late 1970s, which will be examined below. But social studies now appeared to be developing, and this impression was strengthened by the fact that the movement was not confined to the United Kingdom: over most of the world there was a growing tendency to use social studies as an organizing subject within primary education.

Cross-national Trends

Rogers, who had made the first criticisms of Plowden for ignoring the social subjects, was observing the English system from the viewpoint of an American culture that had long stressed the social sciences in school education. Denis Lawton's survey in 1971 had identified the major development that had occurred in the United States since the late 1950s, when the social studies curriculum began to develop through a series of development projects. Lawton estimated that there were fifty to sixty of these in 1971, and described three of the best known projects in some detail: the Massachusetts EDC Social Studies Project, with which Jerome Bruner was associated in the development of the MACOS scheme for Grade 5 children (10-year-olds); the Contra Costa Social Studies Project in San Francisco, sometimes known as the Taba Project, after Hilda Taba; and the Elkhart Indiana Experiment in Economic Education, also known as Our Working World, led by Laurence Senesh.

The development of social studies as a curriculum area became a world wide phenomena, both at primary and secondary levels of schooling. Its growth was such that a UNESCO handbook was compiled to help the development of a common sense of what the subject was concerned with (Mehlinger, 1981). The editor defined the area as comprising 'courses of study at the primary and secondary levels of schooling presenting components of history, geography, economics and moral and civic education, prescribed and taught either as an integrated discipline or as separate curriculum subjects with an interdisciplinary emphasis' (*ibid.*, p. iii). A survey of social studies in different countries noted that 'the most prevalent worldwide view of social studies sees the field as consisting of separate subjects' (Wronski, 1981, p. 21), with 'history and geography as the core — and sometimes the only — subjects subsumed under social studies . . . (which) may also include civics (or political education), economics (or political economy), anthropology, sociology and psychology, or some variation of these courses' (*ibid.*, p. 18).

Denis Lawton (1981) contributed a strongly argued defence of social studies, drawing from his British experience of primary and secondary education. Because 'the world is increasingly . . . "social scientific" in its orientation . . . young people need to acquire accurate knowledge of certain aspects of their own society if they are to participate effectively within it. By this argument, all children have a right to certain kinds of political, social and economic education' (p. 56).

A more quantitative analysis of global trends in the development of primary social studies was produced by the team led by John Meyer at Stanford University. They developed a major collection of data on primary school curricular categories from across the world, stretching back, in many cases, into the mid-nineteenth century. Their analysis shows that in curricular outlines, using standard categories, that national variations are surprisingly unimportant. Variations in national power structures and functional pressures tend only to affect content and practice within standard categories: 'the overall outlines of school curricula are remarkably similar in style and structure. If we are to speak of the evolution of the mass curriculum . . . we are talking about a process that is world-wide as much as national in character' (Meyer, 1992, p. 7). They examined the subject descriptions, and the amounts of timetabled time give to each of these, in some 125 countries between 1970 and 1986, 105 countries between 1945 and 1969, sixty countries between 1920 and 1944, and a small number of countries in earlier periods, back in some cases to 1800.

One of the major historical changes to emerge from the study was 'the remarkable devaluation' of the pre-'social studies' subjects of geography, history and civics. In the 1920s, they found some 90 per cent of their sample offering these as separate subjects. By 1986, 'social studies has become the instructional category encompassing these older subjects' (Kamens, 1992, p. 76). Their speculations on the reasons for this will be of particular interest later in this chapter, when we come to examine the situation in the United Kingdom, where social studies are uniquely in decline, against the worldwide trend. They argue that generally nationalism has changed in the later part of the twentieth century:

> The construction of national myths, symbols and monuments has given way to the prosaic work of institution building based on internationally available models, such as setting up health care systems, mass schooling

Table 3.2: The percentage of time given to instruction in selected subjects, all available countries

Subject	1920s	1930s	1940s	1950s	1960s	1970s	1980s
History	2.7	2.8	2.6	2.5	1.5	0.7	1.5
Geography	3.4	3.4	2.9	2.7	1.7	1.1	1.4
Civics	0.8	1.3	0.4	1.2	0.8	0.2	1.0
Social studies	0.1	1.1	1.5	2.0	4.7	5.7	4.8
n	29	32	38	94	52	40	110

(adapted from Wong, 1992, table 9.1(a))

and pension funds. This change affects the legitimacy of local and national history and geography as subjects children must learn. As the sacredness of the 'nation' declines, learning facts, names and dates becomes a less compelling task of schooling. Furthermore, under conditions of desacrilization, the nation itself — and its traditions — become appropriate objects of study. Similarly, as institutions are seen as 'man [sic] made' and not 'natural', other cultures and societies gain credibility as objects of analysis, from whom useful lessons may be drawn . . . modern social studies becomes possible and taken-for-granted as a curricular topic. (*ibid.*, p. 77)

Wong (1991) presents the specific data for the social subjects. Looking first at all the countries for which data is available, there seems to be a clear increase in the time given to social studies worldwide (table 3.2).

This effect is not caused merely because different countries have been sampled at different times. Using constant panels of countries, it is possible to trace changes over time in the same countries (table 3.3).

Three trends emerge. Firstly, the total amount of time given to the social subjects (however they are designated) remains fairly constant: these subjects have been taught in nearly all countries in the world, for about 8–9 per cent of the total time, over the past half century. Secondly, the emphasis has dramatically shifted from separate instruction in history and geography (falling from about 3 per cent to 1.3 per cent) towards combined social studies (rising from 0.65 to 4.8 per cent). Thirdly, civics has remained fairly stable. Wong speculates that there has been a trade-off between the two forms of curricular organization and description, and that the data also represents a marked tendency towards the standardization of a dominant form of modern culture.

It is also possible to determine some regional variations in these patterns. Table 3.4 compares the amount of time given to three subjects in different periods over different regions of the world.

The British experience up to the early 1980s, as described in the previous section, thus appears to be simply conforming to a worldwide trend to develop a single-subject social studies curriculum, that probably in most cases sought to prepare responsible and rational citizens, rather than national patriots. However, the

Table 3.3 (a): The percentage of time given to instruction in selected subjects, constant panels

Subject	1920/44	1945/69	1945/69	1970/8
History	3.0	2.1	2.3	1.3
Geography	3.7	2.7	2.6	1.3
Civics	1.4	1.3	1.1	0.7
Social studies	0.6	2.6	2.1	4.8
n		37		74

Table 3.3 (b): Proportions of countries offering instruction in selected subjects, constant panels

Subject	1920/44	1945/69	1945/69	1970/86
History	81	70	73	47
Geography	87	72	73	44
Civics	40	45	35	27
Social studies	11	26	26	60
n		37		74

(adapted from Wong, 1992, table 9.1(b))

Table 3.4: Percentages of instructional time given to history, geography and social studies by world region

Region	Subject	1920/44	1945/69	1970/86
Sub-Saharan Africa	History	0.0	2.1	1.4
	Geography	0.0	2.3	1.6
	Social studies	0.0	1.2	3.3
Mid East/N Africa	History	2.6	2.9	1.0
	Geography	3.1	2.6	1.0
	Social studies	0.0	0.2	3.8
Asia	History	2.3	1.3	0.7
	Geography	2.7	1.3	0.6
	Social studies	0.3	5.3	6.0
Latin America	History	1.9	1.9	1.7
	Geography	2.1	2.0	1.3
	Social studies	3.9	6.9	8.7
Caribbean	History	1.1	3.1	2.1
	Geography	4.4	2.9	1.8
	Social studies	0.3	3.7	7.2
Eastern Europe	History	5.0	3.6	3.0
	Geography	4.9	3.5	2.8
	Social studies	0.3	0.0	0.0
W Europe/N America	History	3.0	2.2	1.3
	Geography	3.8	3.2	1.3
	Social studies	0.6	1.3	5.0

(adapted from Wong, 1992, table 9.2)

growth of primary school social studies was about to be checked and reversed, in a sharp reversal to move in the opposite direction to the rest of the world.

The Attack on the Social: Decline and Fall

In the 1960s the educational changes brought about by the incoming Labour government had attracted the criticisms of the right. But, perhaps because these changes had been largely with the structure of educational provision, the criticisms of the early Black Paperites had been shrugged off or ignored without much difficulty. The educational innovations brought about by the Schools Council (and by bodies such as the Nuffield Foundation) were rather different: they were concerned with the curriculum, with ways of learning. It is remarkable that most of these innovations were ignored by the right for a long period of time. With the exception of occasional critiques of 'new maths' and, less often, of the teaching of reading, the attacks on educational innovations were confined to other matters.

For example, the first 'Black Paper' (Cox and Dyson, 1969) made virtually no criticism of the curriculum in schools, apart from a few remarks about 'free play methods' in primary schools, and 'taking to an extreme' 'discovery methods'. The two papers on primary education presented calls for concentration on the literacy and greater planning and teacher-directed work, but had virtually no references to curriculum content (Johnson, 1969; Browne, 1969). The main thrusts of the articles were concerned with the introduction of comprehensive education, student involvement in the management of higher education institutions, and the expansion of higher education. The two side-swipes at the curriculum were the exception: Kingsley Amis (1969) attacked higher education courses that were promoted as 'challenging' or 'exciting' in which 'a non-subject or two, like sociology, social psychology, etc., is thrown in to alleviate the burden of concentrating on a real subject' (p. 10), and Robert Conquest (1969), also attacking some university degree courses, identified 'sociology as the bastion of . . . barbarism'. While acknowledging that there was a 'genuine sociology . . . concerned with social philosophy . . . or . . . a definable set of facts . . . treated with numerical rigour', he dismissed the rest as 'preconceived notions of a notably shallow type' (pp. 17–8). But the significance of these is that, in the general right-wing attack on educational change in the late 1960s, they were lone voices: the great preponderance of complaint was not about the curriculum innovations that were being introduced, but about comprehensivization, allegations of falling standards, the move away from formal examinations, and student representation. The second 'Black Paper' (Cox and Dyson, 1970) was very similar in its approach: the curriculum debate in primary education was confined to modern mathematics and to the teaching of reading (Crawford, 1970; Froome, 1970). There *was* a critical curriculum debate at the time, but this was primarily within academic circles (for example, Dearden, 1969).

Boyson was one of the first to express a concern over the direction of curriculum changes brought about by the innovations of the 1960s and 1970s. In 1975 he claimed there had been a 'breakdown in the "understood" curriculum' in schools, and described 'compulsory education (as) a farce unless all schools follow the same basic syllabus as preparation for society' (Boyson, 1975a). He argued that if schools were to be made more accountable, then there needed to be 'either a nationally enforced curriculum or parental choice or a combination of both' (Boyson, 1975b, p. 141), presciently identifying the distinction that was to emerge between the neo-conservative and the neo-liberal wings of the new right (below). Callaghan, in his speech at Ruskin College the following year, picked up elements of these themes. But while he was concerned with 'new informal methods of teaching' (particularly when these are carried out by those without 'well-qualified hands'), he specifically limited any criticism of curricular diversity: 'I have been very impressed by . . . the variety of courses that are offered . . . there is little wrong with the range and diversity of our courses. But is there sufficient thoroughness and depth in those required in after life to make a living?' (Callaghan, 1976).

While concern about the changing nature of the curriculum was confined among politicians at this stage to Rhodes Boyson, the status of subjects in the curriculum was an issue for HMI and the Department of Education and Science in the late 1970s. The HMI Report on Primary Education made at the first ten-year post-Plowden survey (HMI, 1978) put much emphasis on the need for some specialist subject teachers in primary schools (paras 8.40–8.65), with numerous references to teachers having particular subject knowledge. These were repeated elsewhere. The DES, in its consultative documents issued for the 'Great Debate' that followed Callaghan's speech, noted, in terms expressed more strongly than those of the Prime Minister, 'the curriculum has become overcrowded in response to constantly expanding demands, and arguably the attempt to meet social needs has been at the expense of the more strictly educational' (DES, 1977a, p. 3). This particular quotation is a particularly obvious attempt to equate the 'academic' educational tradition described earlier with 'the strictly educational', at the expense of preparatory or developmental traditions. The Green Paper of the same year, also issued in support of the 'Great Debate', drew attention to 'the background of strongly critical comment in the press and elsewhere on education . . . (that) the curriculum . . . was overloaded with fringe subjects' (DES, 1977b, p. 2). Five years later, the DES was proposing new criteria for courses in initial teacher education, and required that prospective students must have or acquire a 'subject' of study relevant to the age that they would be teaching: it was argued that this would recognise 'teachers' needs for subject expertise if they are to have the confidence and ability to enthuse pupils and respond to their curiosity in their chosen subject fields' (DES, 1983, para 64). Goodson (1989) points to the circularity in this argument: this Circular was also used to prevent most social science graduates taking postgraduate professional teaching qualifications for primary schools, on the grounds that social sciences were not taught in the primary school. The HMI *Survey of Middle Schools* (HMI, 1985c) returned to the need to 'extend teachers' subject knowledge', which Rowland (1987) argued 'may well be interpreted by teachers and others as recommending yet another means in the trend towards a more schematised approach to learning in which the focus is placed even more firmly on the subject matter than the child' (p. 90).

And still the new right was relatively silent on the curriculum. As late as 1981, the contributors to the Social Affairs Unit's *The Pied Pipers of Education* (Anderson *et al*, 1981) were primarily concerned with educational structures and the machinery of education — voucher systems, academic tenure, teacher education, and the like. Only O'Keeffe (1981) raised curricular issues for schools,[2] in his discussion on truancy: interestingly, he suggested that truancy could be analyzed as a rational response to irrelevant curriculum subjects. He identified post-registration truancy, where school children selectively absent themselves from particular lessons, and suggests that children make curricular decisions (to attend lessons) either for reasons of investment in their future employment (for example, technical drawing) or for consumption arising from the intrinsic interest of the material (for example, O'Keeffe suggests, sociology) (p. 33). What is significant is that O'Keeffe writes from the neo-liberal wing (or faction) of the new right, not from the neo-conservative wing (Rawling, 1990).

The major challenge to the school curriculum was in the publication of *The Wayward Curriculum* in 1986, edited by O'Keeffe. This combined O'Keeffe's own libertarian view, that the curriculum should be diverse and that parents should be able to exercise some genuine choice over which subjects were appropriate or useful for their children, with the academic elitism shown by a number of his contributors. O'Keeffe himself attempts to straddle both positions: he is with the neo-liberals that there should be a curricular choice, and that the discipline of such 'market forces' will determine the variety and quantities of the various subjects, but at the same time he is concerned that the current curriculum was no longer adequately transmitting 'the history and culture of society' (O'Keeffe, 1986, p. 12). Some of his contributors show the same confusion: Bantock (1986) argues first that the 'non-academic pupil' should have a curricular offering that 'takes his [sic] needs seriously', arguing that it is 'ideological confusion (that) all must follow the same curriculum (and), must take the same examination' (pp. 20–1); and at the same time asserts that there is a core culture that must be enshrined in the curriculum of all. Other contributors were more decidedly neo-conservative, arguing, for example, that English teaching should explicitly develop first utilitarian skills, and then stress the cultural heritage that English is claimed to enshrine, eschewing notions of personal and social growth that many English teachers were alleged to have adopted — 'in some schools, English has become a ragbag of social topics, a substitute sociology, even a form of therapy' (Barcan, 1986, p. 42).

The position of the neo-liberals was that they generally favoured exposing all elements of education to the disciplines of the market, thus offering a degree of choice to the 'consumer' (though with some lack of clarity as to whether 'the consumer' of education was the pupils, the parents, the employers, or some wider community). Most of them argued this case particularly for a range of structural aspects in the provision of educational services — for the abolition of the LEAs, for vouchers, for open enrolment, and so on. Some also argued for offering a wide range of curricular subjects, and some even extended the argument to suggest that school attendance be voluntary from a much younger age. The neo-liberals did, however, have a special position on sociology, or, more precisely, on sociology-as-it-is-taught in schools and higher education. Sociology, they argued, had become politicized, its classical authorities laid aside, and questions and methods chosen from the neo-Marxist agenda. Thinkers of astonishing mediocrity — Althusser, Raymond Williams, Habermas — have become the standard authorities in this field . . . simply because their conclusions are congenial to the left-wing activist, and cloaked in the mysterious jargon that seems to endow them with authority. (Scruton *et al*, 1985, p. 29)

Regan's contribution to O'Keeffe's book continued this theme: sociology and politics would be useful as practical subjects if their role was simply 'to equip pupils for citizenship of a democracy' (Regan, 1986, p. 130), but in practice they had become both academicized and politicized. While Regan portrayed sociology as an essentially utilitarian subject (teaching practical life skills), O'Keeffe (1981) saw it as academic ('curricular consumption', see above): both agree that, suitably purged of left-wing theorists, it should be allowed to compete in the curricular market place. While these neo-liberal arguments were focused on secondary education, they were also applied to primary schools, where 'sociology' was seen to reside in social studies topic work. Hill (1986) makes this relationship specific in his analysis of urban studies in primary and secondary education in the ILEA.[3]

The Hillgate Group (1986) linked the neo-liberal critique of current sociology with the neo-conservative position, arguing that 'the new "soft" subjects have been nurtured by an inadequate and politically biased sociology, whose colonization of the school curriculum . . . is cause for concern' (p. 5). The neo-conservative case derided sociology not because of the way it was taught, but because of its very existence. They grouped sociology together with other 'unsuitable or dubious newer subjects' (O'Keeffe, 1986, p. 12) — peace studies, urban studies, women's studies, anti-racist education and political education. From a completely different perspective, Whitty (1992) characterizes a rather similar list as 'radical curriculum initiatives' (p. 96). The argument was not merely that these were potentially partisan, but that their presence cluttered up the curriculum to the detriment of the traditional subjects, and thus interfered with the transmission of standard cultural values. This was linked to the neo-conservative critique of egalitarian initiatives in education, particularly over multi-culturalism (for example, Flew, 1986). In terms of the primary school curriculum, project work, discovery methods, and learning through play filled the same role, squeezing out teaching of the core basic skills, and thus compromising standards.

For both groups in the new right the curriculum was an issue that developed late and one that developed as a necessary outcome of their major concerns with the educational system. Chitty (1988 and 1992) identified their activities and influence beginning in the mid-1970s, following the economic crises of 1973 and 1976. But their concerns at this juncture were with structures and standards in education. The neo-liberals argued for greater choice and the creation of a market system that would provide the necessary discipline; and the neo-conservatives saw dangers both to basic standards and to cultural and moral norms in educational emphases on equality, anti-racism, cultural pluralism and moral relativism. The neo-liberals were neutral on the effects of these: the neo-conservatives were agin them. But neither group looked to the curriculum implications of their position until the mid 1980s, even though curriculum reform and definition had been by that time on the agenda of the DES and HMI for the best part of a decade.

The effective moment of change with educational traditions did not come until 1987 (Chitty, 1992, p. 39). The new Secretary of State, Kenneth Baker, signalled his intent to initiate major reforms in the structure of education, allowing schools to opt out of local control, the introduction of some form of league tables to allow 'choice' within some framework of comparability, and some control of the curriculum. All of these were, it was claimed, would encourage an increase in 'standards'. The dilemma that faced the Government was that the demands of the two wings of the new right were irreconcilable on the position of a National Curriculum. The neo-liberals (with whom Thatcher sympathized on this point) wanted minimal prescription, of a core of basic subjects; the neo-conservatives sought a much more prescriptive list that excluded all the suspect social subjects. The neo-liberals were given the market mechanism of parental choice, more open enrolment, and the introduction of new forms of schooling through new city technology schools and the opting out of LEA schools to grant-maintained status. But on the National Curriculum, the neo-conservatives were given a traditional curriculum, with the accent almost entirely on the traditional 'academic' subjects. Technology was admitted as a newcomer. History and geography were reinforced as separate subjects: there was a suggestion in the 1987 consultative document that they might be combined in primary schools (DES/WO, 1987), but this was not pursued.

This accorded with the HMI view of 'subjects' that had been developing over the 1980s: for example, their 1983 Report on Middle Schools had already retreated from the 1980 and 1982 positions of 'history and social studies' and 'learning about people' to a plain 'history and geography' (HMI, 1983; see table 4.1).

The very words 'social' and 'society' were not used in the 1987 consultation papers that preceded the Education Reform Act: there would be no place for social studies in the new National Curriculum.

Models of Curriculum Change

But there was a gap, of a sort. The consultative paper included a possible exception: 'some subjects or themes . . . can be taught through other subjects . . . for example, health education' (DES/WO, 1987, para 18). The body at that time responsible for the development of the school curriculum, the Schools Curriculum Development Committee (SCDC) had only three months earlier set up a curriculum development project 'Educating for Economic Awareness', and the Project Coordinator immediately responded by writing to LEAs and schools working on this, suggesting that economic awareness be included as one such 'cross-curricular theme' — the first time that this term was used (Pearce/EEA, 1987). In the period between the consultation document and the passing of the legislation, the possibility of including certain other curricular areas with some demi-official status was clarified. The

Education Reform Act called for a 'broad and balanced' curriculum, of which the National Curriculum with its ten subjects was but a part. The National Curriculum with religious education formed the 'basic curriculum', defined and prescribed by law. But this in turn was but part of the 'whole curriculum', which schools were obliged to deliver. The National Curriculum Council was to offer guidance to schools on what constituted the difference between the 'whole' and the 'basic' (Ross, 1993, explores this in more depth).

The development of the whole curriculum was slow, and hampered by the DES officials who liaised with the National Curriculum Council (Graham, 1993, pp. 19–21). After many delays, the Curriculum Guidance paper *The Whole Curriculum* (NCC, 1990a) was published, in what Duncan Graham, the NCC's first chair, was to describe as the 'Council's finest hour — it fought for the whole curriculum, and won' (Graham, 1992). Five cross-curricular themes were identified, and further guidance papers were issued on each — *Education for Economic and Industrial Understanding* (NCC, 1990b), *Health Education* (NCC, 1990c), *Careers Education and Guidance* (NCC, 1990d), *Environmental Education* (NCC, 1990e) and *Citizenship* (NCC, 1990f). Three cross-curricular dimensions (equal opportunities, multicultural perspectives and the European dimension) received less attention, as did the cross-curricular skills (communication, numeracy, problem-solving, PSE and information technology). These did seem a signal, at least to some commentators, that a social dimension could exist within the framework of the 1988 Act, and that forms of the radical curriculum initiatives of the 1970s could persist (Whitty, 1992, p. 112).

There was similar hope that the subjects of history and geography might, as they emerged from the subject working parties, have an adequate social dimension (for example, Ross, 1990). But the history group, despite espousing the 'PESC' formula in its interim report — which required every history unit to be explored along political, economic, social-religious and cultural-aesthetic dimensions (DES/WO, 1989) — dropped the emphasis on this in the final report (DES/WO, 1990). Despite his declarations of triumph at ensuring the publication of *The Whole Curriculum,* Graham (1992) was also at times more sanguine about the objectives of the DES: 'what was really wanted was a narrow 'basics' diet, minimally at risk of dilution'.

The primary school curriculum began to reflect this desire. One symptom of this was the way in which a series of subject-based professional journals began to emerge aimed at the primary school teacher reader. Many of these were put out by subject associations, which up until this time had tended to ignore the potential for their subjects in primary education. Now they developed particular missions, interpreting the fact that the nine/ten subject National Curriculum applied to children from the age of 5 as a sign that primary schools were acting as preparatory agents for the subjects in secondary education.

The creation of distinct subjects in the primary school does not necessarily mean that integration and the social studies approaches will be lost. Denis Lawton had much earlier pointed out that 'there is no reason why a curriculum based on disciplines should not be related to the children's own experience and interests. The

Table 3.5:   The growth of subject-specific professional journals in primary education, 1986–91

Date of first publication	Title	Professional association publishing journal
Summer 1986	The Primary Science Review	Association for Science Education
Summer 1989	Primary Geographer	Geography Association
September 1989	Questions: Explanations in Science and Technology 3–13	(Commercial publisher)
October 1990	Primary Historian	Primary History Association (later subsumed by Historical Association)
Summer 1991	Primary Associations: The Journal of Cross-curriculum Primary Practices	National Associate for the Teaching of English (NATE) + Mathematics Association + Association of Teachers of Mathematics + Association for Science Education

fact that so much so-called academic teaching of subjects does tend to neglect children's everyday knowledge . . . is a condemnation of traditional pedagogy or teaching method rather the disciplines themselves as a basis of the curriculum' (Lawton, 1975, p. 85). Lawton was responding to philosophers such as Hirst and Pring, who had suggested that the forms of knowledge that constituted the curriculum were beyond culture and history — Hirst in particular saw the curriculum in terms of the structure and organization of knowledge, which by his analysis was not culturally based, but in some way universal (Hirst, 1965; Pring, 1972). But disciplines are themselves socially created, and in flux. Each is a response to collective experiences and interests, both in terms of the content or subject matter and of the nature of enquiry within the discipline. However, if definition of the curriculum subject is left to those outside the discipline, and in particular to those who seek to impose a particular ideology, then what may well be imposed is the folk-memory of the discipline, the particular interests and specific experiences of an earlier generation. 'Rarely have the fundamentals of curriculum construction been so palpably political in nature' (Hargreaves, 1994a, p. 4).

Conclusion

The description and practice of the social elements of the curriculum has changed radically with the imposition of the National Curriculum. One view might be that they were, in effect, disposed of: firstly subject to 'benign neglect', then frozen out of discussion, and finally legislated into oblivion. A counter view might be that they were translated into other disciplines, and other forms, by interested professionals acting in a subversive manner to colonize the new curriculum. But an alternative might be that many of the themes and concerns that were hitherto located within the social parts of the curriculum were subtly reformulated and reintroduced to the curriculum in the cross-curricular themes.

This alternative will be explored in the next chapter: the idea of the social that is espoused in the cross-curricular themes is not the same as that which was lost in the 1980s. There was a significant shift to the emphasis of the role and responsibility of the individual, at the expense of group or social action. As Hargreaves (1994b) has recently noted of teacher's work and culture, 'the preoccupation with the personal, and the relative neglect of the social and political is a chronic feature of our post-modern social condition'.

> The irony . . . is that now, when the practice of curriculum reform has rarely been more profoundly social, systematic and political in nature (in the pervasive preoccupations of national curricula, subject knowledge and the like), most of the curriculum field remains anachronistically anchored to issues of interpretation and implementation. (Hargreaves, 1994a, p. 3)

Notes

1 Personal communication with the author, summer 1981.
2 Dawson (1981), in the same volume, criticized the inclusion of the sociology of education within the curriculum of student teachers: 'it is more than unnecessary, it is harmful. It unfits teachers to teach' (p. 43), and argues that the way that it was taught expressed 'values inimical to education and industrial enterprise' (p. 44).
3 The specific questioning of the social sciences was not confined to the school curriculum. The Council that had funded research into the social sciences had been the Social Science Research Council. Sir Keith Joseph, when Secreatry of State for Education and Science, anguished publically and at length as to whether the study of society could be properly called a science. Eventually he concluded that it could not, and the Coumcil was redesignated as the Economic and Social Research Council in 1984. Nigel Foreman, a Conservative MP with a social science background, later suggested that Joseph, with Margaret Thatcher, had (erroneously) 'equate(d) the social sciences with social engineering', and has swept both away as part of their campaign against the statist and corporatist assumptions of the 1960s and 1970s (Foreman, 1991). Joseph had a mild obsession about the need to teach all children what he saw as the economic realities of life, and initiated the process that led to the Educating for Economic Awareness Programme under the Schools Curriculum Development Council and then the National Curriculum Council: Craft (in chapter 8) describes some of the outcomes of this and its relationship with the NCC curriculum guidance paper *Education for Economic and Industrial Understanding* (NCC, 1990b).

Chapter 4

The Whole Curriculum, the National Curriculum and Social Studies

Alistair Ross

In the National Curriculum Council's guidance paper, the Whole Curriculum was defined as something greater than the National Curriculum (NCC, 1990a). It was admitted from the outset that the nine or ten foundation subjects alone could not provide the breadth necessary to meet the requirements of Section 1 of the Education Reform Act —

> to provide a broad and balanced curriculum which
> * promotes the spiritual, moral, cultural, mental and physical development of pupils at the school and of society
> * prepares pupils for the opportunities, responsibilities and experiences of adult life. (p. 1)

The realization that the ten-subject National Curriculum alone could not meet this brief led to the addition of religious education as part of the 'Basic Curriculum', and then the creation of the device of the 'Whole Curriculum' — something broader than the Basic Curriculum, to be defined by the new National Curriculum Council. The first Chair of the Council, Duncan Graham, has described how the Whole Curriculum Working Party was established, and struggled against obfuscatory DES officials to identify and define the 'cross-curricular elements' (Graham, 1992 and 1993). The elements were described as 'ingredients which tie together the broad education of the individual and augment what comes from the basic curriculum' (NCC, 1990a, p. 2), of which dimensions, skills and themes were identified. Although there was a promise to provide further guidance on all of these, only the five cross-curricular themes were elaborated upon in subsequent guidance papers. Of these five, it was claimed that 'it is reasonable to assume at this stage that they are essential parts of the whole curriculum' (*ibid.*, p. 4). The status of the themes is thus ambiguously presented: they are statutory where they are part of a National Curriculum programme, but 'other aspects, whilst not statutory, are clearly required if schools are to provide an education which promotes the aims defined in Section 1 of the Education Reform Act' (NCC, 1989, para 16). It is not clear how the requirement to comply with an Act can be regarded as non-statutory.

The five themes — and quite possibly religious education — represent a grouping of areas all of which have social characteristics, so that they could be considered as permitting the social studies curriculum that is so clearly lacking in the foundation subjects of the National Curriculum. Clearly, many teachers will elect to treat them in that way (Whitty, 1992), but there is also evidence that most schools have been under such pressure from the foundation subjects that they have given little or no attention or classroom time to the themes (Jamieson and Harris, 1992; Rowe *et al.*, 1993). If the composition of the whole curriculum is the only possible way for the social subjects to be maintained within the school curriculum, it is essential that some clarity is thrown on what the cross-curricular themes and other elements represent. The argument of this chapter is that although they may well represent the social — the missing link of the National Curriculum — the way in which they have been framed offers a subtly new and distorted version of the social, and one that has been constructed for two particular political ends. Firstly, they attempt to satisfy neo-liberal demands for a redefinition of the relationship of rights, duties and responsibilities between the individual and society. Secondly, that when the cross-curricular themes are taken with the foundation subjects, they reinvent neo-conservative aspirations of a national tradition.

How should the concept of this additional material, judged necessary to make the National Curriculum 'whole', be analyzed? The various models that Goodson suggested (1987, see previous chapter) allow some alternative schemata. The academic model, for example, could be used to view many of the cross-curricular themes as simply an alternative way of including some traditional (and some not-so-traditional) subjects that were overlooked when the original list of foundation subjects was being drawn up:

Economic and industrial understanding	Economics
Health education	Public health
Careers education and guidance	—
Environmental education	Environmental studies
Citizenship	Politics/civics

The utilitarian model, on the other hand, could explain the cross-curricular themes in a quite different way. While the traditional disciplines represented in the foundation subjects represented the academic tradition, the themes represented necessary social competencies or life-skills. Each is concerned with empowering the individual with the abilities necessary to be effective in adult (and pre-adult) life. This may seem a more accurate description than the 'academic' model of a collection of left-overs, and one that may, despite the hierarchy usually associated with the academic (subject/ examinable) — utilitarian (non-subject/non-examinable) divide, allow the possibility of giving independent status to the cross-curricular themes.

Each of the cross-curricular themes is concerned with some practical aspect of everyday life. They represent strategies to make each individual able to manage these aspects, to empower them to take some responsibility for them. The NCC was rather coy about what the themes might have in common, and managed to describe them avoiding the word society: they were 'elements that enrich the educational experience of pupils' (NCC, 1989, para 15), and which 'explore the values and beliefs which influence the individual and his or her relationship with others and the wider world; . . . help pupils respond to their present lives and prepare them for work and adult life; emphasize practical activities, decision making, learning through experience, and the development of close links between the school and the wider world' (para 17). The emphasis within each of the themes is to stress the role of the individual, rather than any corporate role: duties, responsibilities and obligations (of the individual to the state) are placed before any rights or expectations the individual might have of the state.

Because the cross-curricular themes are designed to develop and exercise practical skills and competencies, rather than the more remote cognitive attainment targets of the National Curriculum, this can in many ways be seen as a more invidious attempt at social engineering than the jockeying over the inclusion or not of various pieces of subject matter in various foundation subjects. It will be argued in the first section of this chapter that these themes provided a pattern with the potential to construct an aggregation of individuals, all taught to see their primary communal functions as being to assume maximum responsibility for their own individual needs, and only being required to contribute a residuum to the commonwealth. Although words like 'society' are very largely avoided, it will be seen when each theme is examined in turn that the themes have been used to construct an understanding of 'society' very different from that which has developed in modern times. In this sense, the themes are radical and even post-modern.

But the second part of this chapter will argue that the Whole Curriculum — the statutory foundation subjects and all the various additions — also had another social intention, which was to reiterate the supposed forms of the traditional English or British nation (the confusion between the two, as will be shown, is not mine). This may seem to contradict the earlier contention that the purpose was to create a changed relationship between the individual and their society. Is it possible for the same programme to be responsible for both change and tradition? However, it will be argued that the sense of national heritage that is being engendered is largely — if perhaps not wholly — an invented fiction, designed to clothe the frame of the post-welfare state in what appear to be the robes of antiquity. The sense of nationality that had existed, by-and-large, up to some thirty to forty years ago was itself a myth. This myth had collapsed from a whole variety of pressures: the development of consumerism, the collapse of full employment, the growth of a plural society, changes in domestic/family structures and the way in which other nations had so clearly demonstrated their greater economic and political powers. Compounded with self-doubt about the characteristics of post-modernity and the growth of moral relativism, the new sense of nationhood offered in our 'national' curriculum can be seen as an attempted atavistic reaffirmation of national identity through the invention of a fabricated tradition. Neo-liberal radicalism and neo-conservative nostalgia comfortably combine in the contrivances of the new society of the cross-curricular themes.

Alistair Ross

New Social Contract in the Curriculum

When the Department of Education and Science issued a *Draft Statement of Principles on the Teaching of Politically Controversial Issues in Schools and Colleges* in 1986 it identified political education as 'one of the principal functions of education'. The press release that accompanied the publication referred to the need for pupils to understand the 'rights and duties' of citizenship — except that those two words have been carefully deleted, and the words 'duties and rights' substituted, in a hand very similar to that of the signatory, Sir Keith Joseph, Secretary of State (DES, 1986).

Though the change pre-dates the construction of the cross-curricular themes, it is indicative of the changed emphasis that the Conservative right aspired to establish. The cross-curricular themes were drawn up by the Whole Curriculum Working Party of the NCC: taken together, they encourage pupils to 'explore the values and beliefs which influence the individual and his or her relationship with others and the wider world' in a very particular way. The individual is generally portrayed as being responsible for ensuring his or her own well-being (acting to preserve their own property, health, and welfare, making themselves fit for and seeking employment, and owing duties towards the state), and is mirrored by the reciprocal view of society and the state as having minimal obligations to preserve rights or to provide services.

The first set of guidance to be published for a cross-curricular theme was *Education for Economic and Industrial Understanding* (NCC, 1990b). It is possible to construct a very direct link between the concern to include 'economic realities' in the curriculum expressed by Sir Keith Joseph in a consultative letter on economic awareness, of March 1985, and the publication of the Curriculum Guidance document in 1990. Sir Keith's Circular suggested a particular list of items be included under the heading of economic awareness, which reveals more of his preoccupations:

> ... some understanding of such matters as the operation of supply and demand, price, quality, profit and loss, competition and monopoly; such aspects as the creation of the nation's private and public wealth, customer satisfaction, enterprise, management and productivity and taxation ...
> (quoted in SCDC/EEA, 1987)

Many of the responses to the consultative letter pointed to the narrowness of the range of topics: nevertheless, the Schools Curriculum Development Council held a Consultative Conference on Economic Awareness in July 1986. The report (SCDC, 1986) suggested wider, more liberal, definitions of the economic, including, for example, the need to equip children to be consumers and citizens, as well as producers, and led to the SCDC project 'Educating for Economic Awareness' (EEA). Funded by both SCDC and the Department of Trade and Industry, the project ran from 1987 to 1990, in the latter part under the NCC. When Kenneth Baker published detailed proposals for the National Curriculum, it offered no place for economic awareness, but it was later able to emerge as a cross-curricular theme, with industry added as a somewhat strange bed-fellow (Blyth, 1994). Within this incorporation, the 'Educating for Economic Awareness' project became largely subverted to preparing and drafting the *Education for Economic and Industrial Understanding* document. But the clear line of descent can be seen, from Joseph's obsession with what he saw as a lack of capitalistic *virtu* in the nation's schooling to the eventual cross-curricular theme to the cross-curricular theme that in many places is no more than a front for inculcating monetarist economics in the young — despite the coalition of interests that has temporarily masked this ideological origin (Blyth, 1990).

The foreword of the document outlines its purpose: to '. . . prepare (pupils) for life and work in a rapidly changing, economically competitive world' (NCC, 1990b, foreword). In the first pages of the document it becomes clear that it is based on a mixture of neo-liberal and pre-Keynesian economics. Throughout, it accepts the traditional economists' assumptions that economic activity is determined by the individual decision maker. This person is presumed to make rational choices, in a spirit of (enlightened) self-interest. The document stresses the active contribution to the national economy that can be made by the individual actor — for example, 'pupils will face choices about *how they contribute to the economy* through their work' (*ibid.*, p. 1, my emphasis). We are reminded in several places that Britain is an advanced industrial nation: we need this theme, we are told, 'to help them contribute to an industrialized, highly technological society' (*ibid.*). Comparing our industrial output and technological capacity to that of other nations, perhaps it is necessary that we are assured of this assertion. Why must they contribute? Because 'the nation's prosperity depends more than ever on . . . knowledge, understanding and skills'. Thus *national* self-interest determines that children should be prepared in this way, and be taught that their role as producers will be their 'contribution'. It is as a secondary feature that they are also prepared to make decisions as consumers ('how to organize their finances and which goods and services to spend money on') — and the act of consumption is also, of course, of importance to an economy dependent on consumerism.

We are told that it is 'to meet this challenge [that] pupils need to understand enterprise and wealth creation and develop entrepreneurial skills'. This is not true: neither these understandings nor this skill are required by most children in order for them to become producers or consumers. Perhaps the intention was not so much that people 'understand' enterprise and wealth creation, but a desire that the population appreciate the need for the 'entrepreneur and wealth-creator' to be allowed free rein to get on with it, untrammelled by regulation or other considerations, and be given proper respect by the rest of the population: it is teaching acquiescence to the 'trickle-down' theory of wealth distribution. Even accepting the ideological premises of the government, entrepreneurial skills only need to be developed in a very small proportion of the population as a whole. Most people do not need the skills *per se*. However, it may be convenient if they develop the attitude that the outcomes of the application of these skills are so important that those exercising them should be held in proper esteem and privilege.

The language of the document is very carefully chosen (as it is in all the themes). Words like 'balance' and 'controversial' are used, so that it apparently seems that there is encouragement to explore a diversity of views. Few examples of such diversity are indicated to the teacher, and the 'choices' that are offered are largely illusory. For example, given the premises of the 'need' for economic education, outlined in the previous paragraph, what diversity of views can result when industrial relations are considered (which is one of the few examples given of a diverse issue that might be considered). The document exemplifies the notion of 'balance' by suggesting teachers contrast 'the needs of producers' to 'the rights of consumers', when in the national socioeconomic context these two groups very frequently are in an implicit conspiracy against the needs of third-world producers abroad, or of minorities and the less powerful at home.

Much of the detailed provisions of the document are less contentious. There are important omissions — of the nature of property, for example (see the chapter by Ahier in this volume). It is not economic and industrial understanding in itself that is suspect, but the ideological framework within which it is set. This determines the overall ethos of the approach, which is to stress the need for the individual to produce and consume, to make decisions that accept the 'rational' system of the market, and to understand that (despite their own hard work and effort) the entrepreneurial business person will be properly rewarded with far greater wealth, and that they should accept this.

The second cross-curricular theme is health education. Only a decade ago this would have seemed an unlikely area for sociopolitical controversy. However, in areas in which health education can particularly impact on the lives of young people — sex and drugs — there is a strong moral agenda being set by the neo-conservative right (perhaps unsurprisingly, the neo-liberal and libertarian right have not been allowed influence on these issues) (Stears *et al.* take up these issues in detail in chapter 9). But what is of concern here is the way in which the health education document again shifts the emphasis from communal responsibility for health matters to the obligation of the individual to be dutiful in preserving their own health. Health education 'protects pupils from illness and risk, and promotes the development of healthy lifestyles' (NCC, 1990c, foreword).

The overriding focus of *Health Education* is on individual choice and responsibility (uncontentious in itself), but this must be set within the contemporary context of health-consumerism. Children are to be educated so that they 'acquire the ability to make healthy choices' and 'establish healthy patterns of behaviour' (*ibid.*, p. 1), but it is not acknowledged that they will be attempting to make these choices within a competitive market that freely promotes alternative visions. Sometimes these are alternatives to healthy living (alcohol and tobacco consumption, for example), and sometimes alternative health-related life-styles are advocated (in aspects of diet, weight control and exercise, for example). The onus is thrown on the individual to make choices, but in a situation in which information is manipulated and presented to make informed choice near-impossible.

Individual aspects of health are emphasized. 'Essential features of health education are ... the physical social and mental well-being of the individual. It ... involves the development of skills which will help individuals use their knowledge effectively' (*ibid.*). Why is it necessary to stress the role of individuals in responsibility for health? The reasons given concern the creation of national wealth: 'healthy living must be an issue of major importance . . . as society can be affected by one health crisis after another. People's health is . . . one of the most important resources required for the creation of any other kind of wealth.' Much less emphasis is given to the responsibilities of society as a whole, either to provide health care, or to control, through legislation and regulation, environmental health dangers. But while everyone is exposed to health hazards, the document makes extravagant claims that 'individuals can do much to lessen those risks and to improve the quality of their lives'. If 'everyone' is at risk, what has become of the notion of 'public' health, or that society as a whole has an obligation to regulate and control risks and hazards common to all? But a regulatory ethos is inimicable to the neo-liberal ideology that pervades the curriculum guidance document.

As in so many areas of social life, the document is part of the movement that seeks to make the individual the author of his/her own misfortune:

> . . . much unnecessary illness injury and death is caused by specific behaviour patterns . . . established during childhood and adolescence', and the role of schools is to 'bring about positive changes which are demonstrated in responsible attitudes and behaviour'. (*ibid.*, p. 2)

Not that it is always the individual who is to blame: society itself, unsurprisingly, can be another villain: 'during adolescence . . . skills concerned with resisting social pressures . . . can prove to be as important'. (*ibid.*, p. 3)

Nine components are identified as the framework for health education, and in each of these there is a far greater emphasis on the individual's responsibilities and duties than there is on society's obligations to the individual, and virtually nothing on any rights that the individual might have to health care. Table 4.1 identifies a range of references that stress the individual's duties and responsibilities in the field. There are some other references — for example, to knowing about health agencies and the NHS, but the pervasive thrust is towards individualism.

The third cross-curricular theme document is *Careers Education and Guidance*. Again, it is Duncan Graham's foreword to the document that emphasizes the duty of the individual: careers education and guidance is 'a prerequisite to pupils making well-informed educational, vocational and training choices' (NCC, 1990d, foreword). The implied corollary of this statement might be that if pupils do not find careers and employment, this is a consequence of poorly-informed choices, but the document is very careful *not* to suggest that employment is the objective of careers education. Instead, pupils are to be prepared for 'the opportunities, responsibilities and experiences of adult life . . . (and) for the choices, changes and transitions affecting their future education, training and life as adults' (*ibid.*, p. 1). 'Opportunities' embraces employment, 'responsibilities' refer to keeping in employment (if one has work) or seeking employment (if one has not), and 'experience' is an all-embracing term for both work and unemployment.

Table 4.1: Stresses on individual responsibilities within **Health Education**

Component of Health Education	Reference to individual responsibilities
Substance use and misuse	'. . . consider the effects . . . on themselves . . . and . . . make informed and healthy decisions . . .' (p. 4); 'know how to make . . . choices . . . resisting pressure from friends and others' (p. 14); '. . . personal responsibility for decisions' (p. 16); 'recognize that individuals are responsible for choices they make about drug use' (p. 18)
Sex education	'. . . understand individuals are in charge of and responsible for their own bodies. . . . skills and attitudes . . . to manage their relationships in a responsible . . . manner' (p. 4); '. . . the importance of personal choice' (p. 16)
Family life education	'. . . the central role of the family as an institution . . .' (p. 4)
Safety	'. . . accept responsibility for the safety of themselves and others . . .' (p. 14); '. . . know that individuals play an important part in the maintenance of safe, healthy environments' (p. 16)
Health-related exercise	'. . . to make positive choices about their own responsibilities' (p. 5)
Food and nutrition	'. . . pupils to make healthy choices' (p. 5)
Personal hygiene	'. . . personal cleanliness helps to reduce transmission of communicable diseases . . .' (p. 5); 'accept responsibility for personal cleanliness . .' (p. 15)
Environmental aspects	'. . . know that individuals . . . have some responsibility for care [of the environment]' (p. 13); 'accept responsibility for and be able to justify personal choices and decisions about health' (p. 20)
Psychological aspects	'. . . the development of self-awareness . . . necessary to act' (p. 5); '. . . understand that actions have consequences for oneself and others' (p. 15)

Source: NCC, 1990c

The responsibilities of the individual are brought out in most of the five strands described in *Careers Education and Guidance*. The first of these is 'self': pupils must develop a knowledge of themselves, including their strengths, abilities and limitations. Such self-knowledge will usefully excuse a whole variety of future career experiences: the more the unemployed are aware of their own limitations and lack of strengths and abilities, the more they will realize that they are responsible for their own situation. Similarly, the second strand of 'roles' relates to pupils' 'position and expectations in relation to family, community and employment' (*ibid.*, p. 2). This form of expression allows for a fairly wide latitude of possible outcomes. The third strand, 'work', is also very broadly defined, as 'application of productive effort, including paid employment and unpaid work in the community and at home'. This seems to be asking schools to ensure that their pupils learn to acept that whatever their future roles might be, they simply need to make 'productive effort' and accept any particular context in which it occurs (as employee, volunteer or home-maker). The fourth strand of 'career' is more limited, for though this is concerned with the 'sequence of roles undertaken through working life' (which, given the earlier definition of work is all-embracing) it then refers to 'the personal success, rewards and enjoyment it brings'. Careers are therefore limited to only certain kinds of work, unless schools are expected to show children that a 'sequence of roles' that includes involuntary unemployment brings with it certain 'personal success, rewards and enjoyment'. But these attitudes are probably included within the fifth strand, 'transition', where children develop 'qualities and skills which enable [them] to adjust to and cope with change'.

Environmental education is the NCC's fourth cross-curricular theme. This seems to be a particularly perverse area in which to put such stress on the responsibility of the individual, especially in a global and market-based political economy. The environmental consequences of a myriad of consumer-producer relationships *can* be of global significance, yet on the level of the individual transaction the outcomes are apparently small-scale, insignificant and distant in effect. Environmental protection seems to be the area *par excellence* in which national and supranational agreement and regulation is required to limit the individual's immediate self-interest. But *Environmental Education* (NCC, 1990e) asks schools to ensure children are led to 'informed concern for and active participation in resolving environmental problems' (foreword). This may be sufficient in terms of litter control, but does not seem to be a very realistic approach to global warming or to acidic rain. To state, as this document does, that 'young people are (the environment's) custodians, and will be responsible for the world' (p. 1) is either hyperbole or an attempt to provide an alibi for corporate, governmental or intergovernmental action.

Environmental education also '. . . has strong links with education for citizenship as it introduces pupils to political processes and encourages them to take on social responsibility' (*ibid.*, p. 4). *Education for Citizenship* (NCC, 1990f) was the guidance document for the final cross-curricular theme. The slimmest of all the guidance documents, it nevertheless puts the greatest stress on the duties and responsibilities of the individual as antecedent to rights. Indeed, in the first nine pages there are thirteen references to the 'duties, responsibilities and rights' or the 'responsibilities and rights' of individuals. There are references to rights in isolation, but these are few in number, and we are clearly informed that 'rights are accompanied by duties and responsibilities. This component ['Being a Citizen'] helps pupils to recognise and understand the nature of their duties and responsibilities, both present and future' (*ibid.*, p. 6). Contrast this with the objectives of the French civic education programme for secondary schools of 1985:

> Civic education presupposes an understanding of the rules of democratic life, how they were bought into being, an understanding of the institutions with their historic background and *a reflection on the conditions and the means by which respect of the individual human being and his rights is exercised*: by tolerance and solidarity, by refusal of racist behaviour, in a wish to live together under democratic rules. It should *enable pupils to*

> *respond to questions about rights.* (quoted in Corbett, 1990, pp. 138–9, my
> emphasis)

Why do the British cross-curricular themes all place such emphasis on the responsibilities of individuals? Taken together, the Curriculum Guidance documents
read like the panic-stricken response of an elite to the rising political demands from
a disempowered underclass. Clearly, in any polity in which power is not distributed
equally, those with power will seek to emphasize the duties that those with less
power owe the state, and to remind them of their responsibilities. But most mature
democracies are more relaxed in their acceptance of the trade-off between the rights
and the duties of citizens than the near-paranoia shown here. The social contract
that is being suggested in *Education for Citizenship* is not that of Locke and Rousseau,
but an attempt to resurrect Hobbes's Leviathan, in which the contract is between
the governed, and is a contract to equally subject themselves to the duties and
responsibilities that they owe the government.

But one of the most curious aspects of *Education for Citizenship* is that it
never informs its readers of what they are citizens. Admittedly, the 'National'
Curriculum Council was itself something of an absurdity, in that it dealt with two
countries — England and Wales — neither of which is a political state. But there
are a mere eight references to what state this citizenship might refer, all of which
are extraordinarily mixed and tangential (my emphasis).

'No school in *England* would deny its responsibilities for educating pupils
for citizenship' (p. 1)

'*Britain* as a multicultural, multiethnic, multifaith and multilingual society' (p. 6)

'The means by which *Britain* . . . ensure(s) the rights of . . . citizens' (p. 7)

'*Britain's* political system . . .' (p. 7)

'The roles of the *UK* government . . .' (p. 9)

'Understand . . . that the laws of the *UK* are influenced by European
laws . . .' (p. 19)

the 'links *Britain* has with communities elsewhere in the world . . .' (p. 26)

'the welfare state in twentieth-century *Britain*' (p. 27)

There is also a mixture of references to 'national communities', 'national organizations', and 'the nation'. But it requires no constitutional lawyer to point out that
Britain is currently a mere geographical expression, and that England is not the

United Kingdom. There are twice as many references to the European Community than there are to the state of which the readers of this document are citizens.

In part this confusion must stem from the muddled status of the National Curriculum that only operates in a fraction of the political state. In the other parts of the United Kingdom, other cross-curricular themes operate. In Wales, the Education Reform Act applies the same National Curriculum as in England, but it is called *Curriculum Cymreig*, which translates as 'the Welsh Curriculum'. There are still five cross-curricular themes, four of them with the same titles as in England (but with different Curriculum Guidance documents, and with different emphases). However, the English 'Citizenship' is replaced with the Welsh 'Community Understanding'. In Scotland, there is no National Curriculum, but a Curriculum Development Programme, in which there is a much looser definition of 'the social subjects' (SOED, 1993). In Northern Ireland there can be no 'National' Curriculum, because of the nationalist overtones that this would carry. Instead there is the Common Curriculum, with four cross-curricular themes enforced by a Statutory Order: education for mutual understanding, cultural heritage, information technology and health education (DENI, 1992; Marriott, 1994). And the United Kingdom also includes the self-governing dependencies of the Isle of Man, Guernsey and Jersey, where the National Curriculum has no legal status: it appears to be followed in a locally modified way by default in the first two dependencies, but Jersey has a formal Jersey Curriculum (Blyth, 1993).

Given this confusion, it might be useful to stand back from a more narrow focus on the social subjects as seen through the cross-curricular themes, and examine what social description is given to the nation in the National Curriculum/ Curriculum Cymreig/Curriculum Development Programme/Common Curriculum/ Jersey Curriculum.

The Invention of a National Heritage Through the Curriculum

There is a significant ambiguity in the title of Linda Colley's study *Britons: Forging the Nation 1707–1837* (1992). She points out that the concept of the British nation is of considerably less antiquity than is commonly depicted in recent and contemporary political rhetoric. Indeed, the current formulation of the United Kingdom is just 73 years old, dating from when the Irish Free State was unfettered from the former United Kingdom. That earlier state was itself only formed by the union of Great Britain and Ireland in 1800, while Great Britain, formed by combining the Kingdom of England and the Principality of Wales (themselves combined in 1536) with Scotland was created in 1707. Colley scrutinizes the various strategies that were employed to create the new nation of England, Wales and Scotland after 1707, and the ways in which a sense of being a Briton was constructed. In that there was no pre-existing national identity, the nation was forged, both in the sense of being hammered out into a single object and in the sense of being an invented counterfeit.

The concept that nations and states are invented, rather than being organic, is not new: *The Invention of Tradition* (Hobsbawm and Ranger, 1983) brought together several examples of seemingly long-standing national traditions that were shown not only to be of very recent origin, but also to be deliberate contrivances, including case studies from Scotland (Trevor-Roper) and Wales (Morgan). Hobsbawm points out in his introduction to this collection that

> invented traditions . . . are highly relevant to that comparatively recent historical innovation, the 'nation', with its associated phenomena: nationalism, the nation-state, national symbols, histories and the rest. All these rest on exercises in social engineering which are often deliberate and always innovative. (p. 13)

Colley defines the characteristics that were selected as the basis for the new nation in the eighteenth century, and it will be possible to analyze the twentieth century National Curriculum in very similar terms. The debate that has surrounded what should or should not be included in the various subjects of the National Curriculum, together with the problematic redefinition of individualism and communality in the cross-curricular themes, suggests that the state is currently attempting to reinvent its concept of nationhood, in part through the definition of a 'national' curriculum. This reinvention is partly through a selective retelling of the various myths that Colley shows to have been employed in the eighteenth century, when the state was first invented, and partly by asserting the new relationship between the individual (with more responsibilities and duties) and society (offering rather fewer rights in return), as described in the previous section of this chapter.

Some of the most contentious parts of the National Curriculum debate have been over the inclusion of aspects of cultures that define identity: usually of a 'British' culture (particularly in the history and the English literature selections), sometimes of a less defined Western or European culture (for example, in the majority of the examples given in art and music). The debate over religious education, and its 'predominantly Christian' nature can be seen as part of this same movement. This contention is one of the symptoms of a lack of certainty and of identity, and the emphatic inclusions and definitions within the various Orders is a response to the insecurity in contemporary society. This is true both of the original Orders, that came from the NCC consultation processes in the 1988–91 period, and of the proposed revisions made in the Dearing review (SCAA, 1994a). The appeals about the inclusion of the 'British' characteristics of the history curriculum, and the debates over which poetry, drama and novels (particularly from before 1900) should be included in the English curriculum are evidence enough that the old order is not holding:

> The very appearance of movements for the defence or revival of traditions, 'traditionalist' or otherwise, indicates such a break. . . . where the old ways are alive, traditions need to be neither revived nor invented. (Hobsbawm, 1983, pp. 7–8)

It is argued that such a moment of invention is occurring now, because the

> ... factors that provided for the forging of a British nation in the past have largely ceased to operate. ... no more can Britons reassure themselves of their distinct and privileged identity by contrasting themselves with impoverished Europeans (real or imaginary), or by exercising authority over manifestly alien peoples. (Colley, 1992, p. 374)

The older certainties have evaporated, and contemporary society is pluralist in its composition and in its values. The 'old' strengths that Colley shows were used in the construction of the idea of the nation can be compared with the invention of the current National Curriculum, in which the 'new' strengths are invented afresh. Such moments of invention should be expected, Hobsbawm (1983) reminds us,

> ... to occur more frequently when a rapid transformation of society weakens or destroys the social patterns for which 'old' traditions had been designed, producing new ones to which they were not applicable, or when such old traditions and their institutional carriers and promulgators no longer prove sufficiently adaptable and flexible, or are otherwise eliminated ... (p. 4)

The processes by which national identity is defined are not necessarily the positive identification of a set of shared characteristics. It is just as possible to define the nation, or any other social group, by a process of exclusion, of contrasting it against 'the other'. The nation is defined not as having particular characteristics, not as behaving in a certain way, but simply as *not being the other*. In his study of the history of nationality and identity in the Pyrenees, Peter Sahlins (1989) pointed out that

> ... national identity, like ethnic or communal identity, is contingent and relational: it is defined by the social or territorial boundaries drawn to distinguish the collective self and its implicit negation, the other. (p. 271)

Colley (1992) argues that Britons in the eighteenth century constructed their national identity in precisely this manner, by defining themselves as being not Europeans, not Catholic, not subjects within the Empire, as much as they identified their own particular characteristics. The exclusion of 'the other' was an essential element in the forging of the nation. She identifies four major foundations to the construction: Protestantism, the profits of trade and commerce, the peripheries of empire, and the power structure of the new state. These no longer hold:

> as an invented nation heavily dependent for its *raison d'être* on a broadly Protestant culture, on the threat and tonic of recurrent war, particularly war with France, and in the triumphs, profits and Otherness represented by a massive overseas empire, Britain is bound now to be under tremendous pressure ... It has had to adjust to the loss of its empire ... Protestantism is now only a residual part of its culture ... it is fast becoming part of an

> increasingly federal Europe . . . The Other . . . is no longer available to make
> Britons feel that — by contrast — they have an identity in common. The
> predictable result has been a revival of internal divisions. (pp. 6–7)

The response to these pressures has been to devise new 'traditions' that define the
nation in a new way, but to do so by constructing, in the late twentieth century,
very similar pillars to those identified by Linda Colley as having been fabricated
in the eighteenth century. These constructions have, perhaps not surprisingly, found
their way into the National Curriculum that was being manufactured at the same
time. Not only has the curriculum been used to transmit a particularist cultural
heritage, one that embellishes the artifice of the nation in the past, but it has also
been constructed to re-invent a very similar set of foundations.

Protestantism and Religious Education

The first of the cornerstones of the new eighteenth century British nation that
Colley describes is Protestantism. This was not a religious identity as such, but a
mark of distinction from the Catholic other in Europe, and particularly in France.
It marked out the dominant new order in Great Britain, against both the external
enemies of the state and the potential internal dissidents of the old faith, the Jacobites.
Protestantism was also used to affirm the moral superiority of the British, to both
bind them together and to mark the nation out as in some way the elect of God.
As Colley points out, Britain was 'not a confessional state in any narrow sense.
Instead, its laws proclaimed it to be a pluralist yet aggressively Protestant polity'
(*ibid.*, p. 19). This sectarian device was used to unite the majority of individuals
into a new grouping, by emphasizing an element that they had in common, but
had not previously regarded as a mark of unity. There was a cost, particularly to
the Catholic minorities, but although

> the Protestant construction of a British identity involved the unprivileging
> of the minorities who would not conform . . . there are few more effective
> ways of bonding together a highly disparate people than by encouraging
> it to unite against its own and other outsiders. (p. 53)

It was also used to mark out the nation as different, and imbue it with a sense of
divine providence, almost as the new Israel. As the words of *Rule Britannia* make
clear it was '. . . at *heaven's* command [when Britain] arose from out the azure main'.[1]
Protestantism was also practised in a way that gave an important sense of contrived
historical identity to the patriots of the new nation. A wide variety of Protestant
almanacs were published, often in very large quantities. These reminded ordinary
people of a large number of anniversaries to be celebrated: for example, *The
Protestant Almanack* of 1700, published in London, reminded its readers of the
time '. . . since Our first delivery from Popery by K. Edward VI; Our second

deliverance from Popery by Q. Elizabeth; The horrid design of the Gun-Powder Plot . . .': each date was given to be remembered during the year. David Cressy (1989) described this reiteration of past tribulations as though 'time past was a soap opera written by God, a succession of warning disasters and providential escapes acted out afresh each year as a way of reminding themselves who they were'. This has particular parallels with contemporary society, and the development of a 'heritage industry' that moulds and retails views of the past that are at best semifictional. A Ministry of National Heritage devises public anniversaries of past tribulations in precisely the same way as did the Protestant almanacs three centuries before. For the new Britons of the eighteenth century, 'Protestantism . . . gave (them) . . . a sense of place in history and a sense of worth. It allowed them to feel pride in such advantages as they genuinely did enjoy, and helped them endure when hardship and danger threatened. It gave them identity' (Colley, 1992, p. 53).

In contemporary Britain, the reemphasis of a 'predominantly Christian' society has taken on the mantle assumed by Protestantism in that earlier period. This conception has the same lack of confessional precision as did Protestantism: it is considered to be sufficient to unite the majority of the population, and to distinguish it from 'the other' — in this case, an other that is portrayed as the fundamentalism or fanaticism of other religions. And, just as before, it also conveniently demarcates a minority 'enemy within', of other faiths and of those with no faith, who can be seen as subversives. The imposition of this 'predominantly Christian' conception is incorporated into the curriculum both through the inclusion of religious education, of which at least half is Christian, and through the requirement for schools to hold daily assemblies that are acts of worship of a predominantly Christian nature. These are justified by the Secretary of State for Education on two grounds: firstly, it is asserted that 'Christianity is the predominant religion in Great Britain' (DFE, 1994a, para 16), and secondly that only religion can provide the necessary moral code. John Patten claims that '. . . no civilized society has ever been able to survive without a strong moral code that individuals understand and share', and that 'values are virtues . . . not open to choice or change' (quoted in Roberts, 1994). The first ground is not that the majority of the population *is* Christian, but that 'traditionally' it was, and this is an adequate reason to require it now. The regulations enforcing both religious education and school acts of worship refer to the 'heritage' that will thus be transmitted: 'a thorough knowledge of Christianity reflecting the Christian heritage of this country' (DFE, 1994a, para 7). Although there has been a requirement for state schools to include religion since the 1944 Act, it was until the late 1980s widely accepted that there was some considerable latitude in interpretation. It is only since the 1988 Act, and particularly since the 1994 Circular on Acts of Worship and Religious Education, that this has been pursued with vigour and with rigorous interpretation.

The link with the concept of the nation is not merely that the 'predominantly Christian' characteristic is imposed in association with the National Curriculum. More significant are the facts that firstly, it is imposed in the face of an increasing diversity of faiths, secondly, it is required because it represents one of the traditions of the state in earlier times, and thirdly it is demanded in the belief that this will reinstil a lost (or at least an imperilled) moral virtue to the country. It is not a confessional requirement, because there is a very wide variety of confessional practices within the various Christian denominations: it is being used, as Protestantism was used before, to identify and provide a locus for a set of values that can now be said to be shared, and that provide a mark of distinction from the other. It becomes part of the way in which the nation is to be redefined in the face of (or in defiance of) the growth of cultural and moral pluralism in the previous three or four decades.

Profits and Education for Economic and Industrial Understanding

The second foundation of the new nation of Britons in the eighteenth century was trade and profits. Colley (1992) argues that it was in their self-interest to preserve the new unitary British state, because only this would preserve their growing economic well-being. The large internal market, with no barriers to trade between regions or towns, and the protection to external trade afforded by the Royal Navy, and the growing interest of the state in entrepreneurial activity led to growing commercial activity. And this activity bred support for the nation:

> Men and women living in or near towns with some access to print, *particularly those caught up in the mesh of the nation's internal and foreign trade*, seem always to have been among the busiest and most reliable of patriots. They might not approve of the men in power in London, but they still had a stake in the nation's security and were acutely sensitive to its dangers. (p. 369, my emphasis)

The state protected the growing trading and commercial interests (for among other reasons, they provided, through taxation, a useful source of governmental income), and began to respond to mercantile interests in an increasingly active manner. The Society for the Encouragement of Arts, Manufactures and Commerce (latter the Royal Society for Arts, the RSA) for example, was founded in 1754 to promote the interests of manufacturers through economic nationalism, seeking in many ways 'an interventionist state closely attuned to the needs of traders and entrepreneurs' (p. 93). The RSA's founder wrote that his aim was 'to render Great Britain the school of instruction as it is already the centre of traffic to the greatest part of the known world' (in Colley, 1992, p. 91). The corollary of the process by which 'the machinery of the state . . . opened up opportunities, something that could . . . be used to [the entrepreneur's] own profit' (*ibid.*, p. 68) was that the entrepreneur became a patriotic supporter of the state. The reason for suppressing forms of civil unrest and minorities (for example, the Jacobite risings) was that they threatened both stability and profits.

Colley suggests that a new and broader definition of active patriotism emerged at this time, and that it became 'the willingness to participate that marked out the true Briton' (*ibid.*, p. 94). 'The authentic voice of the bourgeois patriot [was one] who believed that his individual prosperity and the country's good are forever twinned' (*ibid.*, p. 97).

In contemporary Britain, economic nationalism has reemerged as an important theme as politicians become increasingly obsessed with the UK's position in the economic league of nations. Prosperity is seen as relative, rather than absolute. Wiener's thesis, in *English Culture and the Decline of the Industrial Spirit 1850–1980* (1981), was that the entrepreneurial vibrancy of the eighteenth and early nineteenth century (that Colley identified as a cornerstone of the new British nation) had evaporated into a complacent acceptance of economic superiority and the elite's disdain for the processes by which it was achieved. Wiener's analysis, as his title indicates, was of *English* attitudes, but it was taken up with some alacrity by a Southern English-based ruling party as an explanation for the whole of the UK's relative position. The book was adopted by Sir Keith Joseph, at the time Secretary of State for Trade and Industry, and circulated by him as recommended reading to his senior civil servants (along with Adam Smith's *The Wealth of Nations*). It went with Joseph when he moved to the Department of Education and Science, where those sections of Wiener's thesis that castigated the educational establishment for promoting an anti-science, anti-manufacturing ethos formed part of the impetus behind his consultative letter on economic education in schools, issued in March 1985 (see p. 82).

It was the National Curriculum project that resulted from this letter that was charged with drafting the cross-curricular theme education for economic and industrial understanding (NCC, 1990b) (see above, also chapters 3 (note 3) and 9). Similar perceptions led the RSA to organize Industry Year in 1986: 'in Britain we hold industrial activity in low social esteem and the causes of our relative industrial decline are deeply embedded in our cultural attitudes' (RSA, 1985). Industry in this context was defined to include manufacturing and services, publicly and privately owned. Industry Year, and the successor Industry Matters organization focused their activities on education, aspiring to achieve long-term changes in attitudes.

The development of the economic and industrial cross-curricular theme thus has its origins in a concern with the nation — its 'private and public wealth' and its 'relative industrial decline' — rather than any pedagogic concern. It too can be seen as part of the concerted attempt to revivify national identity, as an antidote to relative economic decline.

Peripheries — Europe as 'The Other'

The third cornerstone that Colley identified as the basis of the new nation was its concern with its peripheries: the growth of empire. The peripheral North Britain became fully incorporated into the United Kingdom, not merely constitutionally, but also by the process of intermarriage between the landed gentry, so that the land-owning and political classes had property and interests in all parts of the United

Kingdom, and by the inclusion of Scots into the professions that staffed the overseas empire. The periphery of the empire also underwent a significant change in the first century of the new nation: the American colonies, conceived of in the metropole as a mere extension of England, were lost, and replaced with a new and much more vast empire, that in no way could be seen as encompassed within the Protestantism and mercantilism of the United Kingdom. Instead of a small Atlantic-based trading empire, 'the beneficent creation of a [single] liberty-loving and commercial people' (Colley, 1992, p. 102), the new empire included Catholic Quebec and South Asia (non-Christian, and non-white). The post Seven Years War empire could no longer be justified in the same way as the earlier arrangements with the American colonists: if the United Kingdom professed itself to be uniquely free, it would need other grounds to justify its domination over a large and clearly unfree set of very different peoples.

At one level, the notion of the other, and the demonstration of what were seen as the unique qualities of the British, were used to account for British hegemony: the very attributes of Protestantism and commerce marked out Britons to assume and maintain powers on behalf of those exotic subjects who were without these characteristics. At another, the existence of the overseas empire provided an opportune way of promoting and incorporating the ambitious Scots into administrative, professional and commercial positions, without dispossessing any of the English in the process.

The loss of Empire in the recent past has again been a source of identity problems for the British. Unlike Protestantism, which can be widened to some imprecise notion of broad Christianity, or commerce, which can be urged to revive, there is no readily available substitute for the Empire in sustaining national identity. Instead, Britons are in many ways offered a contrast with Europe as the Other, notwithstanding UK membership of the European Community. In terms of the school curriculum, Europe becomes conspicuous by its absence. The separateness of Europe, its distinction from Britain, is underlined by the way in which most of the National Curriculum is defined to ignore Europe.

Dominance, Majesty and Education for Citizenship

The fourth foundation of the patriotism of the new Nation of Great Britain in the eighteenth century was the system of political and social relationships that was established. A ruling class, initially landed and aloof, developed characteristics that made it appear to be similar to the emergent middle classes and professions. That the same class largely maintained their positions of domination was made to appear as meeting an obligation to the nation, rather than a clinging to power, a form of *noblesse oblige*. The institution of monarchy was similarly transformed, and many aspects of the pomp of the absolutist monarchies were transformed to the ritual of national occasions.

Colley (1992) takes her readers through many examples of these processes, all of which had the effect of creating the appearance of a more common sense of purpose and identity between the rulers and the ruled, at a time when many such divisions were widening elsewhere. The cult of manly heroism, the counterfeit pastoralism of fox-hunting, the comparative drabness of the everyday dress of the non-military elite — these are all shown as how the ruling classes 'assumed many of the characteristics of a service elite ... without conceding much in way of meritocratic change' (p. 192). The style and appearance of the ruling class changed so that it became difficult to distinguish them from those of the middle classes. It was at this time, for example, that concepts of 'national art treasures' emerged:

> the quite extraordinary idea that even if an art object comes from abroad, and even if it remains securely in private ownership, as long as it resides in a country house it must somehow belong to the nation and enhance it. ... In virtually every Continental state at this time, aristocracies had to live with the risk that their property might be pillaged or confiscated. Only in Great Britain did it prove possible to float the idea that aristocratic property was in some magical and strictly intangible way *the people's property also.* (*ibid.*, pp. 176–7)

The way in which the dominant class maintained its hegemony was through its ability to stress the responsibilities and duties that it owed the nation: it was their obligation to contribute to and aid the administration of the state. The popular perception of an active citizen and patriot was one who served the nation, not one who was owed rights by the nation. The fact that by so reserving disproportionate powers for themselves as a group they laid claim to concomitant rights of access to wealth was not made distinct. But citizenship was increasingly to become a status for all, because the recurrent threat of French invasion of the British mainland required the frequent need to evoke active loyalty on a larger scale than in previous centuries. Subjects had to become citizens if the nation was to succeed. The forms of citizenship were inevitably contrived and linked to the inventions of nationalism:

> Most of the occasions when people become conscious of citizenship as such remain associated with symbols and semi-ritualized practices (for instance, elections), most of which are historically novel and invented: flags, images, ceremonies and music. (Hobsbawm, 1983, p. 12)[2]

Turning from the eighteenth century's invention of the nation to the contemporary situation, the advocacy of education for citizenship can be seen in a rather different light. Alienation and political apathy suggest a disillusionment with the state, and one that is as potentially challenging and undermining to the ruling classes now as was the possibility of working class indifference to threats of French invasion in the eighteenth century. Citizenship can be used to instil a sense of participation and belonging. But such participation needs to stress the obligations of citizenship, rather than raise expectations of rights, as *Education for Citizenship* makes so manifest.

The thrust of this chapter has been to suggest that the National Curriculum with its associated cross-curricular themes, and particularly the social science aspects of these, needs to be interpreted in a wider context of social and political change. Contemporary social movement in Britain is not seen by the government as simply post-modernist phenomena, but as a breakdown of the old order and certainties, an unacceptable moral pluralism, a lack of identity associated with the loss of Empire, the disintegration of the welfare state and relative economic decline. Faced with the collapse of what had formerly constituted the nation, the government is now part of a movement to invent a new nation in its place. Anderson (1983) suggests that a nation is 'an imagined political community' (p. 6); the National Curriculum is part of the process of imagining a new nation, founded on cornerstones that parallel those on which the original nation of Great Britain was first forged — 'predominant' Christianity, economic participation and entrepreneurship, a lack of integration with Europe, and a citizenship that emphasizes duties and responsibilities over rights. In each of these attributes, we are reminded of the traditions which they represent. But, as Hobsbawm (1983) reminds us,

> the peculiarity of 'invented' traditions is that the continuity with (the historic past) is largely factious. In short, they are responses to novel situations which take the form of reference to old situations, or which establish their own past by quasi-obligatory repetition. (p. 2)

There does not need to be any attempt at objectivity in this. When there is an attempt to construct an 'imagined political community', image is all.

> The attitudes of individuals and groups of individuals to their own situation in society and the conduct these attitudes dictate are determined not so much by actual economic conditions as by the image in the minds of the individuals and groups. (Duby, quoted in Briggs, 1985, p. v)

It is on the social subjects that the weight of this new conception falls, even though these are never formally included within the curriculum. But in the cross-curricular themes in particular, together with large elements of the history curriculum, parts of geography, much of the literature in English, and religious education, we are confronted with the curriculum elements that are grounded in the social fabric of the communities of the nation. But these elements do not simply offer a framework that mirrors the social experiences of our communities. They reorder the curriculum, so that children will learn more about their own individual obligations and responsibilities than about the social organizations that offer them rights, and they are based on an attempt to define a new sense of the nation, through a nationality that excludes the other, stresses entrepreneurial activity, and focuses on civic duty as the proper activity of the citizen. The National Curriculum, and the Whole Curriculum that surrounds it, is an attempt to invent traditions that deny community, welfare and social action.

Notes

1 Composed by James Thompson, 1740; my emphasis.
2 This process was not confined to Britain, of course. For example, it was replicated in revolutionary France, as the state sought to legitimate its powers by the active incorporation of subjects as citizens. Writing of the nature of state power at that time, Lynn Hunt (1984) observes that it 'expanded at every level as people of various stations invented and learned new political "micro-techniques". Taking minutes, sitting in a club meeting, reading a republican poem, wearing a cockade, sewing a banner, singing a song, filling out a form, making a patriotic donation, electing an official — all these actions converged to produce a republican citizenry and a legitimate government' (p. 72).

Part 3

Reactions to the Cross-curricular Themes

Chapter 5

Cross-curricular Integration and the Construction of the Self in the Primary Curriculum

Anna Craft

Introduction

Primary teachers often refer to the education of young children as 'holistic', or 'integrated'; they consider themselves to be educating 'the whole person' and their own relationship with individual children as a central aspect of this. Jennifer Nias (1989) cites a variety of evidence which suggests 'many primary school teachers still see the personal relationships which they have with individual children not just as a means of establishing control and increasing motivation but also as the means by which education itself takes place' (p. 15). She refers to a concern built into many primary teachers' training, based on the teachings of Froebel, for 'the centrality of wholeness and [the] belief that education should be an organic process, free of artificial and damaging divisions' (*ibid.*, p. 15). Indeed, one set of worries held by primary practitioners at the inception of the National Curriculum was that an overemphasis on a fragmented curriculum could shift the process of teaching and learning away from educating the whole child to a much narrower process; a process traditionally associated with older children and perhaps inappropriate for primary pupils. At one level these fears were ungrounded, in that the Education Reform Act itself indicates that the National Curriculum is not the whole curriculum, and the series of Curriculum Guidance documents describing cross-curricular themes within the whole curriculum, issued by the National Curriculum Council (NCC, 1990a-f), are intended to codify aspects of children's personal and social education; aspects of the education of the whole child.

Having said this, the 'slimming down' of the core and foundation subjects to a 'core core' recommended by Sir Ron Dearing in July 1993 (NCC/SEAC, 1993) and in detail in his final report (SCAA, 1994a), and subsequently accepted as an agenda for change by the Department for Education, together with the absence of discussion of the social in the curriculum, does rather suggest a lack of commitment to the whole child at the level of policymaking on the curriculum.

It is conceivable that, in principle however, the cross-curricular themes could continue to be considered to be a way of educating the whole child. But what is meant by the whole person, or the 'self'? This chapter considers the conceptions of self which are embedded in that early model of the whole curriculum which included the five cross-curricular themes; in particular the identity and values which they embody. The implications are explored of the integration and the codification of the curriculum, including cross-curricular themes, using current sociological frameworks of modernism/post-modernism, examining in particular where the centralized curriculum — and all that it embodies — leaves traditional approaches to the holistic education of young children.

Within this context, the chapter also attempts to define and exemplify cross-curricular work in primary schools, examining why this is considered by so many teachers to be an appropriate way to learn. With the publication of the Dearing Review of the National Curriculum (*ibid.*) questions of the whole curriculum have been submerged under the concern to slim down the National Curriculum subjects, casting speculation on to what the 'entitlement' curriculum (as defined within the 1988 Education Reform Act and in the whole curriculum statements by NCC) might now mean.

What *is* cross-curricular work beginning to mean in England within the 1988 Education Reform Act and whole curriculum guidance from the National Curriculum Council? The changing meaning of cross-curricular work will be examined in particular through the example of economic and industrial understanding, together with some of the implications of the emerging approach of cross-curricular work for teachers and schools.

Two Types of Cross-curricular Work

Cross-curricular work has a multiplicity of meanings in primary practice, but if we try to broadly classify these, there seem to be two distinct types; those which revolve around a *central theme*, and those which involve *curriculum overlap*.

Central Theme

This is work which revolves around a central theme, and which involves study and investigation in a number of different subject areas, chosen either by the teacher, the teacher in consultation with the children, or the children/child with the teacher, and ranging over any length of time from a few days to a term, involving anything from the whole class to just one child, and taking up anything from virtually the whole timetable to just a fraction of it. This kind of cross-curricularity centres around a context for learning. Common or central themes can form 'unifiers' for work across the curriculum.

Curriculum Overlap

Cross-curricular work can also involve overlap of subjects. In other words, some parts of the curriculum can themselves form unifiers for other parts of the curriculum.

These include areas of the curriculum which require a context for learning, such as English and technology, and areas of the curriculum which can be seen as inherently involving other domains such as geography (which involves a great deal of science) or music (which, being a social artefact, actually encapsulates historical data). As well as providing a way of 'unifying' curriculum areas, this sort of cross curricularity is also context-*dependent*. This is different from being context-*centred*, in that it is the subject learning which is emphasized, rather than the context, although for the learning to be cross-curricular, the context needs to be a shared one. Thus, children may be learning about rock-formation in geography and about using fossil evidence in history. In this way, they depend on the same context for learning aspects of the subject, rather than centring on exploring how the earth's crust came to be the way it is.

This second model is more common in secondary schools than in primary, if only because timetabling using subjects lends itself far more easily to this kind of 'non-intrusive' cross-curricular work than it does to central theme work. Nevertheless, it is not exclusively the domain of secondary teachers and indeed some argue that with a very full subject-oriented National Curriculum, 'curriculum overlap' may become a more common form of organizing cross-curricular work in primary schools.

Common Key Features of Cross-curricular Work

Certain key features of cross-curricular work can be identified in both central theme or curriculum overlap types.

Interest-centred or Context-dependent

Cross-curricular work attempts to work through a focus which enables pupils to draw on different kinds of knowledge and skills in order to deepen their understanding of the focus. The following snippet case studies may help to illustrate this.

> In a Newcastle primary school, year 6 children learned for a term through the focus of a project on the Quayside, a riverside part of Newcastle-upon-Tyne. The main curriculum areas developed were history, English, music, drama and art, although other subjects were also to some extent developed. Activities included visits to the Quayside; deciphering and trying to understand a nineteenth century document written by a keelman; singing and interpreting local folksongs from the Quayside, inviting a local historian into the classroom and working wih him; researching the history of the Quayside using his books and others; making a large appliqué wall hanging representing the Quayside through the ages.

> In a London primary school a year 2 class project on transport involved learning in English, mathematics and geography. Activities included survey

work at the local bus stop, finding out where people were going to and from, asking about value for money and generally exploring the customer satisfaction. They subsequently travelled on the bus all the way along its route, and visited the garage to talk to workers about their work, and about the findings of their survey. They mapped out their journey and deciphered bus and road maps. Children's understanding and skills were deepened and developed through the focus of transport, which acted as a common context for learning in the three subjects of maths, English and geography.

In each of these examples, learning in the contributory subjects was focused around a common context, rather than there being a different learning context for each subject.

Cross-curricular Work as a Unifier

The notion of thinking of the curriculum as involving a number of different kinds or 'forms' of knowledge, each with its own specialized forms of enquiry, which was put forward by Paul Hirst (1965), has been developed by HMI (1985) into the notion of there being 'areas of experience' in the curriculum, each of which is quite distinct. The notion of the different and distinct kinds of knowledge was carried forward into the 1988 National Curriculum (table 5.1).

Cross-curricular work acts as a 'curriculum unifier'; it provides a way of 'overlapping' different subjects or areas of experience, providing a common focus for study. Thus in the examples given above, the Key Stage 1 class project on transport formed a unifier for learning in English, mathematics and geography, and the Key Stage 2 project on the Quayside enabled history, music, English, art and drama to be developed.

The linking through a focus which draws on two or more different 'forms' of knowledge raises questions about how real the links between the forms are. Cross-curricular work offers potential for enhancing real links and overlaps, where the flow of curriculum and of learning is directly related to questions and issues arising from the focus of study, rather than being artificially created. Thus, in the project on the Newcastle Quayside, the children were led, through trying to understand why the building layout as it is, and through exploring the social and economic activity of the Quayside, into the oral and written history of the area. The common focus here was sufficiently rich in potential to enable the development of natural curricular links between geographical and historical enquiry, musical experience and composition and the handling and analysis of literature.

Rationales for Cross-curricular Work

Traditionally, reasons for working in a cross-curricular way have centred around three sets of principles; learning, knowledge and practical organization.

Table 5.1: The development of the primary curriculum in England

Hirst (1965) Forms of Knowledge	DES (1985) Areas of experience	Education Reform Act (1988) National Curriculum	National Curriculum Council (1990) Whole Curriculum	Key Stage 1	Key Stage 2
mathematical knowledge	mathematical	mathematics	mathematics		
physical sciences	scientific	science	science		
human sciences	technological	technology	techology		
history	human and social	history	history		
literature/fine arts	aesthetic and creative	geography	geography		
philosophy	linguistic and literary	English	English		
religion	moral	(Welsh)	(Welsh)		
	physical	music	music		
	spiritual	art	art		
		PE	PE		
		+ religious education	+ religious education		

cross-curricular themes, skills + dimensions

Source: Craft and Clarir, 1993

Cross-curricular Work and Approaches to Learning

Reasons often given include the pupil-centred belief that pupils (especially young children) do not distinguish between subjects, but rather learn through their interest in the context. The context for learning is thus very important as a motivator. A second kind of argument often given from this pupil-centred perspective is the idea that pupils learn by making their own connections between experiences, and that compartmentalizing experiences is not meaningful for them. A third kind of reason concerning learning is that working across the curriculum through some kind of curriculum focus enables skills and processes to be developed and applied more meaningfully (CACE, 1967; Dearden, 1968).

Cross-curricular Work and the Nature of Knowledge

There seem to be three kinds of arguments concerning the nature of knowledge. Firstly, the familiar Plowden view that 'knowledge is a seamless web', and that therefore cutting it into discrete subjects for learners is inappropriate. The second kind of argument is the one put forward by Michael Young (1971), that splitting the curriculum into subjects means imposing one's own values about what should constitute curriculum subjects. Working *across* the curriculum and encouraging a kind of fluidity in its definition, and in who is entitled to define it, might thus be seen as desirable by those who share Young's views. The third kind of argument is the one put forward by Pring (1976), recognizing that 'subjects' do indeed move and weld over time. He notes that new 'subjects' have emerged which are interdisciplinary and conceptually linked: 'Environmental studies' is an example of this.

Cross-curricular Work as a Practical Response

Practical reasons for cross-curricular work include those rooted in views of learning (such as if children are to learn by discovery, they need to be given practical freedom to do so, and to rove across the subject boundaries); those concerning classroom management (it is easier to organize the class so that several activities can take place at once related to the same theme); those which highlight resources (resources can be pooled for use across subject boundaries) and those which concern the outcomes (the displays and other work created is more stimulating and creative, and feeds back into the pupils' interest).

The Reality of Cross-curricular Work in Primary Classrooms

Traditionally, the sorts of cross-curricular work described so far have been something which teachers have or have not opted for, according to their own views of curriculum and learning, together with the influences of their working context.

In primary schools, it has not been uncommon for children to experience very different kinds of curriculum organization, and to experience different forms of cross-curricular and non-cross-curricular work from year to year. Children in primary schools have also often experienced cross-curricular work in connection with special events, such as residential and day field trips. However, research from the early 1980s onward in primary schools, attempting to look under the surface of these cross-curricular models at what children actually experienced (Bennett *et al.*, 1984; Tizard *et al.*, 1988; Alexander, 1992) suggested that, in fact, little of the curriculum was actually integrated; although time and space frequently were. The attempt, however, to redefine in legal terms what children's school education should be about has significantly altered the picture.

Theories of Self

It is interesting to consider the weight of influence of the theories and practice of early educationalists such as Rousseau, Pestalozzi and Froebel, and to consider how the concept of 'self' which they embodied (as individual, whole and active) has become a part of traditional primary practice and continues to have an influence on teachers within the political and economic context of the late 1980s and early 1990s in England. Why does this notion of the child hold such sway at a time when some might argue (Johnson, 1992) that the introduction of a knowledge-based National Curriculum implies the political imposition of conformity (and, in such contrast to the initial take-up of progressivism, which Selleck (1972) documents as being one response to authoritarianism)? One could speculate on the extent to which the whole and active view of the child springs from the type of individuals in primary teaching and their values (Ashton *et al.*, 1975). Certainly, the continued emphasis in many aspects of child and adult culture on the autonomy of the individual as a choice maker and a decision maker is a curiously tenacious fact. For it is set against the paradoxical background of conformity in terms of the 'packaging' of identities, whether these be forms of dress, conventions in sports/leisure, kinds of food and food rituals, or the increasing conformity in chain stores, restaurants, garages and other service or retail outlets. And yet, the breakdown of Fordist forms of bureaucratic work structure, to the much more fluid 'post-Fordist' one, does mean an increasing chaos of choice and social identity: later in this chapter the relationship between the curriculum and a post-modern analysis will be considered. Within the political sphere, the continuing influence of individualism is set against an increasing pressure from right-wing political values concerning the relationship between the individual and society, where the appeal is to tradition, authority, the 'back to basics' call, driven by conceptions of 'ought'.

And yet, the line of development of the notion of 'self' as incorporated into primary teaching as traced so far is not an unbroken one. Over more recent years, certain theories of the child and of learning have dominated. These can be divided into three main approaches: learning as growth, learning by association and learning as constructivism.

'*Learning as growth*' can be traced back to Pestalozzi and Froebel to Rousseau (Boyd, 1956; Courthope Bowen, 1903; Froebel, 1887 and 1895; Lawrence, 1952; Lilley, 1967; Pierrepoint-Graves, 1936); its main precepts seem to involve:

- viewing the child as a collection of innate qualities that are 'good';
- considering people to have innately different qualities from one another;
- believing the development of these qualities (i.e. 'learning') consists of a process of 'growth' or 'getting bigger';
- believing that this requires action or experience which the child chooses; and
- believing this entails giving the child complete freedom'. (adapted from *Curriculum and Learning*, Open University course E271, block B pt 1)

This was taken up in extreme form by 'progressive' educators such as A.S. Neill in the experimental secondary school he founded in the 1930s — but many of these assumptions have also been incorporated into primary teaching (Nias, 1989) since the 1950s and are manifest in the organization of classrooms as emotional, cognitive and physical learning centres. Maria Montessori (1914) and Susan Isaacs (1930) among others contributed to these developments in primary teaching. It is unlikely that many primary teachers are wholly influenced by the theory of learning as growth today, but elements of it can be found in classroom management, particularly for younger children (3–7-year-olds) where 'choosing' is often a feature of the school day. Underpinning the decision to allow children to self-select activities for all or part of the day must surely be a belief in the child as innately good — and a trust in the child, a recognition of individual differences, a belief that the child will learn without direct instruction, but through chosen experiences, and that the freedom to choose is an important aspect of helping children to develop or to learn.

On a more theoretical level, the notion of learning as growth has been developed since the late 1970s into the notion of 'learning as rationalism', particularly in the area of language, by individuals such as Noam Chomsky. This is based on the notion of individuals being born with innate capacities in each form of knowing (such as the linguistic, logico-mathematical, musical, spatial, bodily-kinaesthetic, and personal intelligences, as Gardner (1993) has identified them). Chomsky (1980) has developed the rationalist theory of learning with respect to language, and considers that 'we may usefully think of the language faculty, the number faculty and others as "mental organs"' (p. 39). One implication of the rationalist approach to learning is that learning is seen as fulfilling an innate potential particularly in the cognitive sphere. Whereas earlier 'growth' theorists stressed the all-round emotional or affective characteristics of children, rationalists stress the cognitive. Within the historical view of learning as growth, we have two similar but different conceptions of 'self' — both involving the unfolding of innate potential but one also involving the emotional aspects of the person.

One of the criticisms of growth-derived theories of the individual and of learning is that these approaches can become a catch-all explanation for underachievement or failure, and can in effect endorse low teacher expectations. This may have contributed to the demise of purely 'learning as growth' oriented classrooms in primary schools (if they ever existed beyond the nursery, though as argued earlier, elements of the theory seem to exist in many teachers' practice).

'*Learning by association*' is based on the idea that events which tend to occur together in experience will be represented together in the mind. Learning is considered to involve the acquisition of associations and the storage of them in the memory. The idea comes from ancient Greece, but was developed further by eighteenth and nineteenth century British associationists: Locke, Hume, James Mill, John Stuart Mill and others. To these writers, all learning was based on associations. As some commentators have pointed out, the concept of 'self' implicit in such theories is a mechanistic one, where reason involves the associative compounding of ideas rather than involving voluntary control.

These ideas of the self have been incorporated into education through *behaviourism*. Versions of behaviourism influenced learning theory in England from around 1910 right through to the 1960s when growth theories began to dominate. The notion of association was combined with the idea of rewarding correct learning and thus conditioning children through association of correct learning with some kind of pleasure.

One of the dominant criticisms of behaviourism and the concept of self which it embodied was that it disregarded the will and the autonomy of the individual, at an ethical level. It appeared to condone the institutionalization and control of human behaviour. Nevertheless, I would suggest that many elements perhaps of primary practice incorporate aspects of the behaviourist view of 'self' and approach to learning, although teachers may not always choose to recognize it as such. Many classroom rituals, such as putting hands up to speak, sitting up straight on the carpet, lining up at the door and setting work out neatly are examples. Learning spellings and multiplication tables are examples from the formal curriculum. All involve reward for 'doing it right' or 'getting it right'.

The approach to 'self' which has had the most impact on the legacy of 'learning as growth' and the innately good self which unfolds given individualized circumstances, combines elements of learning as growth with new elements of autonomy and sense-making.

'*Learning as development and growth*' is based on the idea of the construction of experience of representations and schema of action. Constructivist views of learning tend to reject both associationist views of learning (resulting in passive copies) and also the idea that knowledge is innate and will unfold. On the other hand, they do on the whole embrace 'growth' notions of the 'self' as being whole, and developing through active experiences with the world. Where constructivists depart from 'growth' theorists in their conception of the self is that they reject the notion that children are born with innate knowledge. Instead these theorists contend that the 'self' contains basic ways of sorting and responding to sensory data which serve as building bricks for mental constructions. Piaget is probably the best known and most influential constructivist, and although he began to publish his ideas in the 1920s, they only became incorporated widely into educational theory and practice in the 1960s, and has been further developed since to incorporate the following elements:

- active experience;
- relevance to the learner;
- social interaction with other children;
- challenging, 'scaffolded' talk with adults;
- 'modelling' by adults; and
- negotiation of meaning with adults and other children. (from Wood, 1988)

The 'self' is seen by constructivists to be an individual, autonomous, active, social, sense-maker. There is clearly a contrast between the individual as sense-maker and the right-wing conformity-oriented influence on the social aspects of the curriculum. On the other hand, the notion of the individual constructivist learner resonates with many of the ideas in the growing 'new age' spirituality or philosophy of living, which has recently found an increasing voice in some of the popular culture of children and teenagers as well as adults. Such aspects of culture include music, clothes, dance, food and 'events' involving celebration, the exploration of personal creativity and personal growth (Edwards, 1991 and 1993; Gawain, 1993). Here the individual is seen as having the capacity to explore and interpret the world around them, integrating the experience into their own lives, by 'making sense' of them. Although the material of New Age spirituality is music, rhythm, voice, dance, touch and other kinaesthetic and emotional experience, the process and the focus on the individual are very close to the constructivist view of the child learning in the more intellectual environment of the classroom. Indeed, the very nature of 'post-modern' living, with its fragmentation of 'discourses', or ways of being, the proliferation of choice and personal autonomy, has as one of its premises that individuals make their own sense of their world. As Rob Gilbert (1992) has argued, this is not unproblematic. His view is that the 'pervasive informationalism', the 'universal but fragmenting organizational forms', and the 'views of knowledge which dissolve history's grand narratives' actually 'shape identity' (p. 55). And his view is that individuals as a consequence draw on a vast array of sub-cultural combinations, in a schizophrenic fashion, which, in terms of schooling, produces at least two kinds of problems. Firstly, that aspects of post-modern life do not necessarily demand conscious sense-making or position-adopting, which means that attempts to encourage pupils to adopt and argue a personal viewpoint may potentially involve a conflict of style/demand. Secondly, there is an inherent conflict between the individual's capacity to *choose what* to take in, as well as how to make sense of it, and any uniform curriculum; an issue returned to later in this chapter under 'implications of senses of self'.

So what kind of impact have constructivist views of learning had on the practice of teaching and learning? Piagetian views of the self and learning have certainly had a wide effect on primary teaching, and it can be contended that many teachers, intentionally or not, incorporate aspects of Piagetian constructivism into the way they organize and manage learning, particularly in the infant years, and with regard to certain concepts such as egocentricity and conservation of number and quantity. However, as Galton *et al.* (1980) showed in their survey of primary practice, few teachers at that time applied it strictly, perhaps because of the resource and organizational implications for teaching large classes of children in a constructivist way for all of the time. I would suggest that if a survey was carried our now, similar results would be found; in that teachers might well identify with the active and autonomous conception of self embedded in constructivism, but that they might in fact incorporate less of it into their practice than they imagined.

Having traced some of the theoretical background to the senses of self which primary teachers perhaps incorporate into their practice and related this to firstly post-modernist individualism, secondly to the conformity apparent in the economic and political context and thirdly the growing movement toward a philosophy of individual spiritualism, I will now consider conceptions of self embedded in the written curriculum of the cross-curricular themes. The five cross-curricular themes identified by the NCC embody much of the personal and social aspects of children's learning.

A Changing Approach: The Cross-curricular Themes

The Education Reform Act (1988) brought with it a statutory curriculum within a curriculum framework which must be:

- broad and balanced, and must
- promote the spiritual, moral, cultural, mental and physical development of pupils at school and in society; and
- prepare pupils for the opportunities, responsibilities and experiences of adult life. (Education Reform Act, 1988)

The Act was significant in that it made reference to both the breadth of the curriculum and its relevance to pupils' lives in the present and as adults. This was presented as a curriculum to which all children were entitled. The National Curriculum itself was strikingly similar to the sort of whole curriculum suggested by Hirst in 1965, claiming that these 'forms of knowledge' constituted the entire range of ways of knowing about the world used by humankind, as table 5.1 showed. NCC's interpretation of the Education Reform Act seems to recognize and represent a slightly different sort of cross-curricular work. The whole curriculum suggested by NCC also gives value to certain elements of the curriculum which were previously perhaps not as visible.

NCC's Cross-curricular Elements

The philosophy behind the cross-curricular elements was that they should permeate the statutory curriculum and make a significant contribution towards personal and social development. The National Curriculum Council (1990a) distinguished three kinds of cross-curricular element while recognizing that 'it would be possible to construct a list of an almost infinite number of cross-curricular elements' (p. 2).

Dimensions

The cross-curricular dimensions identified by NCC included a commitment to providing equal opportunities for all pupils and education for life in a multicultural society.

Skills

The NCC identified six 'core skills', which are transferable and can be developed in different contexts across the whole curriculum:

- communication
- numeracy
- study
- problem-solving
- personal and social
- information technology

NCC 'considered it absolutely essential that these skills are fostered across the whole curriculum in a measured and planned way' (*ibid.*, p. 3).

Themes

It is the cross-curricular themes which are most significant in understanding the development in meaning of cross-curricular work. NCC identified five major themes which formed a necessary part of the whole curriculum. They were concerned with the social, moral, physical, sexual and vocational self, and involved the application of school knowledge and skills to the real world.

They could be seen as an empowering part of the curriculum, enabling children to understand themselves and the world of which they are a part. They involved children in exploring values and beliefs and encouraged practical activities and decision-making and developed the relationship between the individual and the community. They were each concerned with human and social activity and behaviour, in a way that most of the foundation subjects were not. The five themes summarized from the NCC's guidance are as follows.

The first of the cross-curricular theme Curriculum Guidance papers to be published was *Education for Economic and Industrial Understanding* (NCC, 1990b). It is concerned with equipping children to make economic decisions now and as adults, and to fulfil future economic roles — as producers, consumers and citizens. It focuses on the individual, encompasses business, commerce, finance and consumer affairs from the point of view of the world of work, economic ideas, technological developments and for primary children predominantly involves study at local level and, where appropriate, at regional, national, European and global levels.

The curriculum area is described in terms of knowledge, understanding, skills and attitudes; and direct experience of industry and the world of work is seen as essential. Central to economic and industrial understanding is the development of analytical, personal and social skills, 'including the ability to:

- collect, analyze and interpret economic and industrial data;
- think carefully about different ways of solving economic problems and making economic decisions;
- distinguish between statements of fact and value in economic situations;
- communicate economic ideas accurately and clearly;
- establish working relationships with adults outside school;
- cooperate as part of a team in enterprise activities;
- lead and take the initiative;
- handle differences of economic interest and opinion in a group;
- communicate effectively and listen to the views of others on economic and industrial issues' (NCC, 1990b, pp. 4–5)

These aspects imply an active, social approach to learning which encourages children to make sense of learning for themselves: they embody a constructivist approach to self and learning.

The second Curriculum Guidance paper was *Health Education* (*NCC, 1990c*). This focused mainly on the individual: 'essential features of health education are the promotion of quality of life and the physical, social and mental well-being of the individual' (p. 1). Through the education and behaviour of the individual, the NCC considered that the well-being of society at large could be influenced: 'it is clear that healthy living must be an issue of major influence for everyone, particularly as society can be affected by one health crisis after another' (*ibid.*) — and it also refers to the responsibility which individuals have both to themselves and to others: 'while everyone is exposed to potential risks to good health, individuals can do much to lessen those risks and to improve the quality of their lives and their environment' (*ibid.*). Some of the examples of learning activities are described as having an individual, group and community focus.

The components of health education are described in terms not only of knowledge and understanding, but also skills. For example, safety is one component of the curriculum: 'the acquisition of knowledge and understanding of safety in different environments, together with the development of associated skills and strategies, helps pupils to maintain their personal safety and that of others' (*ibid.*, p. 4). *Doing* is an important part of learning health education. Examples are given throughout the document of pupils engaging in active learning experiences.

The approach to self embedded in the health education curriculum is constructivist. The emphasis is on helping children to develop the capacity to make informed and meaningful choices; this is quite explicit: 'The emphasis . . . is on encouraging individual responsibility, awareness and informed decision-making . . . The participation of pupils is essential . . . Opportunities should be provided for pupils to assess evidence, make decisions, negotiate, listen, make and deal with relationships, solve problems and work independently and with confidence' (*ibid.*, p. 7). The notion of the child constructing meaning through active, social and mediated engagement in their learning seems quite clearly to be a constructivist one. It is not a curriculum which implies the unfolding of innate knowledge, nor the reproduction of facts by rote or association learning.

Careers Education and Guidance, the third Curriculum Guidance document to be published (NCC, 1990d), focuses strongly on the development of the individual child's autonomy: 'in promoting self-awareness, it is a prerequisite to pupils making well-informed educational, vocational and training choices, and to managing transition from education to new roles, including employment' (foreword).

Five strands of development are suggested:

- *Self*:   Knowledge of self — qualities, attitudes, values, abilities, strengths, limitations, potential and needs;
- *Roles*:   Position and expectations in relation to family, community and employment
- *Work*:   Application of productive effort, including paid employment and unpaid work in the community and at home
- *Career*:   Sequence of roles undertaken through working life and the personal success, rewards and enjoyment it brings
- *Transition*: Development of qualities and skills which enable pupils to adjust to and cope with change, for example, self-reliance, flexibility, decision-making, problem-solving. (*ibid.*, p. 2)

The learning aims emphasize children's active involvement in the curriculum and, in the primary years, developing a greater understanding of each strand. Examples of activities all involve children working with others, finding out and negotiating understandings. Many examples involve visits beyond the classroom or inviting people into the school.

The notion of self which appears to underlie this theme is again a constructivist one, in which children are encouraged to make personal sense of their environment through active and social exploration. There is no sense of self as the unfolding of innate qualities through the child's selection of choices, as growth theories would have it, nor of learning by association, the self as a regurgitator of information or methods.

Environmental Education, the fourth Curriculum Guidance document to be published (NCC, 1990e), provides a contrast. Unlike the other themes, the NCC promotes environmental education as being concerned less with the development of the whole child as an individual than the development of collective responsibility for the environment. For example, in urgently stressing the fragility of the biosphere, the document argues 'never has there been a greater need for young children to be aware of the necessity to look after the environment. They are its custodians, and will be responsible for the world in which, in turn, their children will grow up. It is essential that all those with influence over the environment work together towards its conservation and improvement. This means that schools must assume their responsibilities for environmental education' (*ibid.*, p. 1).

Aims for environmental education are expressed in terms of knowledge, skills and attitudes, and emphasize active involvement in learning and critical reflection: 'Environmental education aims to:

- provide opportunities to acquire the knowledge, values, attitudes, commitment and skills needed to protect and improve the environment;
- encourage pupils to examine and interpret the environment from a variety of perspectives — physical, geographical, biological, sociological, economic, political, technological, historical, aesthetic, ethical and spiritual;
- arouse pupils' awareness and curiosity about the environment and encourage active participation in resolving environmental problems. (*ibid.*, p. 3)

Again, there seems to be no trace of the kind of selfhood which is embodied in growth theories of primary education. On the other hand, there are strong constructivist tones. Children are to engage actively and socially with the environment, and environmental issues, to develop their understanding of it. In addition, we can perhaps see also elements of learning by association, since there is a strong basic value position underneath this curriculum which is environmental preservation. In effect, the curriculum represents an explicit attempt to socialise children to care for and about their environment; a much more associationist or behaviourist approach, it could be argued, than is adopted in economic and industrial understanding, health education or careers education and guidance.

Education for Citizenship, the final cross-curricular theme on which the NCC issued guidance (NCC, 1990f) again emphasizes the development of the individual, emphasizing the relationship of the individual to wider society: 'it helps each of them understand the duties, responsibilities and rights of every citizen and promotes concern for the values by which a civilized society is identified — justice, democracy, respect for the rule of law' (foreword).

The curriculum area is expressed in terms of knowledge, cross-curricular skills, attitudes and moral codes and values, and there are a number of different component levels: the nature of community; roles and relationships in a pluralist society; and the duties, responsibilities and rights of being a citizen. These are to be explored through the contexts of the family, democracy in action, the citizen and the law, work, employment and leisure, and public services. The emphasis is on participative citizenship (Quicke, 1992).

Although the document acknowledges that 'pupils' own experiences provide the starting point in education for citizenship' (NCC, 1990f, p. 15), and for pupils to explore controversial issues and viewpoints dissimilar to their own, through both learning knowledge and understanding and by active involvement within the school community, there is a strong and explicit emphasis on socializing children for Britain, Europe and the world-wide community: 'Curriculum provision should build on personal experience and encourage pupils to see citizenship as something which extends beyond their immediate experiences and relationships. Individuals have obligations, to and relationships with, national, European and worldwide communities. Citizens in the 1990s and beyond will require an appreciation of the significance of the economic, social and political changes taking place in Europe and of the need for international cooperation' (*ibid.*).

Although there are elements of a constructivist self embedded in this curriculum, I would suggest there are also elements of an associationist self where learning includes conditioning to behave in a certain way given certain circumstances.

The NCC Cross-curricular Themes as Social Enquiry

Learning in each of the NCC cross-curricular themes, like the traditional work described earlier, has the potential to provide a context for interest-centred and unifying work across the curriculum. However, there are significant differences between the NCC cross-curricular themes and traditional cross-curricular work. Firstly, the choice of themes. They each involve the application of school knowledge to the real world. They can be seen as an empowering part of the curriculum, enabling children to understand themselves and the world of which they are a part. They involve children in exploring values and beliefs and encourage practical activities and decision-making and develop the relationship between the individual and the community. The themes thus provide some of the 'relevance' mentioned in the 1988 Education Reform Act and therefore form an essential part of the whole curriculum. This brings us to the second difference; they *cannot* be seen as optional — indeed, I would suggest we have to view the systematic planning and evaluating of learning within each of these themes as part of every child's entitlement. Thirdly, the themes are more than contexts; they each involve specific knowledge, understanding, skills and attitudes, to be introduced in each key stage, through and alongside other subjects. This requires a commitment to systematic planning of specific learning experiences which will involve the introduction of specific ideas, understanding and skills, throughout the years of compulsory schooling.

The NCC themes challenge the notion of pursuing 'virtually any' unifying centre of interest. The themes can be seen as an essential part of the whole curriculum; as an entitlement. This semi-statutory status, together with the substantial content involved in each, requires them to be fully planned for. This semi-statutory aspect of the whole curriculum comes on top of a bursting statutory primary curriculum (now acknowledged by both Dearing and the Department for Education). Each is almost like an extra 'subject' in its own right. And perhaps because each is concerned with human and social activity and behaviour, each is controversial in its nature.

Looking at One Theme: Economic and Industrial Understanding

In addition to using economic and industrial issues as a focus through which to develop learning in foundation subjects, the NCC suggests 'schools may wish to consider supplementary provision outside foundation subjects' (NCC, 1990b, p. 10). This might involve blocks of time in primary schools focused on for example, enterprise activities, or visits to a local workplace.

Economic and industrial understanding is possibly fairly unfamiliar to many primary practitioners. In essence, it involves helping children learn about and critically appraise five basic areas: economic ideas, industry and the world of work, enterprise, consumer affairs and public affairs — using economic and industrial contexts as a focus for developing the subjects of the National Curriculum — and using the subjects as contexts for developing understanding about economics and industry. The following snapshot case studies of economic and industrial projects and activities illustrate what it can involve. Most of these were developed by the SCDC/NCC curriculum development project *Educating for Economic Awareness*, working in over forty LEAs with pupils between the ages of 5 and 19, from 1987 to 1990.

Economic Ideas and Consumer Affairs

The problem faced by year 5 and year 6 pupils in a south east London primary school was what was to be done about the old school site? How could it be best used to the benefit of the local community? A systematic enquiry approach was adopted. Pupils carried out survey and interview work in the community. Contacts were made with many local professionals and residents.

Global Links in Industry and Work

A teacher with an interest in global education decided to add a global dimension to the topic on our neighbourhood with her year 5 class. She devised a global town trail. The pupils examined shop windows and supermarket shelves for overseas goods. They visited local industries to find out about exports and imports. They contacted local tourist information offices to enquire about foreign visitors. A large-scale wall map was drawn to show the extent of the local/global links.

Economic Ideas and Consumer Affairs: Understanding Different Viewpoints

As well as exploring their local rail network, year 5 Haringay pupils spent a week in Wales as part of a project on railways. To enrich the work, the teacher devised two simulations: the coming of the railway, individuals taking on the roles of different interest groups in an area designated for railway development; and stuck in the underground, in which groups of children seated in the tube were given roles. The train gets stranded between stations and the passengers begin to talk to each other and how the situation affects them.

A Mini-enterprise

Pupils in a North Wales primary school seeded plants, using fertilizer products produced by a local company and sold them to parents and local residents. They approached the bank for a £50 loan, having calculated how much money they needed to go into production. As the seedlings grew, yield and initial outlay were assessed by pupils in order to set appropriate prices.

Consumer Affairs

Some 7 and 8-year-olds in a Bristol school were working on various aspects of the topic 'Underground'. One group was investigating potatoes in all their aspects. They investigated the 'healthy eating' involved in the various ways of eating potatoes. They compared the price and relative weight of frozen chips to a bag of potatoes, looked at the price of a bag of chips at the local chip shop and discussed the convenience aspect.

Community Enterprise and Teamwork

Year 5 children in a Lancashire school planned a tea party for elderly people in the neighbourhood. Planning issues were addressed and included who should be invited, where the party would be held, what would be needed, how would it be organized and how would tasks be allocated.

Industry and Work

Year 1 pupils in a Leicestershire infant school had the opportunity to enhance their work on feet and shoes by a visit to a local shoe factory owned by the parents of a child in the class. The visit focused on the 'making process' and the children followed the shoes around the production line from start to finish.

Consumer Affairs

Infants in an Avon school were involved in a topic on food. They planned and carried out a survey to find out which sort of crisps people preferred.

Public Affairs and Consumer Affairs

A response to a request from a local councillor interested to hear children's views on a proposed local leisure facility led to the involvement of Avon pupils in a major piece of work. They sought the opinions of a range of people, formed sub-committees to consider the whole idea and became involved with planners, architects and others involved in the decision process.

Industry and the World of Work

As part of a project on people who help us, children in year 1 in a Northumberland first school invited the school nurse to their classroom to advise them on how to set up a doctor's surgery in the home corner. They prepared questions to ask her about aspects of her job and created a collage of their interviews afterwards showing key words and phrases learned through the experience.

Economic Ideas

Year 2 children in a Berkshire school visited a number of shops to compare prices for the same products. They interviewed shopkeepers about their pricing policies.

Year 4 children in a Lancashire school visited a local wallpaper factory where they investigated the technology required for measuring, rolling, wrapping and sealing the finished wallpaper. On their return to school pupils designed their own wallpaper.

In a small group discussion, year 3 pupils in a Newcastle school debated whether Smarties count as a 'need' or a 'want' and began to classify their own needs and wants.

(It could well be asked whether the introduction of further content and skills through the cross-curricular themes [which are concerned with values and attitudes] represents an entitlement curriculum, as opposed to a form of indoctrination. This is considered in chapter 8.)

It is contended here that educating for economic and industrial understanding represents a process of empowerment and entitlement, rather than of indoctrination, and that the general principles of critical awareness, independent-mindedness, respect for rationality and the necessity for balance, are applicable across the themes — and that treated in this, each theme has the potential to empower rather than to indoctrinate.

Implications of the Cross-curricular Themes as part of the
Changing Approach to Cross-curricular Work

A number of curriculum, learning and practical reasons for working in a cross-curricular way have been noted: *learning reasons*, concerning the personal way in which pupils, especially young children, make sense of the world (not necessarily compartmentalized), *curriculum reasons*, concerning the nature of domain overlap, and *practical reasons*, concerning classroom organization, management and resourcing, and also relating to views about the nature of learning.

The spirit of the 1988 Education Reform Act as interpreted in the NCC whole curriculum model brings two additional sets of reasons, one philosophical and the other moral. The *philosophical* reasons for cross-curricular work revolve around the notion of a curriculum which must in law be relevant, in order to enable and empower children. This is a philosophical position on curriculum which recognizes very explicitly the extrinsic purpose of education — in other words, the purpose of education being to prepare pupils for life beyond school in their present and future lives.

The *moral* reasons for cross-curricular work are built on the philosophical ones; that if the curriculum is seen as having extrinsic purposes (as opposed to being there for its intrinsic reasons, i.e. for its own sake), then themes which help to connect school knowledge with the real world, are each child's *entitlement*.

An entitlement approach to cross-curricular work means something very different from randomly planning the odd theme here or curriculum overlap activity there. It means a commitment to planning for balance, breadth, continuity and progression in each theme, throughout the school. There are all kinds of implications here, for teaching and learning, and also for planning, management and coordination of the cross-curricular themes.

Implications for Teaching and Learning

Each of the cross-curricular themes is concerned with active, investigative and often collaborative approaches to learning. This can mean, at a superficial level, developing strategies for classroom management and organization, including the grouping of pupils and the encouragement of genuinely cooperative work; as well as building and strengthening links wth members of the community, taking visits out of the school and inviting specialists in to the classroom to work with pupils. But at a deeper level, it means developing a view of teaching and learning which values these kinds of learning experiences, which may involve a more open-ended approach to solving problems, which may offer pupils more autonomy in learning than otherwise offered, and which may at times (but does not necessarily need to) involve a noisier classroom than usual.

Each of the cross-curricular themes is also concerned with values, attitudes and beliefs and therefore inevitably involves controversial issues. Learning experiences which pupils engage in offer opportunities for considering a range of viewpoints and perspectives, to enable pupils to form their own judgments on issues. This is inevitably going to involve teachers in adopting very deliberate strategies for handling controversial issues with respect to their own views on them. It may be that different learning situations and issues involve different strategies. For instance, it may sometimes be appropriate to take a neutral chair position on issues, not revealing one's own views, whereas at other times it may seem more appropriate to give one's own view — or to play a devil's advocate role (Carrington and Troyna, 1988). But it will always be necessary to ensure pupils consider a range of views. This can be most effectively achieved by inviting representatives of different viewpoints to work with the pupils; or through structured role play.

Implications of 'Senses of Self'

It has been suggested earlier that all of the cross-curricular themes described in Curriculum Guidance documents have a 'constructivist' sense of self embedded within them; and that *Environmental Education* (NCC, 1990e) and *Education for Citizenship* (NCC, 1990f) also have an associationist concept of self embedded within them. None of the themes appears to incorporate the traditional primary philosophy of self as embodying 'growth'.

How significant is it that the traditional 'growth' concept of self is absent from each of the themes? My impression from visiting schools is that middle and secondary schools have taken up the challenge of planning for and providing learning experiences in the cross-curricular themes, more so than primary schools. Reasons range from not knowing that the series of Curriculum Guidance documents exist (because the member of staff responsible for them is also responsible for several foundation subjects and is a full-time class teacher and consequently overloaded) to having difficulty reconciling the themes with the learning of primary children. In addition, I would argue that the absence of the 'growth' concept of self from these curriculum documents contributes to this feeling of dislocation. For many primary teachers, the breaking of this continuous thread, stretching back to Rousseau, may constitute a form of identity crisis. For although constructivist views of learning have become integrated into primary teaching since Piaget, the social constructivist approach in these documents is not necessarily one which all primary teachers will find easy to adopt at a philosophical level; the tendency to think of the class as groups or as a whole group as far as cognitive learning is concerned, is still quite strong — and partly perhaps the result of managing large numbers of children. And though many primary teachers incorporate more associationist learning into their classrooms than they might consciously acknowledge, concerns over the passive concept of self which underlies these themes may account for some possible discomfort with aspects of them. Yet the one theme which seems to include an associationist concept of learning and self is environmental education — which has perhaps been the most accessible for primary teachers in terms of classroom practice. Why?

One way of understanding the answer to this is by considering *teachers'* own values (Nias, 1989). Teachers' own pesonal values are likely to come into the picture, and it may well be that the environmental education curriculum poses teachers less problem than the education for citizenship curriculum, although both have strong elements of socializing children into a particular set of views and behaviours. The difference in teachers' perceptions may relate to the match between the contentions of the curriculum and teachers' own self-concepts.

According to this analysis, different and apparently contradictory senses of self are embedded in two of the themes. The autonomous, individual thinker and sense-maker view of 'self' embodied in the constructivist view of learning seems at odds with the passive, receptive view of 'self' embodied in the associationist view. How can environmental education and citizenship involve both senses of self simultaneously? One way of approaching the problem is to separate the curriculum from the learning and teaching methods advocated. In both themes it is the pedagogy which is constructivist; and it is the knowledge content of this curriculum which has associationist learning embedded within it. In practice, the extent to which children act as passive recipients of environmental education or citizenship will depend on the extent to which learning is active and requires them to be critically reflective, or to make their own, conscious understandings.

Taking a psychological analysis of the themes shows, then, that apparently different emphases in learning theory underpin each. Analyzing the themes sociologically, in terms of their cultural capital, they each represent an agenda of items which, with consultation, have been selected by those with some power in society as worthwhile and important for children to study. A form of hegemony is produced; a structure which disseminates key ideas and values from adults with power to children and young people with less. The model is apparently a linear one, and implies a uniformity in culture and in values. As a political act, this jars with the 1990s.

The very publication of the Curriculum Guidance series (and the publication of the statutory curriculum itself) is a modernist act, in that it presents a set of values which assume a mutual acceptance between producers and audience. Modernity assumes interaction with and reflection on 'socially defined and available roles, norms, customs, and expectations, among which one must choose, appropriate and reproduce in order to gain identity in a complex process of mutual recognition' (Kellner, 1992). Indeed, since one of the features of post-modern society is its instability, complexity, lack of conformity and that 'it has become increasingly difficulty to confidently assume the identity or significance of particular events' (Grossberg, 1989), and given the consequent fragmentation of the individual-society contractual relationship, it seems odd, or contrary, to produce documents which imply 'appropriate social discourse'. It is as though the documents offering guidance on the social in the curriculum come from a modernist, rather than a post-modernist, framework.

As Smart (1993) argues, post-modern life involves relational values, rather than absolute ones, in part perhaps because it is 'continually in a state of flux, perpetually in motion or processual in character'. Though not all sociologists agree to define contemporary society as 'post-modern' (Giddens, 1990, for example, argues that we 'are currently living in a period of *high* modernity' (my emphasis), by which he means the institutionalization of doubt at the social, political and economic levels of everyday life), what I observe is that the certitude of shared values implied in the act of publishing both statutory and guidance documents on the school curriculum does not reflect the actual social political and economic context.

On the other hand, there is some parallel between the values-uniformity implied within a centralized school curriculum and the particular consumer aspects of post-modern life, such as what George Ritzer (1993) has called 'McDonaldization' — in other words, the domination of homogenous products, technologies and work routines as one finds in multinational product chains such as the McDonald's hamburger chain. As Ritzer has pointed out, the existence of classic Fordist work organisations such as McDonalds's, with its rigidity, rationality and lack of flexibility, suggests that alongside the differentiation and flexibility that supposedly characterizes the post-modern era, forms of modernist life continue to exist. The co-existence of a modernist educational policy within a partially post-modern social context is perhaps unsurprising and unremarkable. However, there is a difference between making policy on how children should socially define themselves, and operating a workplace whose mission statement is geared ultimately to making a profit. The modernist or Fordist nature of McDonald's, although not unproblematic in terms of what it embodies and fosters in the social identity of its employees and its customers, nevertheless is not charged with the same level of responsibility as policymakers wanting to influence the thinking and actions of young children. Policymakers claim to hold up a mirror of society to young children. This mirror is like a joke fairground one, distorted, but the difference is that children — and teachers — are not necessarily aware of this.

Conclusion

It has been argued that the emerging model of cross-curricular work can be viewed as representing an empowerment curriculum and therefore should be seen as each pupil's entitlement; and some of the implications of taking this view have been outlined for teaching and learning. Some of the implications of the notion of 'self' in relation to 'social' which are embedded in the themes have been explored, and it has been argued that the existence of the cross-curricular themes at all as forms of knowledge suggest a dated approach to personal identity, in that a curriculum of social values implying mutual recognition and acceptance is set out within them.

For them to facilitate the learner as an active sense-maker in the whirl of post-modern culture, the possibilities of wider interpretation and extension must be acknowledged. To some extent, teachers' own concept of 'self' may influence the ways (if at all) the cross-curricular themes are implemented in their classrooms. The approach to selfhood which is emphasized will depend on the sorts of learning experiences children are offered as well as what is implicit in the written curriculum. And for some children, this will mean being offered a post-modern framework for exploring ideas in each of the themes; 'flexibility' and 'differentiation' in values rather than bureaucratization and uniformity. The question remains, however, how many children *will* in fact experience this flexibility within the whole curriculum; statutory subjects and cross-curricular themes included. A demoralized profession which the government has tried systematically to turn into 'technocrats' combined with a particular form of cultural acceptance within staffroom sub-culture in the primary school as documented by Nias (1989) may combine to prevent some teachers from recognizing the distortion in the mirror they are offered. Those that do, and who also go beyond the subjects in the statutory curriculum in their classrooms, may be far less inclined to reflect critically and to offer pupils that opportunity.

Many of these implications involve staff development and INSET, but others may lie beyond schools — for example, it may be that research is required on the assessment of pupils' understandings of each of the themes (but see Blyth, 1990). Accepting the primacy of the individual may require a political shift which can only happen in integration with teachers' own personal lives. Questions need to be asked, such as are the five cross-curricular themes which the NCC identified appropriate and sufficient? *Are* they empowering, or do they indoctrinate? How far do they reflect a post-modern society of variety, anachronisms, flux, choice and immense diversity? How far do they in fact imply a shared set of accepted values?

All of the implications for schools and teachers take for granted a common starting point, where teachers recognize and accept that the cross-curricular themes, like equal opportunities, are every teacher's responsibility. Achieving this recognition and accepting it will be a great challenge for the development of this emerging model of cross-curricular work. Just as difficult may be the acceptance of a model of the social as the individual's responsibility.

Chapter 6

Citizenship in the Primary Curriculum

Keith Crawford

The theme of this chapter is that *Curriculum Guidance 8: Education for Citizenship* (NCC, 1990f) is a controversial document. This is for two reasons: firstly because the issues it deals with are controversial, and secondly because of the manner in which it deals with those issues. While the document is certainly less muddled than *Educating for Economic and Industrial Understanding* (NCC, 1990b), it is not as helpful as *Environmental Education* (NCC, 1990d) or *Health Education* (NCC, 1990c). It is weak on the how, but perhaps more than any other of the curriculum guidance series, it is strong on the what and the why. This document is controversial because it is full of statements which focus upon values and value judgments. Nor are these implicit values, hidden away: the reader does not have to search very far for the document's opening statement, written by Duncan Graham, which clearly establishes its ideological perspective:

> *Education for Citizenship* is essential for every pupil. It helps each of them to understand the duties, responsibilities and rights of every citizen and promotes concern for the values by which a civilised society is identified — justice, democracy, respect for the rule of law. (NCC, 1990f, Foreword)

Throughout the pages of *Education for Citizenship* it is this relationship between duties, responsibilities and rights which form the cornerstone of the document's ideology. There is an expectation that the active promotion of, and support for, a democratic society will form part of a child's curriculum entitlement, and that it is preparation for adult citizenship that will be a central feature of that entitlement. *Education for Citizenship* also places emphasis upon the concept of the individual citizen who, assuming responsibility for their own actions, is encouraged to act in support of the principles and practices of a democratic society. Although the guidance document supports the promotion of attitudes and modes of behaviour that focus on personal initiative, enterprise and wealth creation, the development of individual moral codes and patterns of behaviour are acceptable only within a context of shared values and beliefs which are said to function in order to reproduce a democratic society:

> Education for citizenship develops the knowledge, skills and attitudes necessary for exploring, making informed decisions about and exercising

responsibilities and rights within a democratic society. (NCC, 1990f, p. 2)

Key principles include the process of democratic decision-making, the development of shared values and the identification of common ground. It is difficult to turn a page without being reminded that as well as having rights, individual citizens also have legal and moral obligations as members of a community. The necessity of encouraging '. . . respect for the law' (*ibid.*, p. 6) is identified as is the need to create a balance '. . . between individual rights, duties and responsibilities' (*ibid.*, p. 7).

The inclusion of such statements within a curriculum document begs a number of questions. Lest what follows should be accused of being an assault on the fundamental principles of a democratic society let me say at the outset that it is not the purpose of this chapter to mount an attack on a belief in the rule of law, to cast doubts upon a concept of justice or to argue that rights, duties and responsibilities within a democratic framework are not important. However, inherent in such statements are sets of assumptions about society which require analysis, for there are more fundamental questions which underpin the realization and practical experience of such values in everyday life. These assumptions, and the questions they raise, are not presented for discussion in *Education for Citizenship*. This chapter seeks to draw attention to that omission and to suggest alternative directions in the study of citizenship.

What are the origins of the concept of citizenship presented in the curriculum guidance document, and how can we contextualize its emergence as part of the curriculum? These are important questions, for although they may seem divorced from the daily experience of teachers and children, they provide a very real context for those experiences. Schools do not exist independently of society. School organization and management, the way in which the curriculum is selected, structured and presented — all are responses to the way in which the society of the school is influenced by the society outside the school. Upon what socioeconomic and political set of values is *Education for Citizenship* based?

Citizenship: Competing Models

Education for Citizenship does not deal explicitly with the debate behind the emergence of citizenship as a curriculum area and it shares this omission with other publications in the series of curriculum guidance papers. But this does not mean that it presents no evidence as to why citizenship is considered to be an important feature of the curriculum. There are two sources of evidence:

- from the context provided by the wider debate over citizenship;
- from what *Education for Citizenship* contains, and importantly, omits.

The second of these two sources will be discussed later, within the context of empowerment and indoctrination; this first section will explore the underlying theoretical framework of *Education for Citizenship* through an analysis which takes the concept of class as a defining characteristic of society. Such a base for analysis would not be the sole property of the Left. But for almost any social and political analysis which emphasises the importance of class divisions, the framework suggested in *Education for Citizenship* presents problems.

The concept of class as the framework within which socioeconomic and political struggle takes place has a powerful, important and well-established historical pedigree. Even amongst its critics — and there are many — it is accepted as an explanation which merits proper consideration while for its supporters it provides the context for explanation of the social, economic and political structures of contemporary Britain. The theory is centred on questions concerning the legitimacy of unevenly distributed power and authority, and these must be central concerns in any discussion of citizenship. For some, power and authority has been appropriated by the capitalist class, and it is only through struggle, over generations, that the working class has established its entitlement to particular rights. The possession of these rights is seen to be continually under attack from the structure of a capitalist society, and workers are encouraged to be on their guard against their erosion.

A good example of this is provided by successive Conservative governments' concerns with trade union power, and the amount of parliamentary legislation enacted during the 1980s to check that power. Conservatives see such action as politically justifiable and necessary within their mandate from the electorate: trade unionists view it as an unwarranted attack upon legal rights which they have fought to establish during the previous ninety years.

Class theory also provides an explanation of the social problems which confront particular members of society such as economic and political discrimination and inequality. Some analysts see these problems as a consequence of the way in which society is organized, in which 'true' and 'democratic' equality is denied to all but a few. These issues are of crucial concern to the development of an active and informed citizenry. This is particularly so when those who seek to sustain class divisions perceive individuals as being members of classes, and not as citizens.

An alternative view of social organization is based upon the concept of functional integration, which challenges the centrality of class in social differentiation. Here the concept of citizenship in the NCC Curriculum Guidance document takes shape and is given meaning. In a classic study Marshall (1950) defines citizenship as a 'status', which is coupled with full membership of a community. Citizenship bestows upon individuals equal rights before the law, such as civil, political and social duties, powers and responsibilities. Halsey (1981) identifies two forms of social division based upon occupation and status patterns. Halsey argues that it is possible to group together certain occupations through the identification of shared interests and common working situations and conditions. In this way Halsey identifies three classes, a middle class, a lower middle class and a working class adding that the consequences of such divisions are extensive economic inequalities. He then poses the question: given that there is so much economic inequality why, as a consequence, is there not greater social conflict?

For Halsey, the answer is that, despite economic inequalities, other equalities have been created between all members of society in three key areas, and these marginalize economic inequality. These areas are:

- legal equality focusing upon civil rights;
- political citizenship based upon universal suffrage; and
- social citizenship based upon the benefits of a welfare state, to which all are entitled.

This results in limiting social conflict and clashes of interests on class grounds, because of the quality of the status provided by these basic principles of citizenship. Halsey suggests that we should see ourselves as British citizens rather than class members. The contrast between this and a class model of social organization is clear. While the citizenship of Halsey and Marshal is a *social* identity, the Marxist two class model poses an *economic* identity. The concepts of citizenship and class can thus be seen to be in conflict: while citizenship unites, class divides. Citizenship is presented as an overriding status, shared by all members of society, which places the conflict of class inequalities on the periphery of social concern.

In what sense do these models compete to explain the state of British society, and where are the ideas within *Education for Citizenship* located in this argument? The empirical validity and coherence of both models can be explored within a context provided by the socioeconomic and political changes which have taken place in British society during the past thirty years but particularly during the period 1970 to 1990.

This period has been one of rapid social, political and economic change. Fundamental questions were being asked about the existence and the nature of British society, and what it might mean to be a full and equal member of this — and, most critically for the present discussion, what might be the role of education in shaping society's values. Woven into the fabric of many of the various explanations that were put forward to account for Britain's social and economic difficulties, throughout the 1970s and 1980s, were criticisms of education. In contrast to the view of education in the 1950s and 1960s, that it could provide the answer to many social and economic problems, there was great disillusionment with education in the following two decades. The argument from the earlier period, that increased spending on education was an investment in the nation's economic prosperity, had a hollow ring about it in the later period.

These economic, social and political changes were the agents in the radical reappraisal of the education service which followed in the late 1980s, and it is within this context that we can locate the origins of *Education for Citizenship*. This is illustrated in the document's content, as one looks for answers to these questions: is *Education for Citizenship* a vehicle for empowerment or for indoctrination? Is it a liberal and pluralist document, which encourages discussion and diversity? Or is it a document designed to assist in the process of cultural reproduction, an instrument through which to maintain the socioeconomic and political hegemony of conservatism?

Citizenship: Empowerment or Indoctrination?

The concept of empowerment is part of a well-established educational orthodoxy about the way in which the curriculum is structured and implemented, and the way in which children's learning is organized. As its focal point, empowerment has the development of children's powers of critical awareness and understanding. To empower children is to provide them with the knowledge, skills and understanding necessary to explore values, beliefs and taken-for-granted assumptions, through a curriculum which enables them to develop these. It is a process in which children gradually assume a measure of responsibility for their own learning, in which they develop personal confidence and self-esteem, and the ability to make decisions based on rational choices.

For educational liberals this is no wishy-washy radicalism, or a by-product of the Plowdenesque rhetoric of the 1960s, but is a significant element of a child's personal, social and cognitive development. It is not part of a left wing plot or attempt to undermine society. Though such arguments have appeared in the media since the 1960s, they only trivialize an issue which is soundly grounded in educational practice.

Is there any evidence in *Education for Citizenship* that suggests it is a document designed to empower children in the manner described? The document states that children should be encouraged to discuss values and beliefs, and that they should develop '. . . respect for different opinions, beliefs and values'. They should acquire '. . . independence of thought' and explore '. . . cooperation and competition between individuals, groups and communities' (NCC, 1990f, p. 4). While these are clearly important areas of experience, I would suggest that the emphasis of the document is weighted in a different direction, away from notions of empowerment, diversity and difference, and towards conformity and consensus. The exhortation to explore alternatives is only half-hearted, and this call is overwhelmed by the series of statements that children are expected to learn about:

'. . . rights and responsibilities in a democratic society';
'. . . shared values and moral qualities';
'. . . the identification of common ground';
'. . . the maintenance of social stability';
'. . . promotion of respect for the law';
'. . . the importance of family life';
'. . . the public good';
'. . . individual responsibility'.

Through the consistent expression of such values, *Education for Citizenship* has its ideological and theoretical roots within the functionalist paradigm. The basic premise of functionalism is that the interdependence and interrelationship of different parts of the social system combine and balance to produce an integrated society that functions equitably. Such a society is based upon the continued equilibrium of those parts, and in order for society to continue to function effectively, those parts must remain in balance. Change necessarily creates imbalance, uncertainty, tensions and socioeconomic discontinuities. Functionalism is a conservative theory which explains and justifies the established social and economic structure and political order. Its influence can be seen throughout the pages of *Education for Citizenship*.

The functionalist nature of the document can be seen in the primacy it gives to the role of the individual and the family, and the importance attached to 'community'. These core elements are the critical features of a functional view of society, because they provide the basis for social integration. The role of the individual in society is an important feature of conservative ideology. Crudely, individual problems and socioeconomic difficulties are a product of individual inadequacies, and individual successes are the consequence of individual enterprise and initiative. If people are unemployed, it is because they have not looked hard enough for work, or have not qualified themselves with the necessary skills for work. Within such an individualistic ideology, the role of the state in supporting individuals can be marginal, for it must be the individual's responsibility — not society's — to provide for themselves and their families within the market economy.

A similar set of values and assumptions surrounds definitions of the family. The family, a 'central component' in *Education for Citizenship*, is the primary unit in establishing and maintaining social cohesion. Within the context of the family children learn the socioeconomic, gender and power norms, and the rules and expectations which shape their attitudes and guide their behaviour. The roles that children learn within the family are often the prototypes of roles they will adopt in later life. These roles need not necessarily be occupational, and are related to more fundamental issues such as hierarchical relationships of power, authority and the individual responsibilities and duties, which are always an important element of conservative rhetoric. The structural link between the family, family values and behaviour and wider society is recognized and exploited in *Education for Citizenship*. The document may in passing acknowledge the existence of alternative family patterns, but within the central component the issues to be addressed include the '. . . legal and moral responsibilities of parents and children; patterns of marriage and family structure and the challenges facing family units' (*ibid.*, p. 7).

What of 'community', another central component? The stress on the duties, rights and responsibilities of the individual and the way in which combinations of individuals form the basis of communities illustrates a further key aspect of functionalism, that of interdependence. The community is a focal point of integration. In *Education for Citizenship* support for the bonds of community is through the identification and maintenance of common interests and the way in which community identification helps '. . . pupils to recognize how order and stability are maintained' and '. . . the role of the family, education, religion, culture and social structure in maintaining social stability' (*ibid.*, p. 5).

The concerns of *Education for Citizenship* are the products of the political concerns of the new right in the 1980s, and they reflect the analysis of citizenship presented by Halsey and Marshall. Evidence of this comes from the larger educational and political context in which the document originated. There was a perceived need to reestablish a stable and integrated society, to be based upon market choice, the entrepreneurial spirit, individual initiative and popular consumerism. Much of the language of *Education for Citizenship* reflects the writings of Halsey and Marshall, particularly the identification of political, social and legal citizenship which binds communities together, and in the notion of reciprocity between rights and duties, '. . . if citizenship is involved in the defence of rights, the corresponding duties of citizenship cannot be ignored' (Marshall, 1950, p. 112).

Is there any place for social class within this conception of citizenship? *Education for Citizenship* clearly assumes, by its omission, that social class can no longer be considered the primary social division in Britain. Class is seen as an outdated and outmoded concept, which has been replaced by other, more relevant, patterns of social organization such as status. Curriculum documents such as *Education for Citizenship* wean us to the idea that the notion of citizenship will actively dissolve class boundaries. But because the economic, social and political system of Britain has been based upon notions of class difference, *Education for Citizenship* could be presented as an attempt to isolate old antagonisms and devise new ways of thinking about living and working in society.

The Implication for Teachers

This analysis of *Education for Citizenship* poses a number of very important questions for teachers. Does the document's reliance upon a functional view of society provide a comprehensive, coherent and acceptable framework from within which the active citizen may explore contemporary society? I am not convinced that this is the case. The ideological perspective which *Education for Citizenship* adopts marginalizes both the conflicts of interest which arise out of different socio-economic and political experiences and the very idea of social conflict. Every area of social life reveals alternative opinions, values and beliefs — between employers and employees, between educational liberals and conservatives, between supporters of Liverpool and Everton. It is difficult to accept the idea that contemporary society — plural in faith, languages and ethnicity, increasingly stratified in wealth, power and ownership — is functional and integrated. The social and economic experiences of people suggests that it does not work in this way. Halsey's suggestion that 'social citizenship' has reduced social inequalities does not seem to be true in the 1990s.

While we might all wish to support civil, political and economic equality and a pluralist view of society, experience suggests that in practice such equality is an elusive goal. The core values that are unquestioningly presented in *Education for Citizenship*, such as justice and democracy, are highly generalized and abstracted labels, which in practice generate intense disagreement and alternative explanations and definitions. We may agree generally with the concept of justice and with the principles of democracy but disagreement is common about what these labels mean in practice. People's experiences of these fundamental aspects of citizenship are often more ambiguous, complicated and contradictory than *Education for Citizenship* acknowledges. In criticizing the very concept of citizenship, Brown (1991) makes the point that:

> in some curious way citizenship drains the anger away from the much more defiant sounding citizen. Men and women have died for the rights of the citizen — citizenship smothers this history in complacency and smugness. Social and economic equality are as far from being achieved today as they were in the ancien regime — citizenship obscures this, and makes out that our society has reached the pinnacle of justice. (p. 90)

Within the context of contemporary British society, the rights of citizenship may not be positively enjoyed by those citizens who experience them within a framework of anger, frustration and disappointment. Although Britain may be a constitutional and parliamentary democracy, for many members of society it is also a rhetorical and flawed democracy. There is little suggestion within *Education for Citizenship* that British society is riddled with conflict in key areas of social, economic and political life, or that such conflicts should be recognised and included within the curriculum and be worthy of critical investigation.

This is the crux of what is wrong with *Education for Citizenship*. It is a flawed document, because it relies on a set of assumptions about how society should operate which are in many respects questionable. The rhetoric of *Education for Citizenship* hides the fact that for many people the experiences of citizenship take place within a framework of inequality. Although the document acknowledges in passing that inequalities may exist, there is no suggestion that children might perhaps question the idea that Britain is an adequately democratic society. The document focuses upon how society is said to work, and not upon why it works as it does — or even if it 'works'. Yet the why question is crucial for the active and influential citizen, because it encourages the exploration of central questions about political power and democratic choice. *Education for Citizenship* is a reactive document, rather than a proactive one, and it has been decontextualized from the lived reality of ordinary men, women and children.

This argument is not to accept that many of the values presented in *Education for Citizenship* are important and worth protecting. But these values too are worth exploring critically in an effort to help develop a more informed and balanced understanding. The failure of the National Curriculum Council's guidance in this area is that it does not emphasize such an approach. We are left with a narrow view of British society, in a document which, because it neglects to invite serious comparison with alternatives, loses strength, vitality and radical urgency.

This curriculum document can be seen as an attempt to construct a functional hegemony and to engineer and manufacture a fictitious consent: and this damages the democratic process. Social integration, and the realization of democratic principles, might be better achieved not by such a universalistic functional response, but through negotiation, bargaining and the balanced discussion of fundamental and underlying differences, inequalities, and problems. *Education for Citizenship* has greatly underestimated the powerful descriptive analysis of social differentiation: while clichéd class labels may no longer always be the appropriate definition of differentiation, the consequences of differentiation remain. The document fails to acknowledge that the key reason why society does not collapse into chaos or is not openly dictatorial is because power and authority have been, and continue to be, negotiated by citizens.

Negotiation is an important social and political concept, based on the interaction between two or more parties, each with contrasting objectives which they seek to maximize. Negotiation involves fashioning a situational contract based on mutual satisfaction, a kind of fragile and often temporary equilibrium achieved through an arbitrated system of checks and balances. It involves bargaining and compromise, realism and pragmatism. Negotiative encounters are dynamic and ongoing, as participants shift between agreement, conflict and compromise.

Education for Citizenship does not appear to fully recognize this aspect of social life, and therefore does not invite a proper exploration of the processes of socioeconomic and political negotiation. Children should be encouraged to explore the power relationships and politics of citizenship, its concern with competing ethical and ideological values, and its central concern with controversy. It is in this last point that we find a paradox. Although the document indicates that 'education for citizenship involves discussing controversial issues upon which there is no clear consensus' (*ibid.*, p. 14), nowhere is it identified, or even indicated, what these controversial issues might be. It is not even conceded that *Education for Citizenship* itself might be controversial. To only offer implicit identification with diversity and controversy is unsatisfactory and not enough.

This chapter is not advocating a move towards some kind of social utopia. Marxist models of class conflict offer a equally simplistic and reductionist analyses of British society. They will not provide a sufficiently sound explanation of the complex social patterns around us, and this is particularly noticeable in its functional assumption that members of the working class (or the capitalist class) share common economic and social interests. In practice there may be genuine conflicts of interest within the working class, concerning for example degrees of job skill and wage differentials, the type of work people do, their earned income, expectations and status. Competition between firms resulting in price wars and bankruptcies also suggest that capitalists are in conflict. Neither does the two class theory make any reference to a middle class. Gibbins (1989) suggests that the diverse and challenging changes in contemporary society lead to political and cultural values such that:

> ... the emerging character of contemporary political culture is pluralistic, anarchic, disorganized, rhetorical, stylised, ironic and abstruse. (p. 23)

Narrow one-dimensional explanations, functionalist or Marxist, are inadequate for the development of a comprehensive understanding of citizenship and what being a citizen means. There is little intrinsically wrong with the ideas of personal responsibility and enterprise, or with active participation within a democratic framework. What is difficult to understand is the expectation in *Education for Citizenship* that these ideals can be achieved without a proper, balanced understanding of the key issues confronting the citizen. This would be a much truer empowerment. Without such empowerment and the curricular framework necessary to develop a socioeconomic and political critique of society, such ideals will remain elusive.

A Question of Interpretation

The argument so far has been that *Education for Citizenship* is incoherent, because it presents a partial, one-sided, view of British society which either marginalizes or ignores key features of the everyday lives of citizens. Citizenship is not a concept without value, but it represents a far more complex set of ideas than that provided for in *Education for Citizenship*. The document is imbalanced and an additional agenda is missing: it is doubtful whether it itself fulfils the provisions of the 1988 Education Act to provide a 'broad and balanced' curriculum. It may also succeed in infringing the 1986 Education (No. 2) Act (which is even quoted in the document), in that it is forbidden to engage in

> ... partisan political activities in primary schools and the promotion of partisan political views in the teaching of any subject in all schools. Where political issues are brought to the attention of pupils, there is a duty to secure that they are offered a balanced presentation of opposing views. (p. 14)

How might teachers react? What needs to be added to the curriculum agenda laid out in *Education for Citizenship*? The challenge for teachers is to engage in a personal exploration and analysis of the values *Education for Citizenship* supports, as a prelude to implementing a curriculum for citizenship in the classroom. Such an exploration could identify key questions which might offer an alternative perspective to some of the assumptions which have been shown to dominate the document. What might be included?

Section 3 of *Education for Citizenship* lists the objectives for citizenship education. The first part of that section suggests that pupils should develop knowledge and understanding of:

(i)   the nature of community;
(ii)   roles and relationships in a democratic society; and
(iii) the nature and basis of duties, responsibilities and rights.

The suggestions given under each of these labels contain much of interest and importance but, *pace* earlier criticisms, they remain too narrowly focused. Additional issues, such as those suggested below, might help produce a more balanced approach to the critical exploration of citizenship.

The Nature of Community

- How are communities organized in communist nations and in third world states; what are the strengths and weaknesses?
- What do we know and understand about the historical evolution of feudal, tribal and totalitarian societies?
- Why do some communities persist, while others perish or change?
- How can the development of a wider understanding of the sociology of communities help explain contemporary British society?
- What are the alternative sets of values and assumptions about how British society is organized and functions?

Roles and Relationships in a Democratic Society

- To what extent can Britain be described as a democratic society?
- Is Britain a pluralist society?
- How do different socioeconomic, gender and ethnic groups experience democracy?
- What cause political, social and economic conflict and instability and what kinds of responses does society make?
- Who makes society's rules and laws and upon what basis?
- Who governs and exercises power and in whose interests?

The Nature and Basis of Duties, Responsibilities and Rights

- How are social, economic and political inequalities constructed and how are they challenged?
- Are rights within citizenship allocated and earned, or are they civil entitlements?
- Where does conflict emerge from and how can it be tackled?
- Is society 'fair'; if not why not?
- What rights do citizens actually have; are they formal or substantive?
- How can rights be challenged and protected, extended and modified?
- Who decides what is in the common good?
- What role can individuals legitimately take in challenging the power and authority of the rule-makers?
- How, precisely, are the rule-makers accountable to the rule-followers?
- How is society differentiated, and what are the origins of those differentiations?

It could be argued that, inherently and implicitly, there is an expectation in the Curriculum Guidance document that these issues will be explored. This is an inadequate line of reasoning. These kinds of questions, which explore contentious matters central to socioeconomic and political life, need clearly identifying in any document which claims to develop the ideology of the active, informed, reflective and participatory citizen.

Conclusion

This chapter has attempted to illustrate that *Education for Citizenship* has emerged as part of a radical attempt to change the cultural and ideological climate of British society. It is a part of a concerted attempt to redefine and redraw the boundaries of earlier notions about the nature and workings of society. *Education for Citizenship* is part of the new right orthodoxy which challenges the idea that society operates on class lines. Within a framework of participative citizenship, *Education for Citizenship* can be interpreted as an attempt to replace a social class analysis with one which focuses attention upon citizenship, because this concept implies a unity across class boundaries.

It was then suggested that this presented a narrow and limited analysis of contemporary British society, which in practice is anything but functional, but full of inequalities and democratic inconsistencies which need to be addressed. *Education for Citizenship* would become a much more significant document, and might aid the process of empowerment, if it gave encouragement to teachers to raise questions with children about many of the taken-for-granted assumptions about socioeconomic and political life. If children move beyond the surface veneer of *Education for Citizenship*, and critically explore much of what it has to say, then society will be the richer. This may actually help in developing a truly democratic and pluralist society by opening up a public debate through the curriculum.

But in its current form, the claim that citizenship unites, while class divides, is dubious. The hidden purpose of *Education for Citizenship* appears to be to maintain a society characterized by massive differentials of power and equality. The content of the document is weighted towards the uncritical acceptance of this particular type of society, through the development of attitudes which do not develop children's critical awareness. It is claimed that *Education for Citizenship* offers guidance to implementing education about the sociopolitical realities of contemporary British society. The flawed nature of the document makes it doubtful whether such a claim can be justified.

Chapter 7

Hidden Controversies in Two Cross-curricular Themes

John Ahier

Introduction

The intention of this chapter is to explore how two cross-curricular themes, economic and industrial understanding, and environmental education, have been officially constructed within the National Curriculum, with particular reference to curriculum development in the primary school. Two documents, *Curriculum Guidance 4* for the economic (NCC, 1990b), and *Curriculum Guidance 7* for the environmental (NCC, 1990e), were produced by the National Curriculum Council. These claimed to give teachers advice on how to incorporate the two themes within their teaching. The texts attempted to present justifications for the themes, offered suggestions on how to tackle them, and also provide examples of work carried out within the areas, but all within the structure of a National Curriculum made up of traditional school subjects. Thus, for example, the reader was invited to consider the economic and industrial elements within history, geography or English, to use industrial examples and reference points within these subjects, and to incorporate economic data within mathematics.

However, the status of these cross-curricular themes has remained uncertain. They are not areas of knowledge insisted on by law, yet, in comparison with the other cross-curricular issues, they do indicate important areas of intellectual understanding, research and dispute which cannot be contained within the traditional school subjects. The two chosen here are informed by economics, sociology, politics and ecology, which are regarded as separate subjects in institutions of higher education, but not within the National Curriculum. The themes and many of their informing disciplines are not to have the status of subjects within the nation's schools. On the other hand, when compared with the other cross-curricular elements listed in the NCC *Circular Number 6* (NCC, 1989), these themes have definite intellectual content and unavoidable links with the academic.

Perhaps the most useful way of understanding these themes is to see them as encapsulating public concerns, which any educational system proclaiming itself to be about the promotion of 'the spiritual, moral, cultural, mental and physical development of pupils at school and of society' (Education Reform Act, 1988, Part 1, chapter 1, Great Britain) must acknowledge. We do not know whether they will have any long-term future within the administration of the National Curriculum, but because they originated in contemporary public concerns this does make them an important part of its legitimation. They appear to connect this vast bureaucratic and traditional edifice, constructed by the distant central state, to the world of some real local and national public debates. The hope must be that the cross-curricular themes will give some point and coherence to the officially approved collection of separately developed programmes of study in the different subjects. They may also have been intended to provide a palliative to those who suspected that a curriculum made up of separate academic subjects would destroy all that was good in modern school practice.

But, just as there are vital disagreements within the academic subjects which inform the themes, these public concerns themselves are not defined in a consensual way either. There are very definite divisions between the groups who construct the concerns. For example, behind what might be described as the environmental lobby lie a number of serious disagreements on theory, philosophy, tactics, strategy and political perspective. Similarly, the pressures to include industrial understanding in schools arose from a variety of conflicting expressions of the needs of industry and explanations of Britain's economic decline.

In a more confident democracy, acknowledging such disagreements within the discourses from which a national school curriculum is developed, should cause no difficulty. Indeed, if the central state has to take upon itself the task of offering guidance to professional educators in such areas, one would expect that a first step would be to alert them to the contested nature of these areas and, ideally, provide some constructive help in dealing with this. In a less arrogant centralized state another way may be to suggest forms of consultation and representation which might give guidance to schools on how to consult locally on such matters.

In the case of these two cross-curricular themes these were not the approaches chosen by the National Curriculum Council.

True, there is an acceptance in the documents that these themes deal in controversial matters. In *Education for Economic and Industrial Understanding*, for example, it is acknowledged that

> education for economic and industrial understanding involves controversial issues such as the impact of economic activity on the environment

and it goes on to say that

> schools should ensure, where relevant, that there is a balanced presentation of opposing views. Pupils should be encouraged to explore values and beliefs, both their own and those of others. (NCC, 1990b, p. 3)

Similar points are made in *Environmental Education* about the environment being 'the subject of considerable debate' (NCC, 1990e, p. 1).

Unfortunately the documents avoid any mention of the *actual* intellectual or political controversies involved, because disagreement is seen to exist only in the form of value differences in relation to a single issue. They identify no major differences of informed opinion about economic or environmental matters, no 'schools of thought', no theoretical or ideological conflicts. The documents' coyness about what one might call organized oppositions means they can suggest no ways in which teachers within a democratic society should deal with such disagreements and differences.

This point is particularly interesting when applied to an aspect of the curriculum not identified as a conventional academic subject and justified in terms of personal and social development. In geography or history the presence of disputes may not be so problematic because they can be sealed in, and isolated as 'interpretations' or theories. But in a cross-curricular theme such differences could connect with a whole range of understandings, and actually come to mean something more important for the child's life beyond the school. Our thinking about the environment or the economy is likely to have close connections with how we live our personal lives, how we vote, and so on.

Cross-curricularity and Integration

In order to explore the construction of these two cross-curricular themes it is worth comparing notions of cross-curricularity as presented in the two publications with some ideas about integration which have influenced primary school practice in the past. As Marsden (1993) has shown, in the nineteenth and early twentieth century, the space now occupied by cross-curricular themes was dominated by powerful lobbies, including the church, and they promoted their particular messages. Later, however, it has usually been the case that arguments to integrate school subjects and school work in general were associated with a critical attack on educational traditions and practices from what appeared to be an internal, educational-psychological point of view. These arguments were based on various critiques of the 'divided curriculum', its inability to deal with the worlds as experienced by children, its mistaken epistemological or psychological assumptions, its intention to mystify or alienate. Given that much of the promotion of the National Curriculum and other aspects of the Education Reform Act have been informed by attacks on the educational progressivism derived from the 1960s and 1970s, it may be helpful to look back briefly at two different attempts to promote integration then, and compare them with the stance taken on cross-curricularity within the guidance on cross-curricular themes. After all, we are constantly presented with a picture of the 1960s and 1970s as the time when things went wrong with the schools, and the origin of our present social and economic difficulties, so a brief, slightly bemused retrospect might be useful.

Although they were chiefly concerned with integration as an organizational concept, arguments for the integrated day in primary schools provide one useful source for understanding the kinds of ideas which were expressed at the time. Books on the integrated day (Brown and Precious, 1968; Walton, 1971) contained numerous critical references to the artificiality of subject divisions, and how the division of learning into timetabled subjects went against the natural ways in which children learn and develop. In their glowing descriptions of the workings of the integrated day in their own infant and junior schools Brown and Precious (1968) claimed that

> the natural flow of activity, imagination, language, thought and learning which is in itself a continuous process is not interrupted by artificial breaks such as the conventional playtime or subject barriers . . . Subject barriers are extraneous (p. 13)

Later, when describing what they called this 'new adventure' in the infants school they declare that

> subject barriers and divisions of time do not and could not exist in this school with such a dynamic atmosphere. The children's interests and needs are the determining factor, not the timetable and subjects. (*ibid.*, p. 57)

Their arguments presume a vague but persistent conception of how children learn and experience the world, and this produces a continual justification for the abandonment of school subjects;

> As the child explores the real world he relates it to his own inner mental world, he uses his inner mental images to explore reality and he is continually building each in terms of the other. As the young child brings his imagination and his fantasy life to bear in all his activity, the creative, expressive and imaginative activities cannot really be separated from learning such things as mathematics and reading. (*ibid.*, p. 41)

This text directly addresses the classroom teacher. Its persuasiveness rests upon a view of the teacher as an expert in understanding the psychology and life of children, their needs and true nature. This is what was taken as defining the teachers' professionalism and status, and distinguished them from the uninformed parent;

> Teachers stand in *loco parentis* but teachers have had professional training which is not available to the wise and good parent and so their assessment of the children's needs should be more knowledgeable and obviously more objective. (*ibid.*, p. 36)

Consistent with the attacks on the subject-based curriculum, there was no mention of the academic or intellectual aspects of being a successful teacher. Instead the qualities are of a psychological, personal and moral kind. Describing the ideal teacher for the integrated day they declare that,

As well as being intelligent and well trained, the teacher needs to be an adjusted, resilient and sympathetic person having a fund of humour and common sense. (*ibid.*, p. 25)

A second approach to curriculum integration at the primary level which was promoted at the time has direct relevance to environmental education. This maintained that, almost regardless of the way in which children think and live, there is something about various objects of study which make it necessary to deal with them as integrated topics in schools. The environment has been thought to be such an object, and environmental studies has remained a consistent form of integration ever since the 1960s. Not only was it thought motivating and 'realistic' for children to study their locality, but it was also thought impossible to divide the history of a place from its geography, its culture from its economy, and so forth (Rolls, 1969). When combined with the idea that the curriculum must be relevant to the everyday lives of particular groups of children, and have a social purpose, this approach to integration took a variety of radical forms.

Perhaps the most influential of this type of integration was presented by Eric Midwinter in articles and papers arising from his work as Director of the Liverpool Educational Priority Area Project. Here too we find a set of very explicit criticisms of previous educational practice, and a clear invitation to teachers to change, especially those in inner city areas. In comparison with Brown and Precious, however, the arguments rest upon quite different premises. In *Curriculum and the EPA Community School* (1971) he acknowledges that there has already been some major changes in methods, but they have not dealt with the social dimension. Inspired by child-centredness, such changes cannot address the real problems of social, collective regeneration necessary because 'there has not, unhappily, been a similar radicalism in content' (p. 485).

Thus, structural curriculum integration is not seen as the answer of itself, because teachers might continue to teach the same remote, sterile and backward-looking content within an integrated organization. On the other hand, he was certainly critical of what he termed the

bric-a-brac of this and that, bits and pieces of history, shreds and patches of geography, dribs and drabs of scripture, bubbles and squeaks of science . . . (*ibid.*, p. 486)

For him the crucial questions are as follows. Is the content realistic to the children living in the catchment area of the school? Has the curriculum got a clear social purpose? The curriculum must be community oriented, it must be about the problems facing actual children, and it is this which will give children the necessary motivation.

. . . the child is dignified by the acceptance that education can be about him and his environs, that he is an historical character in a geographical situation with social, spiritual, technical and other problems facing him. (*ibid.*, p. 489)

In this approach we have a quite different basis for integration. It is not the interests of the child, or the way he/she thinks and comes to understand, but the *community*. It is the latter which is taken as providing the themes which he lists; 'occupations', 'streets', 'money' 'transport', or 'the city'. (Interestingly, he uses as illustration a project on the supermarket which has remained a favourite over the years, and is now used as a vehicle for teaching economic and industrial understanding in many primary schools.)

If the basis for integration is different, then so is the image of the ideal teacher. In both cases the moral significance of the teacher is paramount, but, for Midwinter, he/she must be a realist, socially committed, politically aware, and able to appreciate the nature of life and culture within the locality. Such a teacher would have to make a radical break with her/his own schooling, its curriculum and its academic pretensions. They must be educationally born again;

> The teachers' conventional support of certain established planks have to be lessened, as they endeavour to conduct an objective examination of the issues facing people today in the city centres. This might include a questioning of, say, the viability of local government procedures or the validity of social and cultural standards. (*ibid.*)

The key aspects of these two previous arguments for the lowering of curriculum boundaries, and many others like them, are as follows. First, they include a critique of previous practice, or the recognition of a definite problem. Second they identify the subject of, or reference point for, integration. In one case it was 'the whole child' and in the other 'the community'. Thirdly, they contain some particular view of the teacher to whom they address their arguments and who they try and persuade. The teacher-reader is a moral figure, open to moral contact and persuasion.

One cannot avoid noticing the contrasts between these approaches and that found in the two publications on cross-curricularity from the NCC with which we are concerned here.

To begin with there are no explicit criticisms of previous educational practice or analysis of wider problems with which such practice was associated. On environmental education there is the hint that when primary school topic work deals with such issues they 'may lack coherence, continuity and progression' (NCC, 1990e, p. 15). There is a list of environmental problems which constitute public concern, but nothing on the ways previous curriculum content and pedagogy may have played their part in hiding or even encouraging environmental degradation. In the case of economic and industrial understanding, the failure to refer to the whole debate about Britain's industrial decline, and the part English education and culture played in this, is even more surprising and irresponsible. The only connection between problems and practice is a brief reference to 'increasing economic competitiveness' and the belief that

> To meet this challenge pupils need to understand enterprise and wealth creation and develop entrepreneurial skills. (NCC, 1990b, p. 1)

From this one can see that the approach is, indeed, informed by a singular, and much contested, cultural explanation of economic decline (Wiener, 1981), but this is hidden in vague references to what understandings individuals need as they live their personal economic lives.

Next, there are very few references to 'the child', 'the community', 'the society' or any equivalent integrating reference points within these documents. There are no mentions of pupils' development, the way they learn, or, indeed, resist being taught. *Curriculum Guidance 4* claims that economic and industrial understanding gives contexts for relevant learning but the orientation is very much directed at future citizens, future producers and consumers. Perhaps it is inevitable that notions of the whole child are even more alien within a National Curriculum which is structured around the divisions between knowledge, attitudes and skills. One might accept that, in a diverse, multiethnic society, constructions such as 'the child' or 'the community' are now as awkward to maintain as 'the family', but it is not the acceptance of diversity and difference which excludes them from the vocabulary of these guidelines. After all, one of the aims of the National Curriculum was to reduce diversity and local difference. *Education for Economic and Industrial Understanding* proclaims a certain kind of universalism when it declares that

> all pupils, regardless of culture, gender or social background, should have equal access to a curriculum which promotes economic and industrial understanding. (*ibid.*, p. 6)

but it says nothing about the different ways the given form of economic understanding is likely to be received by those different groups mentioned, or whether some might be disadvantaged by the learning of such a narrow set of economic concepts.

There are clear differences, too, between the ways in which the earlier, often evangelical texts addressed teachers, and the approach in these guidelines. The latter do not attempt to change individual practice by critical appraisal or persuasive argument. Instead they are addressed more to schools as institutions, where the main problems are those of managing the system. Sentences begin with such phrases as 'Schools should consider . . .' or 'Schools will find it helpful to . . .'. In *Education for Economic and Industrial Understanding* for example, we find references to 'action plans' and 'audits of the whole curriculum', and similar points are made in *Environmental Education* and in the related NCC in-service publication (NCC, 1991). The approach is summed up in the following;

> Whatever provision schools choose to make, it will require careful management, clearly defined responsibilities for coordination, and explicit arrangements for monitoring and evaluation. (NCC, 1990b, p. 11)

In the absence of any integrating holisms like 'the child' or 'the society', these documents cannot try and persuade teachers to enter these forms of cross-curricularity by offering morally significant identities to them beyond their roles as teachers of given subjects. They do try to tell them how important it is to include environmental and economic themes in their teaching but, because of the form of address, such issues appear as being merely good vehicles for managing the whole curriculum and controlling the whole school.

It might be thought that similar government publications would always adopt such a form of address, but this has not been the case. Earlier official publications for the nation's teachers, such as the 1959 replacement for the old Ministry of Education *Handbook of Suggestions for Teachers*, spoke to teachers directly as autonomous, individual professionals. Indeed, there were clear, if rather cloying appreciation of their efforts, and in his foreword the Minister wrote about the 'tradition of independence and vitality among teachers' in this country (Ministry of Education, 1957b, p. iii).

This brings me to what I think is the major difference between the official promotion of cross-curricularity within an already pre-determined National Curriculum of traditional subjects, and arguments for integration in a decentralized school system. The latter allowed the professionals to incorporate a diversity of content, either in accordance with what they perceived to be children's individual interests and development, or in accordance with their views of the pupil's social-cultural situation. It is this professionally-based freedom which the National Curriculum has sought to preclude, and, in doing so, has changed the context for intraprofessional persuasion.

It is not now possible or desirable to defend the particular form of professional autonomy which was presumed by the advocates of the integrated day or the community curriculum referred to above. The former depended upon a certain professional arrogance and self-delusion that teachers, informed by psychologists, could know what children needed, and how they developed (Woodhead, 1991). The second encouraged us to think we could represent the local community in a unified way, as a subject of school study in terms acceptable to all those who lived there. Few could now believe in the roles of teacher as moral educator, child expert and social analyst which are presumed in texts of that sort. Indeed, some of the criticisms of self-appointed moral educators which evolved in the 1970s and 1980s may well have been justified.

But answering the possible excesses of the progressives with a return to the traditional subject curriculum is not justified either. It is based on the unsustainable belief that such subjects, being respectable, long-standing and apparently ideologically diverse, somehow protect the child from the biases of their teachers. This was the mistaken impression created by some of the 'sensible' philosophers of education writing at the same time as others were promoting integration and community curricula. Dearden (1971), for example, using terms which were to become key words in the jargon of the National Curriculum, thought that an integrated curriculum could not give 'the assurance of the balance and progression' which a subject curriculum can provide. He continued,

> An integrated curriculum will necessarily be dominated by some other unifying interest, such as the theme of the project, or the child's special hobby, or the teacher's own bias of mind. (*ibid.*, p. 50)

Similarly, Entwistle (1970), in a book which was very popular in the colleges of education at the time, complained about what he termed 'the integrationist's slogans' (p. 102), attacking their points about the so-called artificialiy of the subject-based curriculum and their largely unexamined assumption about the wholeness of human experience and knowledge implicit in the metaphor of the seamless garment (*ibid.*, p. 103). Nor did he approve of the local curriculum and its 'cultural parochialism' (*ibid.*, p. 107). These may well be justified criticisms, but his support for using a number of separate disciplines to look at one social issue (i.e., the kind of limited cross-curricularity found in the NCC guidance), because this somehow avoids bias is, at best, only partly true. Different subjects do not necessarily represent different value positions, except in the most superficial sense. Indeed, for long periods of time in English education, subjects like history and geography were separate yet mutually supportive in their construction of a particular national identity (Ahier, 1988). In a way, they both did the same ideological work, but accepted an academic division of labour.

No curriculum structures or forms of pedagogy can guarantee freedom from bias, but some forms of educational dialogue which accept openness and difference could still save the educational system from what could possibly be a widespread cynicism. Primary school teachers know that other values do exist, that there are other ways of thinking about economic life, of organizing the public services and so on, and these are supported by millions of people in our society. However, they find themselves having to teach within a curriculum, the structure and ethos of which reflects much from a period of uncompromising political assault on all alternatives to the market and possessive individualism. The two cross-curricular themes, economic and industrial understanding and environmental education, are ideal vehicles for the exploration of different ways of thinking and living. What is now needed is an exploration of the connections between such diversity and curriculum development. This could be seen as an antidote to the preoccupation with merely *managing* the curriculum handed down from central government.

The remainder of this chapter is not intended as a plea to return to the role of teacher as moral exemplar, nor should it be seen as a defence of any particular professional self interest, but as an attempt to suggest how curriculum dialogue could be pursued if the cynical role of teacher as state functionary is to be avoided. I will try to do this by identifying a range of positions within environmental and economic discussion which have quite different curricular implications. By doing so I hope to establish the inadequacies of *Education for Economic and Industrial Understanding* and *Environmental Education* as sources of guidance for teachers.

Different Articulations of Public Concern, Different Curricula

If, as I have attempted to argue, the cross-curricular themes are curricular constructions which are built on, or reflect major public concerns, then it is important to determine the extent to which the guidance offered reflects the range of positions expressed within those concerns.

Taking environmental education first, it is possible to identify some major clusters of different ideas about the nature of current environmental problems and differences of approach and analysis. What follows is not a detailed map of all the various forms of environmentalism but merely an indication of some key oppositions, dualities and differences which may have curricular implications. The most influential attempt to map these positions was originally published by O'Riordan in 1976 and later extended in his postscript to the second edition of his book *Environmentalism* (1981). Here the attempt is made to distinguish two basic positions in environmental discussion, along with certain subdivisions (viz. pp. 12–19 and 375–80). This basic map, together with later additions (for example: Pepper, 1984; Porrit and Winner, 1988) is informed by the following duality.

On one side we find a set of ideas which have been called 'dark green' or 'deep environmentalist' which include extensive criticism of the institutions of modern industrial societies, their centralism, undemocratic nature, and their dependence on technologies which control people and things in a destructive way. This position is generally critical of economic growth and its attendant materialism. Cotgrove (1982) has termed this approach 'catastrophist' on the grounds that those who occupy it believe that without fundamental changes in attitudes and institutions, then life on the planet is doomed. The tenor and emphasis of this general position can vary between those who use more personal, philosophical-religious forms of expression and engagement, and those who concentrate on the forms of social, economic and political life which are to be promoted as alternatives. In general, however, O'Riordan (1976) uses the term 'ecocentric' to identify all these positions which seek to promote the values of reverence, humility, responsibility and care which are based upon a holisitic conception of man and nature (p. 1). The aim of all those campaigning and thinking within this general mode is a state of permanence and sustainability and an escape from the present continual environmental degeneration.

O'Riordan contrasts this ecocentric position within environmentalism with the technocentric one, which has quite different perceptions of nature, method, morality and social-personal life. This position could be seen as continuous with traditional scientific and managerial approaches to problems. It accepts that there are environmental difficulties, but believes that these can be overcome by the tried and tested methods used hitherto to control nature.

Whether one sees this general perspective as optimistic or arrogant rather depends on one's position within O'Riordan's map of environmentalism, but it is maintained that there is an extreme within technocentrism which has an unshakeable belief in man's ingenuity in technological expertise, in the ways of the market, and the ability of economic growth to solve all problems. Others, however, equally given to approaching all environmental issues as technical problems requiring technical solutions, do accept the need for a variety of new legal, economic and managerial mechanisms for ensuring environmental protection (pollution taxes, legal rights to environmental protection, compensation arrangements etc.). O'Riordan describes this position as accommodating to the more radical demands, but uses the methods and ways of thought identified as industrial and technological (*ibid.*, p. 377).

Two points are crucial. The first concerns the way the two positions regard contemporary political institutions and the second relates to the issue of economic calculation.

First, for those who O'Riordan describes as technocentric, the actual political and economic institutions are regarded as acceptable and capable of the modifications necessary to ensure environmental protection. Indeed, many might consider that those institutions have been successful in the face of previous natural and social challenges and can be trusted to deal with the environmental problems of the future. To most ecocentrists, however, it has been these very institutional forms, together with their kinds of calculation, morality and technology, which have brought us to the brink of disaster and, indeed, pushed many in the third world, over the edge.

Second, there is a significant distinction between those who believe that prices can be attached to living things and environmental goods, and those who believe such pricing hopelessly undermines the possibility of changing people's relations with nature. The latter see that this merely maintains an exploitative conception of nature, the reduction of all activity to narrow self-interest and cost-benefit analysis.

Finally there is a general place within environmentalism which is comprehensible only in the terms of the traditional Left-Right political continuum. Described as the 'red-green' , or eco-socialist, this perspective emphasizes the role capitalism, as a system and set of institutions, has played in development of environmental crises. Different aspects of capitalism have been emphasized. For example, because of the competitive nature of the system, this is seen to produce inevitable waste and make the necessary regulation politically almost impossible. Because it must continually stimulate new wants, in order that profits can be made by their satisfaction in the market, then capitalism is seen as necessarily opposed to the acceptance of limits to environmental exploitation. Writers like Pepper (1984), who adopt a more philosophical-historical approach, use Marx's theory of history to trace how nature became a commodity, and how the separation of human beings from nature as well as the alienation of person from person, was the result of *capitalist*, not industrial development;

> We must stress that . . . the man-nature separation and the growth of social alienation which are so decried by ecocentrics took place under a specific (capitalist) organization of production, i.e. it was produced by industrialism under capitalism, not industrialisation *per se*. (*ibid.*, p. 166)

As within the ecocentrist perspective, there are many disagreements on the Left about what can be done. Some writers have accepted the need for economic development, but constructed a socialist approach which advocates a planning system to ensure sustainability (Jacobs, 1991). Others, espousing some aspects of Marxism with regard to the way the capitalist state and political competition works in liberal democracies, think that the promotion of *global* sustainability by these means is almost impossible (Johnston, 1989).

The dualities and distinctions which can be made in the public debates concerning economic and industrial problems are similar but not equivalent. It is possible to contrast those positions which accept and those which refuse the basic institutions and purposes of our current economic system. For example, there is a variety of analyses which take the contemporary national and international economic system as given, but identify different technical, political, and cultural factors which are seen as spoiling its functioning. Standard measures of productivity, consumption, profit, competitiveness and so on, are used to assess national, corporate and personal economic success, and to make the necessary comparisons.

Against that may be posed the perspectives which reject the present political-economic system, on the grounds that it is inevitably self-destructive. From this position, making the economy more productive, more efficient, more competitive, is, at best, contradictory. It may be possible to generate more wealth, but this is bound to produce greater divisions between rich and poor and more exploitation, or more environmental degradation or cultural vulgarity.

These positions are not always reducible to those traditionally identified as Left and Right, nor are they necessarily distinguishable in terms of the depths of changes they advocate. Whilst Marxism and socialism have identified the self-destructive aspects of capitalism and its inherent ability to polarize the rich and the poor, other critical attacks on *consumer* capitalism stem from an appreciation of imagined or real forms of earlier social and cultural life (Lasch, 1991). Furthermore, many self-proclaimed socialists have been only too ready to claim that they could manage and improve the running of a capitalist economy, and many others on the left and centre consider that quite fundamental changes are necessary to the British constitution before any economic advance can be more secure.

It is comparatively easy to show that these ranges of perspectives, and the questions they raise for teaching about economic and environmental matters, are not represented within the guidelines on economic and industrial understanding and environmental education.

In the case of economic and industrial understanding this can be demonstrated by posing the following questions. First, what are identified as the different types of economic actor, and what types of action are acknowledged to exist? Second, what are the different forms of economic relationship accepted within the texts?

Answers to these questions indicate the system of representations within which young people are to be initiated and identified. What we are presented with is a ready-made construction of the economic world for the young, without any explicit debate with the (adult, professional) reader about whether this is the most appropriate or justifiable. It is a world which is essentially demoralized and depoliticized; a construction drived from only one set of economic ideas. The conceptual bases for assessing the adequacy of the economic and political institutions are omitted.

Taking the guidance for Key Stages 1–3, the actors are, in accordance with the foundations of neo-classical economics, *individuals* who choose, decide, buy, forgo one opportunity for another, save, work, gain, lose, and use technology. The representation of communities is weak. There is a reference to the fact that some communities are without the means of satisfying some basic human needs (Key

Stage 2, section 4), and an acceptance that local facilities and planning decisions may be of varying importance to 'different groups' (Key Stage 2, section 9 and 13) but there are no indications of how different groups of individuals can fall foul of the competitive relations between economic institutions. Indeed, important economic actors, whether they be identified as owners, managers, professionals, or various forms of economic enterprise such as companies or corporations, are generally missing. The whole of the economic world in *Education for Economic and Industrial Understanding* is built on the individual, rational, economic calculator. Thus companies are 'workplaces' in which different individuals, protected by the law (Key Stage 3, section 17) do different tasks, and where, with the help of technology, they translate individual consumer wants into new products (Key Stage 3, section 2).

The relationships acknowledged between these actors are equally restricted. There are no references to the control of some by others, nor to the possibilities of exploitation on the one hand, or coordination and integration on the other. Interdependence is referred to (Key Stage 3, section 6) but not dependence. The whole crucial issue of ownership is omitted, as are the concepts of profit and speculation. No guidance is given on how to deal with all those matters concerned with the fairness or otherwise of differences in rewards, about which young children are already aware (Leahy, 1981 and 1983; Emler *et al.*, 1990). Thus, not only are alternative forms of economic organization excluded, but so are the concepts from political economy which enable us to grasp some of the crucial aspects of our own system and compare it with others.

In the case of guidance on environmental education, then similar restrictions can be detected. In particular, no references are made to the need to discuss the whole issue of contemporary Western lifestyles, and the relationship between different environmental problems and the very economic system which is accepted as given in *Education for Economic and Industrial Understanding*. In spite of the fact that one important aspect of the contemporary debate concerns the need for limits to industrial production, there is no mention of that matter. Even the question of sustainability is ignored.

The environmentally aware society depicted in *Environmental Education* is one in which individuals gather together and collect evidence and 'put their case' with regard to the solution of discrete environmental problems. Opposition is recognized, and it is expected that children be made aware of 'the conflicts which can arise about environmental issues' (NCC, 1990e, p. 4), but this opposition is seen as derived from other individuals, with just different sets of attitudes. In its attempt to formalize and codify, this text is unable to include the actual lived predicaments of environmentally aware individuals, be they teachers, children or parents.

Some perspectives would see such individuals as too easily caught within a system which actually uses such a limited form of environmental awareness as a means to promote consumption, albeit of slightly different, and more expensive, 'green' commodities.

Nowhere is the connection made between economic, cultural and political life in this society and its existence within a system of international trade which has destructive environmental effects elsewhere. Again, the relationships are presented only in terms of interdependence. One of the stated objectives is that pupils should know about 'the environmental interdependence of individuals, groups, communities and nations' (*ibid.*) and the examples of good practice balance local projects with an example of a school link with Nigeria (Key Stage 2, pp. 26–7) and a project dealing with the international dimensions to the acid rain problem (Key Stage 3, pp. 30–1).Thus guidance is given on teaching the comparatively easy concept of physical interdependency, but not on the much more difficult notion of economic dependence.

It is quite probable that children at Key Stages 2 or 3 would be genuinely confused by the fact that they can eat food produced in countries where children of their own age remain hungry.

It could be argued in their defence that these are just guidelines to practice, after all, and they therefore can only be expected to have a narrow, pedagogic and technical-managerial function to perform. They are only intended to answer 'how' questions such as, how environmental and economic concerns can be integrated within the curriculum, and how the organization can be set up to ensure that they are. But this fails to appreciate the role that such 'official' documents now play in the definition of what is to count as acceptable educational knowledge. For example, the frequent appearances of unanalyzed case studies of school projects in these documents not only describes and approves a way of teaching something, but also the things which these projects were attempting to teach.

Many of the questions which democratic, sensitive and thoughtful teachers have to address are indeed 'how' questions, but they are of a different kind. For example, how can you help children become aware of the whole range of different ways of organizing economic life? How can you encourage children to develop some critical appreciation of the ways in which their lives can be shaped by advertising, consumerism and the pursuit of more? More personally, perhaps, how can one talk about these issues with pupils of different ages, and what sorts of dialogue are possible?

Perhaps the overall problem with these texts can be understood as follows. Although they are written to provide guidance to professional adults on how to teach about two serious, difficult and contentious public concerns, they prematurely simplify and resolve the content of those concerns. As a result, the actual confusing and problematic social worlds in which both the teachers and their pupils live are forsaken for a politically vacuous, benign context in which rational individuals combine their attitudes, skills and knowledge in the pursuit of their own ends. It cannot be assumed that this is a world temporarily made simple so that it can be understood by children, because children are not the readers of NCC curricular guidance. These are ideological simplifications, in which most of the oppositional and critical positions on the environment and the economy are missing, notably those which are critical of our society's political and economic institutions, and those which see the need for more or less fundamental changes in culture and personal life.

It seems particularly odd that the curriculum guidance *Education for Citizenship*

(NCC, 1990f) should draw our attention to Sections 44 and 45 of the Education (No. 2) Act of 1986 forbidding the promotion of partisan viewpoints in controversial matters, and the need for balance, whilst these other texts present such restricted views of what constitutes two areas of public debate.

Teachers' Reactions to Guidance on Economic and Environmental Education

It is difficult to tell what the reactions of teachers are to these attempts of the NCC to give direction to their teaching of social, moral, personal and political issues across the curriculum. If we concentrate on teachers at the primary stage then it is probable that, in general, they would be much more at ease including environmental themes within their curriculum planning than they would be dealing with the economic and industrial. Indeed, in a national survey of the opinions of students preparing to be primary teachers, environmental education, along with health education, were consistently rated as the most important of the cross curricular themes, with economic and industrial understanding seen as the least (Ross, Ahier and Hutchings, 1991, p. 74).

There are various possible explanations of this preference for environmental education among teachers. When exploring the beliefs and backgrounds of self-declared environmentalists, Cotgrove and Duff (1980) found that a high proportion of them worked in what they called the non-productive service sector, including teaching. They argued that such groups found themselves on the periphery of the institutions of capitalist, industrial society, felt themselves to be political outsiders, and so turned to environmentalism as an alternative to the individualism and competition of the market;

> To the extent that schools, hospitals and welfare agencies operate outside the market place, and those who work in them are dedicated to maximising non-economic values, they constitute non-industrial enclaves within industrial societies and are the carriers of non-economic values. And they may well provide a more congenial environment for those for whom the values and ideology of industrial capitalism do not win unqualified enthusiasm and unquestioning support ... Moreover, such occupations can offer a substantial degree of personal autonomy for those who have little taste for a subordinate role in the predominantly hierarchical structures of industrial society. (p. 344)

One might surmise from this that teachers would not only prefer to coordinate their curriculum around themes represented within environmentalism in general, but that they might also be attracted to the more radical aspects of that set of concerns and be suspicious of the managerial aspects of the cross curricular themes as presented by the NCC.

There are, however, many reasons why this is an inadequate approach to determining what the reactions of teachers to these two officially identified themes might be. Not only does it rely upon a problematic distinction between productive and non-productive work to locate groups such as teachers, but it also distinguishes between private and public enterprises according to their defining values, which, in turn, attract different kinds of people to work in them. Such ideas, although associated with the political Left, have encouraged the now popular view on the political Right, that any opposition to current educational reforms always stem from the traditional self-interest of educationalists. There are other, more productive ways of looking at the particular professional location of teachers in order to discuss the possible reactions to such texts and the ideas contained within them.

If we take the likely reactions of teachers in primary schools to the issues referred to in *Education for Economic and Industrial Understanding* and *Environmental Education*, it may be more interesting to consider what one might call the details of their professional and personal lives than their general class position. Two aspects are noteworthy. First, there is the inevitable and continual involvement with children who are, themselves, at some chronological distance from full participation in the economic system. Second, the ways in which many people, often women, enter and continue their careers in primary teaching mean that, frequently, their domestic and private lives are very close to their public, professional existence. As I have attempted to explore elsewhere (Ahier, 1994) this makes for a certain continuity between the public and the private aspects of life — a continuity of caring for others.

This involvement with young children is likely to alert one to their long-term needs and the problems for future workers and consumers. It is not that such involvement makes one apolitical or naive, but that the economic and environmental effects of industrialists competing for market share, or politicians competing for political power, might well seem rather short-term and short-sighted.

Unfortunately no explicit consideration is given within *Education for Economic and Industrial Understanding* or *Environmental Education* to the genuine reservations with regard to the ethical and moral aspects of teaching about the economic and the environmental which many teachers might have because of their concerns for the futures of their children. Environmental and economic limits, and the whole notion of *sustainability*, are the two conceptions used to explore these matters in contemporary discussions, but they are almost completely missing from *Education for Economic and Industrial Understanding* and *Environmental Education*. In the former there are references to limits, but this is mostly to do with limitations of a given budget (NCC, 1990b, Key Stage 2, section 1), although this section does include the suggestion that children should

> discuss the impact of human activity on limited resources e.g. rain forests.
> (NCC, 1990b, p. 21)

In *Environmental Education* sustainability is not mentioned, partly because 'the environment' is continually represented as a thing to be protected, managed and improved, as though environmental degradation has been the result of individual activities of thoughtless, destructive people, and nothing to do with our economic system and way of life. Nor is this issue of sustainability likely to be raised in connection with economic understanding, because it has an inescapable ethical aspect, and conventional economics upon which *Education for Economic and Industrial Understanding* (*ibid.*) is based has difficulty with including *future* consumers and producers in its models of markets (Jacobs, 1991, chapter 7).

Indeed, the future envisaged in both of these documents is very much like the present, only more technological and more competitive. There is an acceptance of problems (international competition, for example, in *Education for Economic and Industrial Understanding*, and global warming in *Environmental Education*), but this is accompanied by a persistent, shallow optimism. In the case of the economic sphere, the answer is for all future citizens to understand how our economy works and to have the necessary entrepreneurial skills (NCC, 1990b, p. 1). As far as the environment is concerned then what is needed is awareness, reasonableness, knowledge of the facts and 'a positive approach' (NCC, 1990e, p. 1).

In so many ways, and for all its apparent reasonableness, this kind of optimism is very much a product of the enterprising 1980s. There is a persistent assumption that all problems can be solved by technology and the pursuit of wealth, and that the only alternatives to this kind of optimism are what Thatcher and Reagan called the 'prophets of doom' and despair (Lasch, 1991, p. 38). This view of progress, as Lasch shows, dependent as it is upon a belief that the pursuit of personal and national economic wealth will bring universal abundance, always addresses people as consumers and rarely as citizens.

Accepting that there are aspects of the lives of primary school teachers which might make them legitimately suspicious of the approaches outlined within these two documents is not the same as saying that there is no need for suggestions on the teaching of these matters, because the teachers already know what is best for their children. In both these fields there are numerous books and packs for teachers which are related to specific groups and interests, varying from economic awareness packs sponsored by oil companies to inspirational reports on research supported by environmental groups (Grieg *et al.*, 1987 and 1989). The problem is whether it is possible to have authoritative guidance, which is unattached to the particular interest groups currently articulating contemporary economic, industrial and environmental concerns, yet which does not filter out all that is controversial and motivating.

Such guidance must acknowledge openly, both the general problems there are in defining a justifiable moral, personal and political educational programme which includes economic and environmental dimensions in a culturally diverse society, as well as the specific predicaments and contradictions facing teachers in these areas. A vital part of this would seem to be an analysis of how the public concerns about the economy and the environment have been constructed and articulated. Yearley (1991) makes a strong argument for this approach when he examines the historical and social development of environmentalism, claiming that it not only helps us understand the arguments, but also the sources of opposition (p. 185).

It has to be admitted, however, that the chances for the development of such forms of educational discourse are not encouraging. Relatively independent centres from which such guidance may emerge are being rapidly compromised. Institutions concerned with teacher education, for example, have been subject to continuous interference, with direct attacks on their capacity to teach the very courses which might promote an open discussion of these issues.

However, events continually conspire to force teachers and, hopefully, many others, to reconsider the economic and environmental certainties of the 1980s. There can be no greater challenge to those attempting to teach children to be rational about economic and environmental matters than the situation at present. Here we find ordinary people being exhorted to become more profligate consumers in order to rescue their society from an economic crisis which was partly caused by previous excessive borrowing to purchase consumer goods. In the face of such absurdity the NCC guidance on personal, moral and social education, for all its modernity and managerialism, seems no more relevant than the earlier advocacy of an integrated and community curriculum.

Chapter 8

Indoctrination or Empowerment? The Case of Economic and Industrial Understanding

Anna Craft

Introduction and Background

The social elements of the curriculum are arguably its most powerful aspects, given the values and attitudes which they embody. It has been argued earlier (see Craft, chapter 5 in this volume) that the introduction of centralized advice on the values within the curriculum could be seen as an anachronistic act; modernist, in that there seems to be an assumption about social values being uniform and shared — simply not the case in a fragmented and diverse post-modern society. Economic and industrial understanding was introduced at the start of a deep and global recession, which has challenged existing attitudes to work, working practice and the economy at all levels. Can the naming of economic and industrial understanding as part of the whole curriculum be interpreted as another aspect of a government and its quangos trying to hold on to modernist values and structures, and to influence the brand new workforce to recreate and reproduce a known form of indoctrination? Or is it an empowering element to the curriculum, enabling young children as well as secondary-aged pupils access to the people, structures and processes in the economy and giving them a chance to engage actively and critically or reflectively with all of these?

This chapter reflects on developments in the work-related curriculum, and what these developments could signify for pupils. It is written against a changing backdrop of statutory curriculum and an attempt to free the professional judgment of teachers in designing learning experiences and managing the whole curriculum (SCAA, 1994a). Although the cross-curricular themes do not feature in the Dearing Review, the slimming of the curriculum may enable more teachers to try and implement aspects of economic and industrial understanding systematically than have done so to date. However, the main concern in this chapter is with the *principles* embedded in economic and industrial understanding as defined by the National Curriculum Council in *Education for Economic and Industrial Understanding* (NCC, 1990b) and how they are to be interpreted. To what extent can economic and industrial understanding be seen as indoctrination, and to what extent as empowerment?

In working towards some answers, I will consider the way in which economic and industrial understanding is taught and learned in schools. Finally, I will be looking at the extent to which the practical and philosophical implications of social constructivist views of teaching and learning alter the view of economic and industrial understanding either as empowerment or indoctrination.

The Traditional Work-related Curriculum

Traditionally, the work-related curriculum has been for secondary pupils. It has been a pre-vocational track option, but which in practice is more easily available to those who are less able. It has traditionally involved training for skilled manual jobs and business studies. It has involved work experience as well as a workplace- and work skill-related curriculum; and the assessment emphasis has been on pupil-centred formative assessment and on creating some kind of record of achievement or profile. Many forms of the traditional work-related curriculum have been oriented toward a vocational or professional qualification. Pupils have come in contact with this form of learning through pre-vocational courses (for example, BTec, CPVE, NVQs); through PSE courses and through relevant aspects of the GCSE and post-16 curriculum.

In primary schools, the traditional work-related curriculum has been an under-developed and unrecognized aspect of the curriculum for many teachers and schools, although with the work of curriculum developers such as the Schools Curriculum Industry Partnership (SCIP), the Science and Technology Regional Organisations (SATROs), the Geography Schools-Industry Project (GISP), Edge Hill College Primary Industry Centre, the University of North London's Primary Schools and Industry Centre, and so on, some schools and teachers have begun to foster aspects of it. This sort of work in primary schools has often concentrated on specific aspects of the work-related curriculum (such as 'enterprise', or 'industry' or 'work') and has often been of a short-term and one-off nature, sometimes involving only certain teachers and usually not planned together as a whole staff for continuity and progression.

The Emerging Work-related Curriculum

In addition to this traditional work-related or pre-vocational curriculum, a new model began to emerge in the late 1980s. The 1988 Education Reform Act meant many shifts in school foci; and has had implications for the interpretation of the whole curriculum (see chapter 5 in this volume). The notion that the school curriculum of children aged between 5 and 16 should, amongst other things, 'prepare them for the opportunities, responsibilities and experiences of adult life' (from the Education Reform Act, 1988) certainly represents a landmark in our interpretation and understanding of the school curriculum. A direct, statutory connection was made in the 1988 Act, between primary children's schooling and their adult lives.

The programmes of study in National Curriculum subjects make reference to helping children to develop their understandings of the local and wider economy in a variety of ways. For example, the draft proposals for the programme of study for History Key Stage 2 indicates that, during their study of up to twelve history study units throughout the four years of the key stage, children should 'be introduced to the study of history from a variety of perspectives' which include the political and the economic, technological and scientific (SCAA, 1994b). The geography programme of study for Key Stage 2 includes a requirement for children to 'study how goods and services are provided and how this is related to decisions about the use of land'. In the course of this, children will learn 'how goods and services are provided; that land is used in different ways, for example, farming, leisure, manufacturing industry; (and) about . . . issue(s) which demonstrate how conflicts can arise over the use of land' (SCAA, 1994c). Similar (though less economically focused) references can be found in the proposed revised orders for Key Stage 1 in history and geography.

Thus, within parts of the statutory curriculum (and despite Dearing's proposals to slim the curriculum and its assessment) relevance to work and the economy is now something to which all pupils from 5 years upward are entitled by law. In addition, the two cross-curricular themes *Education for Economic and Industrial Understanding* (NCC, 1990b) and *Careers Education and Guidance* (NCC, 1990d), put forward within NCC's whole curriculum model, represent an attempt to codify some of what might be embodied in the primary work-related curriculum.

The NCC (1990a) noted that 'where these themes are embedded in the National Curriculum programmes of study they are statutory. Other aspects, whilst not statutory, are clearly required if schools are to provide an education which promotes the aims defined in Section 1 of the Education Reform Act'. In other words, for the curriculum to be broad balanced and relevant, the NCC's advice was that the themes were an essential component.

The cross-curricular themes were to provide a context for learning the subjects of the statutory and non-statutory curriculum, and to bring relevance to the curriculum. This is particularly significant for Key Stage 1 and Key Stage 2 and to a lesser extent, Key Stage 3 (for many schools this was a new focus). It is significant in Key Stage 4 because the themes are *every* child's entitlement under the broad terms of the Education Reform Act as outlined above; this emerging work-related curriculum is therefore not simply for those pupils who 'choose' a vocational option. The two cross-curricular themes concerning economic and industrial understanding and careers education, as defined by the NCC, had slightly different foci; the former being about setting up an understanding of the world 'out there' through a core of knowledge, understanding, skills and attitudes; the latter being about *understanding one's place* in that world.

How the Emerging Model of the Work-related Curriculum Differs from the Traditional One

Before considering economic and industrial understanding in primary schools in more depth, it is worth reflecting on the ways in which the emerging work-related curriculum differs from the traditional one, both in the way the model is laid out by the NCC and also, where appropriate, in the way the two curricula work in practice.

Firstly, the *access routes* to the emerging work-related curriculum are different. Rather than being available to the less academic upper secondary school pupils as an alternative to academic studies, the cross-curricular themes of economic and industrial understanding and careers education should, in theory, be made available to all children from the age of 5. In practice not all schools have taken on these cross-curricular themes. Those which have often limit the elements which are incorporated into the curriculum for each year group of children, so that the whole economic and industrial understanding curriculum suggested by NCC is explored by pupils during the course of each key stage, but not each year. Other schools again are developing their own economic and industrial understanding curriculum rather than using *Education for Economic and Industrial Understanding* as the basis from which to plan. Despite these different ways of translating the cross-curricular themes into practice, however, the basic access route difference between the traditional and emerging model remains, because elements of the emerging work-related curriculum are embedded in the statutory orders for the core and foundation subjects as outlined earlier.

Secondly, *what the curriculum covers* is, in theory, different. Traditional pre-vocational studies tended to focus on very specific aspects or sectors of work or economic life, but the two themes take (in theory) a far broader approach and are intended to form a foundation for understanding the wider economy and the roles and interrelationships within it, together with encouraging children to become aware of their own roles and potential roles within it. In practice, although some schools attempt to create a broad curriculum, there can be a tendency to concentrate on particular elements of a theme, such as consumer education, or to emphasize specific kinds of work (often because the teachers draw on the resources of the local economy).

There are clearer differences between the traditional and emerging models of the work-related curriculum, however, when it comes to the involvement of adults other than teachers in schools and the organizing of work placements for pupils as part of their studies. While learning in economic and industrial understanding and careers education often involves practice visits out and to the classroom by adults other than teachers, the work-experience which traditional pre-vocational education has often involved is not a part of the learning experiences of children under 15.

Thirdly, the *intended age range* clearly differs. The emerging work-related curriculum is intended to cater for children aged 5 upward, in contrast to the 14+ age range of the traditional work related curriculum. Clearly, the extent to which this is a difference in practice depends on whether teachers in primary schools and teachers in Key Stage 3 take up the challenge of planning for and developing the two themes; this appears by no means to be a widespread pattern yet.

Fourth, the new and old models differ in terms of *purpose*. The emerging model is not about the gaining of vocational qualifications and therefore is not purely oriented toward the development of vocational skills. The emerging model also involves the development of enquiry skills, general social skills and the deepening of pupils' awareness, of the local, regional, national, European and world economy; and of themselves in relation to the economy. In other words, economic and industrial understanding and careers education signify in theory education *about*, *through* and *for* industry and work; rather than being purely for industry and work.

Finally, the emerging model differs from the traditional one in terms of *prescription*. As recently as 1986 it could be said that a traditional feature of pre-vocational education was 'no prescription, no package'; in other words, the curriculum was in many instances flexible, fostering negotiation with local work-places and the local economy and focusing on specific skills or areas of knowledge, depending on the focus of the course or experience. In contrast, the codifying of careers education and economic and industrial understanding for all pupils now signifies an element of prescription, as does its inclusion in statutory orders.

So, although in theory there are clear differences between the traditional and emerging models of the work-related curriculum, in practice they may be harder to distinguish, particularly in terms of access routes, curriculum content and the age range. What similarities are there between the two models?

Similarities Between the Traditional and Emerging Work-related Curriculum

The first similarity concerns *learning approaches*. Both models tend to involve teachers using their outside experience of adult working life in the development of the curriculum as *teachers who are also adults*. Adults other than teachers are also invited to help develop the curriculum. This is the case in theory and also in practice, and learning tends to be active and enquiry-based. Secondly, in terms of *assessment*; forms of profiling and records of achievement are recommended. The breadth and non-job oriented approach of the emerging work-related curriculum means that profiling and records of achievement in the emerging model have a wider scope than the tighter assessment records kept in the traditional model; but nevertheless the principles of learner-centred formative assessment which underpin both are the same. Again, this is a practical as well as a theoretical similarity, although some schools do not record children's achievement in the emerging work-related curriculum at all as yet, except where it forms part of the statutory orders.

What Does the Inclusion of Economic and Industrial Understanding in the Curriculum Signify?

Should we view economic and industrial understanding, part of this new approach to the work-related curriculum, as a form of indoctrination, or as representing empowerment, and thus so positive that it ought to be every child's right? What does the inclusion of economic and industrial understanding within the curriculum signify? Because the introduction of the work-related curriculum into the primary years of schooling represented such a departure from previous tradition, the following remarks draw particularly on the NCC's economic and industrial understanding curriculum for Key Stage 1 and Key Stage 2: the arguments could as easily have been based on the secondary curriculum.

There are two sorts of arguments for viewing economic and industrial understanding as representing indoctrination. Firstly, the view that childhood is sacred and has nothing to do with economic and industrial understanding; secondly the view that the economic and industrial understanding curriculum suggested in *Education for Economic and Industrial Understanding* is itself biased and thus involves socialising children into a particular and biased set of values.

Childhood as Sacred

There is an argument that childhood has nothing to do with the economic structure of society or with industry and the world of work, so why should children, primary children in particular, be learning about these things in school? In response, children of whatever age from birth are already participating in the economy, simply by living in it. Given this, it follows that attempting to develop children's understanding of their economy may have the potential to empower them to analyze and respond to aspects of it as independent-minded people, rather than being the unwitting victims of it.

A Biased Set of Values

Another argument is that the economic and industrial understanding curriculum described in *Education for Economic and Industrial Understanding* has the potential simply to socialize children to accept whole sets of values. Consider an example from this document: one area of study recommended is that of industry and the world of work. Children in Key Stage 1 are to 'know that people work in different kinds of workplaces and do different jobs'; 'know that there are different kinds of work and that these involve different skills' and 'understand how some things are produced, using different resources'. In Key Stage 2 children are to 'understand that workplaces are organised in different ways', have an 'understanding of how goods are produced, distributed and sold', and 'develop an understanding of the nature of work and its place in people's lives'. It might be argued that the study of these areas could involve implying to children that, for example, certain kinds of work roles are 'givens'; together with certain approaches to workplace organization and certain kinds of ownership.

Similar arguments could be put for other aspects suggested in *Education for Economic and Industrial Understanding*, such as enterprise (introducing biased ideas as to what it means, such as successful profit-making and an attitude towards team work which unquestioningly puts the product first); economic ideas (such as that supply, demand, price and value are absolutes in any economy); public affairs (such as that the way public services are organized and the range available is acceptable), and so on. It might also be argued for instance that the notion of technology which forms a part of economic and industrial understanding represents the view that inventing new ways of doing things is inherently a good thing; and that high technology is also a good thing. The counter-arguments to this position which views these as a biased set of values — and thus as indoctrination — centre around the idea that economic and industrial understanding is a controversial and dynamic area of study and understanding.

Children need to be offered opportunities to explore and to understand the different points of view and possibilities in any given situation. For instance, in learning about industry and the world of work, children should have opportunities to explore non-paid work, conflict at work, the role of trade unions and so on, as well as learning about a variety of different kinds of work, workplace organization and means of ownership. If we look back at the learning objectives cited above, they do not in fact preclude this broad approach; indeed one of the example learning activities given in *Education for Economic and Industrial Understanding* for Key Stage 2 involves exploring non-paid work and unemployment. Although the resolution of conflict at work is not made explicit in the document, nor means of ownership, nevertheless the wording of the objectives does not exclude these as areas for focus in the classroom.

Enterprise is another component feature of the curriculum guidance document. This may be seen to have a controversial nature, and a variety of meanings. It should follow that, in learning about enterprise, children question the narrow conception of the meaning of enterprise, to consider different perspectives and to develop much more wide ranging understanding and skills which represents enterprise, or imagination, transferable to any situation. How does this relate to *Education for Economic and Industrial Understanding*? In Key Stage 2, pupils are expected to develop an understanding of local enterprise; for example, they are to 'know about public services, shops, offices and industries in their local community; understand the importance of these to local people'. They are also to 'understand some of the implications of limited resources'. Although all of these could be interpreted narrowly to involve teaching children about business enterprise alone, similarly the two latter statements can also be interpreted much more broadly. Enterprise or imagination, in any context, whether it involves buying and selling, or community schemes, or being creative, or solving a problem, involves recognizing the opportunity cost of each decision and acknowledging the constraints imposed by limited resources. A similar case can be made for the objectives given for Key Stage 1 with regard to enterprise.

Let us turn to a different area of economic and industrial understanding; basic economic ideas. The Key Stage 1 and Key Stage 2 curriculum in *Education for Economic and Industrial Understanding* suggests children should recognize and understand scarcity, choice, price, value and supply and demand. However, although the principle of scarcity may be a 'fact' and that therefore all the other principles of price, value, supply and demand follow logically, this does not mean that they are cultural universals, or value-free. These secondary principles only follow in a market economy; a phenomenon which fits in with certain cultures and not others. The market is not the only way of dealing with the central principle of scarcity, and therefore economic and industrial understanding which is not to be accused of bias and indoctrination needs to include the development of some understanding of alternative ways of coping, such as systems which involve state or societal control over capital. The curriculum guidance document does not exclude this wide approach; particularly in Key Stage 2, where children are, for example, to 'understand the implications of limited resources'. No particular set of implications is spelled out. Similarly, children are to 'understand how money is used in the exchange of goods and services and know some of the factors which affect prices' — again, there is no implication of which factors should be explored.

Similarly, counter-arguments against the claim that learning about public affairs has the capacity to be biased revolve around the *critical enquiry* which should be central to economic and industrial understanding, and which means encouraging children to ask questions about what exists, for whom and why. As future citizens in a democracy, children's understanding and awareness of issues concerning public affairs is critical.

In the same way, economic and industrial understanding ought to involve children in exploring the advantages and disadvantages of the use of technology, in a wide understanding of the meaning of the term technology in the workplace, not a purely high-tech. *Education for Economic and Industrial Understanding* does not constrain this approach; for Key Stage 1, children are to 'understand how tools and technology contribute to pupils' lives at home and at school'. In Key Stage 2, children are to 'develop an awareness of the part played by design and technology in industrial production'; and to 'be aware of some effects of new technology and implications for people and places'. Developing a critical scrutiny of technology may not be explicitly in any but the last of these statements, but similarly the curriculum itself does not exclude this approach either. Similar arguments can be made about the consumer affairs and public affairs elements in the document's version of economic and industrial understanding.

Each of these counter-arguments draws on the involvement of *critical reflection* on the part of children in economic and industrial understanding learning experiences. In several of the cases cited, the potential of the curriculum to empower children through critical reflection has not been explicit. So where is the critical scrutiny element of this theme's curriculum? But the NCC's model of economic and industrial understanding does include the fostering of independent-mindedness. Among the analytical, personal and social skills which the NCC recommends should be developed through economic and industrial understanding are the ability to 'handle differences of interest and opinion in a group . . . listen to the views of others on economic and industrial issues' (NCC, 1990b, pp. 4–5) and among the attitudes recommended: 'respect of alternative economic viewpoints and a willingness to reflect critically on their own economic views and values' (*ibid.*, p. 5). Among the analytical, personal and social skills it lists are the ability to: 'collect, analyze and interpret economic and industrial data . . . think carefully about different ways of solving economic problems and making economic decisions . . . distinguish between statements of fact and value in economic situations' (*ibid.*, pp. 4–5) and among the attitudes 'respect for evidence and rational argument in economic contexts' (*ibid.*, p. 5).

In other words, there certainly are values embedded in economic and industrial understanding as defined by *Education for Economic and Industrial Understanding,* such as those explored here, but children should be encouraged to expose and confront these, and to understand the different perspectives in any given situation. The arguments which can be advanced in favour of economic and industrial understanding as indoctrination can be countered. Indeed, it seems that there are good reasons for viewing the economic and industrial understanding curriculum in the NCC's guidance document as offering potential for empowerment.

Clearly, the intentions of teachers are important in this, since the fostering of critical reflection about economic and industrial issues is an essential part of ensuring that economic and industrial understanding does not become indoctrination. The curriculum in *Education for Economic and Industrial Understanding* can be viewed as a framework rather than as prescriptive or fixed. It offers broad areas of study such as economic ideas, industry and work, consumer affairs, technology and public affairs, which teachers can then translate into learning experiences. My contention is that the framework does offer teachers the potential to foster independent thinking and critical reflection in their pupils. I am suggesting then that the way in which the curriculum is interpreted, taught and learned, is as significant if not more so than the actual curriculum as written. The potential for empowerment rather than indoctrination is there, if teachers choose to develop it.

It has already been argued that children are already participants in the economy. They have and spend pocket money; they consume food, leisure services, toys, clothes (and may have some say in decisions about the consumption of these things); as well as using public services such as health, education and transport. They are surrounded by mass media, including comics, newspapers, TV and radio, which contain and portray opinions and information about the economy in a variety of ways. We know from researchers (for example, Berti and Bombi, 1988; Hutchings, 1989) that children's ideas and understandings about the economy are wide ranging. They often differ from adult interpretations and understandings, and these understandings develop over time. But the developmental picture is not one which makes the economy problematic. What empowers children is not blindly or unquestioningly participating or developing an understanding, but rather exercising choices through recognizing the different viewpoints, tensions and possibilities. This applies to children as consumers — but also as enterprising people, interpreting and responding to all aspects of economic and industrial understanding. Critical reflection empowers them as young adults in making choices about the economy, and where or whether to fit into it (and how), and thus enables them to participate more fully as informed adults in a democracy in an increasingly global economy.

It is my contention that economic and industrial understanding represents the potential for empowerment rather than indoctrination, and that this involves

- *breadth*, i.e. providing a wide range of learning experiences, across economic ideas, consumer affairs, industry and the world of work, enterprise, and public affairs

but more critically,

- *balance*, i.e. encouraging a wide range of viewpoints and interpretations of each; and
- encouraging *critical reflection* and independent-mindedness in children.

Social Constructivism and Economic and Industrial Understanding as Empowerment

The arguments advanced so far for seeing economic and industrial understanding as empowerment rather than as indoctrination have simply accepted that concepts and perspectives in economic and industrial understanding are transmittable to children. We know from a growing body of research (for example, Wood, 1988) that the social construction of meaning is a significant part of learning, and that making sense is an active and personal phenomenon. A social constructivist approach to learning has various implications for learning in economic and industrial understanding. It underlines the importance of finding ways of making learning relevant and practical to children; of scaffolding experiences in helping children make connections from their current understandings to new ones; and of modelling. It draws attention to the importance of negotiating meanings with children and reminds us that we cannot assume that children will share each others' or their teachers' understandings of events, terms or concepts. Conscious and explicit negotiation is therefore necessary.

If we are to understand learning through a social constructivist frame, we need to ask what are the implications of this personal and social construction of meaning for viewing economic and industrial understanding as an entitlement? Recognizing that meanings are personal and social has the effect of reinforcing the way we approach the teaching and learning of economic and industrial understanding. It forces us to take account in a more sensitized way of learning contexts, and to plan ways of supporting and encouraging children through learning experience, and to develop strategies for negotiating meanings with children, rather than assuming that meanings are automatically shared and understood at the same level, or that learning experiences are automatically relevant and practical to children. Social constructivism reminds us that we need to find out and take account of the sense which individual children make of the economic and industrial understanding curriculum.

Social constructivism has implications for the processes of teaching and learning. Teachers must take note of social relations in learning, and try to understand the sense children are making, in order to help them develop and scaffold their thinking and understandings. Both the explicitness of pedagogy, together with sensitivity to learners' sense-making which is so much part of a social constructivist approach, are driven by a central concern to encourage children's autonomy in learning. The implications of social constructivism therefore seem to be in keeping with the view that economic and industrial understanding represents empowerment, rather than indoctrination.

Conclusion

There has been a significant shift in the work-related curriculum from a traditional model to an emerging one; one of the most significant aspects of which has been a codifying of a broad economic and industrial understanding for all primary children, together with careers education and guidance.

Focusing on economic and industrial understanding, it has been argued that this development in primary education can be viewed as a positive enabling of children, and that rather than being seen as indoctrination, it can be seen as empowerment. It can be viewed as offering children ways in to understanding and participating in the continuously changing processes and choices in the structures of post-modern society. However, economic and industrial understanding can only be seen as signifying empowerment if firstly, it involves a wide range of economic and industrial affairs (including consumer and public affairs, enterprise, industry and the world of work, and economic ideas), secondly, if it involves a range of models and views, and thirdly, and most critically, children are strongly encouraged to think independently about these, to reflect and be critical rather than accept the way things are. Drawing on a social constructivist learning framework will enable this broad entitlement to be fully taken up by all children, and the importance and effect of the social and personal construction of meaning must not be underestimated.

Chapter 9

Health, Sex and Drugs Education: Rhetoric and Realities

David Stears, Stephen Clift and Shane Blackman

Introduction

The last thirty years have seen health education traverse a rocky path towards general acceptance as a worthwhile educational activity. Nowhere has this been more graphically portrayed than within the curriculum of English and Welsh schools. From the newly-found status thrust upon it by official reports during the 1960s and 1970s, to its position as a non-statutory cross-curricular area of study in the 1990s, health education has often been the victim of the philosophical ethos and social constraints which surround it. This ethos and these constraints have been politically loaded, and have influenced both the practice and outcome of health education. The rhetoric periodically espoused by politicians to highlight the moral significance of health education has to be balanced by the reality of its practice and position within the curriculum of schools. This chapter gives a brief history of the spirit of health education within the curriculum, before considering two current issues — sex education and drugs education. This will show how good intentions constantly vie with political rhetoric and a reality shaped by political ideology. The fear must be that the constraints and pressures associated with changes in the educational system since the introduction of the National Curriculum have served to undermine the considerable gains that have been made in establishing a holistic model of health education in schools.

A Historical and Philosophical Context

Health education in schools was transformed during the 1960s and early 1970s. The appearance of an official health education handbook from the Ministry of Education (Ministry of Education, 1957a), the introduction of compulsory health education courses for teachers in initial training, and reports from such bodies as the Central Advisory Council on Education and Health Services Committees, expressing the importance of health education in schools (CACE, 1963; Cohen Report, 1964) epitomized the scale of this transformation. Previously health education in schools was restricted to elementary instruction on personal hygiene and at best a medically oriented approach to the prevention of ill-health. The Newsom Report (CACE, 1963) and the Plowden Report (CACE, 1967) were instrumental in challenging secondary and primary schools respectively to make provision for the holistic health and welfare of young people. Health education became a suitable vehicle through which the perceived needs of young people could be met. The simplistic medical model of health education, which had been used up until this time, gave way to an approach which centred upon individual development, holistic health and individual decision-making. Historical reviews of school health education document this transformation (Dalzell-Ward, 1975; Sutherland, 1979; Lewis, 1993).

Throughout the 1970s and well into the next decade many primary and secondary schools responded positively to the challenge of developing health education within the curriculum. This period of development was typified by the appearance in 1977 of curriculum materials produced as part of the Schools Council's Health Education Project (SCHEP). SCHEP was responsible for the development of comprehensive health education curriculum materials and became the prime mover for planned health education in schools. It established the need for the coordination of health education across the curriculum and introduced in-service training for school health education co-ordinators. SCHEP consolidated the educational model of health education by emphasizing the need for teachers to explore young people's feelings, attitudes and experience of health issues before imparting new health knowledge and by stressing the need for skills-based learning as a prerequisite of decision-making.

The late 1970s also saw the recognition of health education as an integral part of the personal and social education of young people. In itself this recognition was not surprising, as the health of young people is intrinsically linked to their personal and social development (Tones, 1987). However, integration of these two discourses saw the health education component move towards the promotion of life skills and the self-empowerment of young people. A self-empowerment approach to health education took root as a development of the personal and social educational model. A general criticism of this life-skills model was that it did not necessarily enhance the capacity of young people to make their own decisions and to put them into action. It has been argued that self-empowerment does not occur as a mere by-product of critical consciousness raising but is a result of training (Tones, Tilford and Robinson, 1990).

The development of specific life skills such as 'assertiveness', 'being positive', and 'influencing systems' are important aspects of good interpersonal communication, and are widely viewed as crucial to personal control and responsibility for health. However, their value within an educational framework may be viewed quite differently from alternative political perspectives. What might be seen as a pathway to autonomy and freedom from one political viewpoint, may be viewed from another as a challenge to traditional values and authority and a first step to disorder and anarchy.

From the mid-1960s through to the mid-1980s it is possible to discern fundamental changes in school-based health education. Whitehead (1989) identifies the degree of progress made in the practice of health education in schools over those two decades:

- a general broadening of the concepts of health employed in many schools;
- more systematic coordination of health education programmes;
- a shift in teaching methods to involve more active learning;
- an upsurge in curriculum development projects; and
- an increased emphasis on the importance of health education in Department of Education and Science and Her Majesty's Inspectorate reports.

It would be reasonable to suggest that a clear shift in approach had taken place. This reflected a move from a predominantly behaviour change approach towards a self-empowerment approach. The overall aim of health education for young people might well have remained the same (that is, to change their health behaviour or encourage them to avoid behaviours which posed risks to health), but a change occurred in thinking about the processes which are effective in achieving this aim.

The National Curriculum and Health Education

The impact of the introduction of the National Curriculum on health education in schools is difficult to assess in precise terms because of the constant reappraisal and alterations, and the lack of systematic comparative research over time. On first inspection, the reforms might appear to have provided a very positive impetus to health education. Firstly, section 1(2) of the Education Reform Act (1988) required that the curriculum should promote the rounded development of each pupil and prepare young people for adult life, and it is clear that education on all aspects of health is essential if this broad requirement is to be met. Secondly, there are many topics relevant to health education which were included as part of the various foundation subjects of the National Curriculum and were therefore compulsory — for example, education about sexual development and reproduction were included within the Science Statutory Orders. And thirdly, health education was clearly identified as a cross-curricular theme and *Curriculum Guidance 5: Health Education* (NCC, 1990c) provided guidance on the fields of study it would be appropriate to cover under nine different headings at each key stage. It also provided guidance on a range of ways in which health education might be organized within a school.

Unfortunately the enormous demands placed on schools by the implementation of the National Curriculum, and the paraphernalia of testing associated with it, together with the non-statutory and non-examinable position of health education, conspired to marginalize its status in the curriculum. Even after the Dearing Review (NCC/SEAC, 1993; SCAA, 1994a), the limited curriculum time available for health education presents major practical problems. Cross-curricular coordination, as advocated in the NCC guidance documents, presents practical problems of adequate professional expertise and motivation. In addition, schools and teachers have had to cope with more recent changes to the legislation and guidance relating to sex and HIV/AIDS education which have sought to impose a specific moral agenda on schools which many teachers do not endorse (Stears and Clift, 1992).

The burdens faced by schools and teachers in relation to the National Curriculum coincided with two further developments which have had significant consequences for health education. The first of these was the removal of central funding for local education authority health education coordinator posts and the consequent loss in many authorities of specialised advisory and training services (LGDF, 1993). One result of this has been the enhanced importance of the training and support offered to schools by district health authorities. The second development was the impact of the White Paper *The Health of the Nation* (Department of Health, 1992), setting out the priorities and methods to be pursued by health promotion specialists. The White Paper sets precise health targets in five key areas (cancers, accidents, HIV/AIDS and sexual health, mental illness and coronary heart disease and strokes). Health education in schools has a contribution to make in each of these areas, but particularly towards the objectives and targets set for HIV/AIDS and sexual health. One such target is to reduce the number of under-16 conceptions by at least 50 per cent by the year 2000. Given that the UK has the highest level of teenage pregnancy in Europe (Smith, 1994) and that international comparisons have shown that teenage pregnancy rates are a reflection of national policies and provision of sex education and services for young people (Jones, Forrest, Goldman *et al.,* 1985) there is clearly considerable room for improvement in the education young people receive. Unfortunately for schools, the health promotion perspective tends to lead to pragmatic strategies for tackling sexual health issues, and this approach conflicts with the emphasis on morality and values that are characteristic of the guidance from the Department for Education.

The issues addressed in health education (from diet, exercise and smoking through to sexual behaviour and drug use) are contentious and problematic. Addressing them effectively requires time, a suitably supportive, non-judgmental learning environment, good relevant resources and committed and well-trained teachers. Given these considerations, and the changing demands that schools faced from the late 1980s onwards, it is probably fair to say that any progress in the development of school health education since then has been achieved despite the National Curriculum rather than because of it. To support this point, it is revealing to examine in more detail recent conflicts between political rhetoric and practical realities in respect of sex and drugs education in schools.

Sex Education in the Curriculum

Few subjects in the curriculum have as much potential for generating controversy as does sex education. Given the appetite of the press for sex education 'scandals', it would be surprising if even the most skilled and experienced of teachers did not approach the topic of sex with considerable caution. A teacher's professional credibility, career and even mental and physical well-being may well be compromised, if they were to find themselves accused of undermining the 'innocence' of children, promoting homosexuality, failing to 'promote family values' or providing individual advice on contraception.

A recent example of this occurred in March 1994, when the then Secretary of State for Education, John Patten was reported as 'incensed' by a programme of sex education operating in a primary school in Leeds. According to *The Times* (Preston and Wilkinson, 1994), 'parents complained that a class of boys and girls acted out roles of people involved in an adulterous love-triangle and were told about sex games using chocolate bars'. From the school's perspective, however, the lesson which caused some parents to complain was part of a programme organized according to sound educational principles, which included allowing young people the freedom to raise issues of concern to them and attempting to answer any questions honestly and accurately. According to the chair of the school's governing body, 'the matters which had offended so many parents . . . had been brought up by the more precocious children . . . For example, one of them asked what a blow-job was'. While she felt that such an expression 'isn't the sort of language you would expect from a 10-year-old', she believed it was entirely appropriate for the nurse taking the lesson to give an explanation 'because it was very clear that other children in the class knew exactly what it meant'. For Mr. Patten and other critics of what is assumed to be the contemporary ethos of sex education, the major problem appears to be that schools are failing to instil basic moral values. According to Mr. Patten, many proponents of sex education for young people 'are very keen indeed to talk about the mechanics and regard it as at best embarrassing and at worst politically incorrect to talk about things like looking after each other, having respect for each other and taking care of each other and have forgotten any religious message'. Not all government ministers appear to share Mr. Patten's views, however, and only a month later, a health minister, Baroness Cumberlege, publicly endorsed the view that under certain circumstances it would be appropriate for a nurse to give condoms to 12-year-old girls without consulting parents, in the interests of avoiding pregnancy.

These examples may be seen as typical of the recurrent political and public debates that have surrounded sex education in recent years. Such debates have exerted a significant impact on the legislation and official guidance affecting sex education which has emerged over the course of the last eight years. Indeed, the status and position of sex education within the curriculum has shifted again as a consequence of Section 241 of the 1993 Education Act and, at the time of writing it is still uncertain how the provision of sex education in schools will be affected by this Act.

Prior to the 1993 Act, sex education in all state schools in England and Wales was governed principally by the Education (No 2) Act (1986) and the Statutory Order outlining the science curriculum (DES/WO, 1991). Section 18(2) of the 1986 Act required that the governing bodies of all county, controlled and maintained special schools decide whether or not sex education should form part of the secular curriculum of their school, and to produce a separate written statement of their policy. More importantly, Section 46 of the Act required that the LEA, governing body and headteacher should ensure that any sex education provided would 'encourage those pupils to have due regard to moral considerations and the value of family life'. It is a mark of the pressures on governing bodies in the late 1980s and early 1990s, and the priority given to sex education, that by 1992, only 54 per cent of primary schools and 82 per cent of secondary schools had produced a written policy (HEA/NFER, 1993) despite there being a statutory duty to do this. It is also clear that LEA monitoring of schools' compliance with their statutory responsibilities to have a written policy was very patchy (Thompson and Scott, 1992). Research on the objectives pursued by secondary teachers in addressing HIV/AIDS also showed that few teachers fully endorsed the moral perspective the government wished to see embodied in sex education in schools (Stears and Clift, 1990; Clift and Stears, 1992).

Coverage of sexual development and reproduction are also part of the National Curriculum science programme of study. Political controversy arose before and after the issuing of the Statutory Order on this (DES/WO, 1991), because the Order included the requirement that, during Key Stage 3, pupils should 'extend their study of the ways in which the healthy functioning of the human body may be affected by diet, lifestyle, bacteria and viruses (including Human Immuno-deficiency Virus)'.

In addition to this legal framework, official guidance on sex education is also presented as one of nine component strands of health education in *Health Education* (NCC, 1990c), as a cross-curricular theme within the whole curriculum. Whatever problems may be faced by schools in addressing sex education, the areas of study for sex education listed for each key stage in this provide clear, official sanction for schools to address a wide range of difficult, sensitive and contentious issues on a spiral curriculum model.

Since these three bases for sex education were established — the 1986 Act, the Science Statutory Order and the NCC cross-curricular theme — the 1993 Education Act has significantly changed the framework for sex education in schools, so that:

- references to HIV/AIDS and sexually transmitted diseases and any aspects of sexual behaviour (other than biological aspects) are removed from the National Curriculum;
- provision of sex education will be a compulsory part of the secular curriculum in all state schools, but outside the National Curriculum framework. Governing bodies no longer have the discretion to decide whether sex education will be taught; and
- parents will have the right to withdraw their children from sex education lessons organized outside the National Curriculum.

These changes stemmed primarily, it seems, from a combination of successful lobbying from fundamentalist religious minorities, the moral sensibilities of John Patten and the government's prioritizing of parental rights over the rights and welfare of young people. The specific target for lobbying was the inclusion of teaching about HIV within the National Curriculum. For most specialists in health and sex education, the apparently innocuous inclusion (in parentheses) of the phrase 'including Human Immuno-deficiency Virus (HIV)' in the 1991 Science Statutory Order represented a tardy and insufficient measure. Teaching about HIV infection in the context of science lessons might help to inform young people about the facts of HIV/AIDS, but would not contribue to the task of addressing problems of prejudice, perceived invulnerability, and the need to foster the self-confidence and skills needed to stay safe in sexual relationships. For some right-wing politicians and at least one fundamentalist religious group, however, not only did it seem to imply that children as young as 11 would be subjected to graphic descriptions of the ways in which HIV could be transmitted, it also represented an attack on 'family values' and the rights and roles of parents in the sexual education of their children. While Kenneth Clark was Secretary of State for Education, the protests against inclusion of education on HIV within the National Curriculum, were held in check by the weight of

> the widely accepted view, that schools have a responsibility to their pupils to offer them at least some education about sexual matters. In particular, pupils may need to know about sexual matters to ensure that education about health is not impaired, and that, for example, they understand about the relationship between certain forms of behaviour and AIDS. (DES, 1987, p. 2)

With the appointment of John Patten, however, the approach of the Department for Education towards sex education became markedly more conservative, and culminated in the Education Act 1993.

A new circular of guidance was prepared by the DFE in the light of the 1993 Act, and sent for consultation in December 1993 to Chief Education Officers and other interested parties (DFE, 1993), before the final circular was issued in the following spring. One aspect of the proposed circular that caused particular concern, and which again highlighted the long running contradictions within the government's health and education policies noted above, was the guidance relating to individual advice on contraception:

> On the specific question of the provision of contraceptive advice to girls under 16, the general rule must be that giving an individual pupil advice on such matters without parental knowledge or consent would be an inappropriate exercise of a teacher's professional responsibilities and could, depending on the circumstances, amount to a criminal offence. (*ibid.*, p. 9)

Even though this part of the proposed guidance corresponds word for word with the guidance contained in *Circular 11/87*, concern about this and other matters arising out of the 1993 Act were sufficiently great to prompt the Family Planning Association (with HEA funding, and in association with six other organizations concerned to promote sex education for young people) to commission a survey of the views young people have of sex education in the light of these changes (BMRB, 1994).

Just over 500 young people aged 13–15 were interviewed by telephone about their experiences of sex education. Of particular relevance, given the guidance in the proposed circular, is the finding that 84 per cent of young people said they would find it helpful to talk to a teacher for advice about contraception, but only a third would do so if the teacher was required to speak to their parents about this. On the issue of the parental right of withdrawal, 99 per cent of the sample agreed that 'everyone should have sex education at school', but a fifth of the group felt that 'parents should be able to make sure that their children are not taught about sex and personal relationships at school' (*ibid.*, p. 6).

The efforts made by groups such as the FPA and the Sex Education Forum to highlight such problems with the proposed circular appeared to have influenced the DFE, since the threatening tone of this guidance on the giving of contraceptive advice was dropped from the final version of the Circular issued in May 1994 as *Circular 5/94* (DFE, 1994b).

It is a matter of considerable concern that so little attention has been given to the findings of research work on the sexual behaviour of young people and the realities of sex education in schools in political and public debate on sex education. A substantial body of research has explored the attitudes of adults and young people towards sex education, the realities of classroom practice and the impact of teaching about sex on young people's knowledge, attitudes and behaviour, and such work ought to be more influential than it appears to have been in setting the agenda for action on sexual health issues in schools.

Allen (1987), in a much quoted study, found that many parents felt ill-equipped and too embarrassed to talk to their own children about sex. No fewer than 96 per cent thought that schools should be the main providers of education about sex. Allen (1992) noted that many parents were uneasy 'talking about something as basic as menstruation to their teenage daughters', and indeed Prendergast (1992) found that over a third of young women in her sample had not been told about menstruation in advance of menarche, and one in ten had not been told anything by anyone. Wyness (1992) argued, on the basis of his interviews with the parents of adolescent children, that 'the problem with sex education is located within the domestic unit as parents had difficulties in initiating discussion on sexual matters', and far from being critical of the school 'most parents saw the school as a crucial source of information and support' (p. 89). Supporting this, the BMBR survey found that for all sexual topics mentioned, 13–15-year-olds were 'considerably more likely to have learned about them at school rather than from their parents' (BMRB, 1994, p. 4). The most extreme examples of this were found for sexually transmitted diseases (90 per cent from school, 22 per cent from parents) and contraception (92 per cent vs 26 per cent). It is also clear that a considerable degree of ignorance and confusion exists among young people regarding sexuality prior to receiving sex education. As members of the Advising Postponement for Adolescents Undertaking Sexual Experience (APAUSE) project noted: 'all our experience in the classroom had not prepared us for the significantly large numbers of year 9 pupils who came up with inaccuracies or wrong ideas' (Phelps, Mellanby and Tripp, 1992, p. 27). When asked to explain menstruation, for instance, only 41 per cent of 13–14-year-olds gave an accurate account and over a third made no reference at all to blood.

The results from such studies have also to be set against the findings from research undertaken in the last ten years to investigate the sexual behaviours of young people (Clift and Stears, 1991). Such research has shown that:

- at least a third of young people have experienced sexual intercourse by the age of 16 (Breakwell and Fife-Schaw, 1992);
- the median age of first intercourse has declined, from 21 in the 1950s to 17 currently (Wellings *et al.*, 1993);
- levels of condom use among young people tend to be quite high early in their sexual careers, but decline with age as longer-term relationships become established and young people shift to using oral contraceptives (Rudat, Ryan and Speed, 1992); and
- young people who are more sexually active are less likely to use condoms and so are at enhanced risk of STDs and HIV infection (*ibid.*).

Young people are often critical of the content, timing and methodology of any sex education they have received (Hutton, Dibb and Lewis, 1992; Woodcock, Stenner and Ingham, 1992; Rudat, Ryan and Speed, 1992), and there is clearly room for considerable improvement in what is offered. There is increasing evidence that the provision of such education does have a positive influence in encouraging young people to delay sexual activity and reduce risky behaviour. The National Survey on Sexual Attitudes and Lifestyles, for example, found that people whose main sex education had been at school were least likely to have been sexually active before the age of 16 (Wellings *et al.*, 1993). A recent international review of the effects of sex education on young people's sexual behaviour also found 'no support for the contention that sex education encourages sexual experimentation or increased activity' (Grunseit and Kippax, 1993, p. 10). In fact, where effects were observed in the studies undertaken, they were almost without exception 'in the di.• ction of postponed initiation of sexual intercourse and/or effective use of contraceptives'.

But a critical commentary on sex education in schools must be balanced by an acknowledgment of the excellent work which has been achieved on a local level. As we have noted, many LEA health education coordinator posts disappeared in March 1993 after the loss of central government funding. Fortunately in some areas posts have been maintained (or even created) with the help of funding from district health authorities (for example, in East Sussex and Kent). In other areas, health authority funding has directly supported the development of sex education in schools. One of the most innovative and well-resourced projects is the Healthwise *Taking Sex Seriously* School Sex Education Project funded by Mersey Health Authority. The Healthwise Organization has produced an excellent teaching resource for secondary schools (Cohen and Wilson, 1993) and provides training and continuing support for using it in the classroom.

Many other organizations have also made substantial contributions in the field of training and resource development for sex and drugs education since the days of the Schools Council Health Education Projects. For example, the Family Planning Association, Brook Advisory Service, the Terence Higgins Trust, the Trust for the Study of Adolescence, and AVERT are all well-known for their contributions in helping teachers tackle the difficulties of educating young people about sexual health issues. Commercial publishing companies such as Daniels have also produced a wide variety of valuable resources designed to help teachers tackle sex and drugs education within the framework of the National Curriculum at all stages (for example, Harvey, 1993).

Drugs Education in the Curriculum

In spite of a growing awareness by the government of the need for effective drugs education, provision is lacking both because sufficient finance has not been made available and because the placement of drugs education in the curriculum detracts from its effectiveness. Furthermore, there are unresolved questions about the nature of drugs education — ranging from unreserved prohibition to various harm minimization approaches — and this has undermined any implementation. This is related to the way in which drug use is perceived by the government as a moral issue, on which it must be seen to act, rather than being seen within a wider social context (Matza, 1964; Young, 1971). The politicizing of drugs education establishes a narrow understanding of the meaning of such education. Firstly, it is only concerned with illicit drugs, and only with the negative aspects of these substances. The heightened political context of drugs education has been counterproductive to the ethos of *Health Education* (NCC, 1990c), which has sought to transcend the arbitrary distinction between legal and illegal substances. The status and purpose of drugs education in the curriculum is thus contradictory. As an area of knowledge it is partial; it suffers from moral, social and economic reductionism and it also carries the burden of being a site for propaganda such as 'Just say no!' (Plant and Plant, 1992).

Drug education in England and Wales has followed a typical British pattern of voluntarism, where lack of central direction has resulted in drug education being (dis)organized at national, regional and school levels. At a national level, the Teachers' Advisory Council for Alcohol and Drug Education (TACADE), formed in 1969 following the raised public profile of drug use among young people in the sixties, has no statutory powers, and its main activity is the generation of educational materials. The Advisory Council on the Misuse of Drugs, (ACMD), was established by the Misuse of Drugs Act 1971. It also has little real power as it can only advise ministers on ways of dealing with drugs and drug-related problems.

Prior to the inclusion of the drug education component within the National Curriculum in 1988, the nature of drugs education was at the discretion of individual schools and local education authorities. As a consequence such education was idiosyncratic: some schools developed drugs education programmes and policies (usually in association with their LEA), while others did not. For example, the Inner London Education Authority (ILEA) had a seven-person Health Education Team which schools could use as a support network. With the introduction of Education Grant Support for INSET in the drugs education area in 1986, nearly all

LEAs appointed a Drug Education Coordinator to manage the development of drug education policy. Such financial support allowed LEAs to prioritize according to their own perceived needs, and was welcomed by schools especially when the initial two-year pump-priming financing was extended for a total of seven years. Lewis (1993) argued of this programme:

> Government rhetoric backed by government cash was not the least of its more successful features. Most crucially, it prepared the ground for the transformation of the scheme from a drugs-specific project to the more comprehensive but no less important, Grant for Education Support and Training for Preventive Health Education scheme (known as GEST). (p. 103)

These changes in government policy on drug education developed from a growing concern with the social problems represented by drug use described in a series of reports from the Advisory Council on the Misuse of Drugs (ACMD). In 1984 ACMD recommended strengthening approaches to drugs education programmes. By 1993 its report sounded a note of new urgency: 'a new impetus is needed' because 'the drug situation in this country appears to have deteriorated' (ACMD, 1993). The report highlights the increased use of illicit drugs by youth, but also documents the problem of collecting accurate and reliable information concerning the increase of illicit drug use by young people. The government's concern about the possible extent of drug use have led to the legitimation of drugs education intervention within the school curriculum. 'Schools are singularly important because of their role in shaping the habits and behaviour of young people' (*ibid.*, p. 6). It is, however, the nature and status of this intervention which is in question.

The then Shadow Home Secretary Tony Blair, with the Home Affairs House of Commons Select Committee, recently argued that a connection exists between drug misuse and crime, using evidence from studies suggesting that use of drugs among young people has increased. Blair claimed this was due to the government's failure to provide an adequate level of drugs education: he argued that financial support for drugs education had fallen since the end of GEST funding (Blair, 1994). This linking of drug use and crime highlights the cost of drug use to society. Without substantiating evidence on the extent of drug use by young people the rhetoric takes precedence. As Parker (1994) argues 'the topic of drug misuse continues to capture media headlines and thus be routinely hijacked by politicians and moral crusaders. Consequently the debate is too often simplistic and muddled'.

Further indications of the government's ambivalence towards drug education is shown in the way in which it has included it in the various curriculum subjects Statutory Orders, and in the non-statutory guidance given on the cross-curricular theme in *Health Education* (NCC, 1990c).

The 1988 Education Reform Act provided for each foundation subject to have a programme of study set out in a Statutory Order, and this has offered a location for drugs education, peppered at each key stage among the various subject orders such as science. There was no secure place for drugs education in the Statutory Orders, in spite of the moral tone adopted by the government when speaking about the decline in the standard of behaviour among young people.

The location of drugs education within the cross-curricular theme of health education significantly downgraded the status of drugs education. The lack of status, from the pupils' perspective, is demonstrated by the fact that the subject is not examined. Health education is experienced as a another timetable problem for headteachers, especially when trained staff are not available to deliver it — in many schools health education may be delivered by any teacher who is available, or by all teachers as part of form tutor periods. The effectiveness of health education is undermined at three levels; firstly, the State fails to confer legitimacy on the subject, secondly teachers fail to give the subject priority and finally, pupils fail to take the subject seriously because it lacks external certification.

The image of health education as a low status subject is sustained by the lack of an acceptable subject base and the fact that it is not examined (Goodson, 1987). This has been compounded by the short-term nature of pump-priming (which suggests support for the subject being related to immediate public consumption rather than long-term commitment) and by the ending of GEST funding. The position of drug education also suffered when the role of drug advisers was broadened to include all health matters, thus leaving less scope for a specific focus on drugs. In 1990/91 the drug support grant was changed to cover wider aspects of preventative health education, largely as a result of the spread of HIV/AIDS. The National Liaison Group of Coordinators for Health and Drugs Education reported that the number of coordinators estimated on its register shrank from 135 to under 75 (reported by Blair, 1994). Stoker (1992) suggests that these educational changes mark the decline and dilution of drugs education in schools: Colquhoun (1993) further argues that drugs education as part of health education has become depoliticized, leading to a neglect of the social, political and economic factors which relate to health.

Approaches to Drugs Education

Drug education programmes currently do not have a common set of learning approaches, nor is there a consensus on the location of drugs education within the curriculum. There is a continuing controversy about the value of different ways of approaching drugs education in schools. This debate tends to be framed in terms of either a hard-line abstinence approach or a harm minimisation approach. In the former, the drug prevention message is judgmental and prescriptive, such as in the 'Just Say No' campaigns. In contrast, the latter approach is less judgmental and claims that if students have greater factual information about drugs, this can reduce the risks to them (Evans and O'Connor, 1992).

Drugs education needs to be both contextual and critical. Pupils will easily notice if a teacher adopts a prescriptive tone, and will be quick to realize that they are being subjected to a moral form of educational instruction. This type of drugs education is readily identifiable by students as a means of social control, especially where pupils are in possession of counter-information which contradicts the message being given. Under such circumstances, pupils can adopt teasing strategies in the classroom, offering forms of misrepresentation on drugs (Blackman, 1994a and 1994b). The prohibition approach to drugs education can be seen as contradictory by young people if it asserts the potential harm of drug-taking only with respect to illegal drugs. When pupils compare the possible ill-effects of cannabis use with those of cigarettes and alcohol, the prohibition approach shows itself to be driven more by an ideological concern than by a will to reduce harm or to educate. Young people who have access to valid experiences of drug use, from acquaintances, friends or even family will interpret such an approach to drugs as an attempt to impose 'moral improvement' on the majority, while allowing the elite to remain free of control (Leitner, Shapland and Wiles, 1993).

The norm for students in the classroom is the dominance of National Curriculum subjects, in terms of activities such as cognitive learning, sitting examinations, testing and formal assessment. Drug education appears to lack the rigour and importance of statutory subjects because it is not an 'academic' subject. Drugs education will often involve discussion, based on experience rather than knowledge, and may not require written work. Negative attitudes will be reinforced if, in addition, pupils are taught by reluctant teachers who are forced into delivering health education without training or an interest in the area. Attempts to use participative and active methods, without the necessary time to establish the skills and classroom climate required, will generate problems of classroom discipline and detract from any perceptions of relevance and value that health education might have. There is also a dilemma here, in that such attempts are counter to the desirability of enhancing the subject through making it examinable. Making health education appear as open (i.e. pupil-led) is quickly perceived as false as it is recognized as a form of social control. Pupils use the learning strategies that they have derived from statutory subjects, and will offer the 'correct' answer, such as 'Just Say No'. Health education can become 'just another lesson to get through', in which students undervalue both the formal content and the different teaching methods and learning experiences they are offered.

Both the prohibition and the harm minimization approaches are questionable, as no research evidence shows that either technique has effectively resulted in reducing drug use. It has now become a commonplace that all forms of drug education are ineffective. The lack of reliable information about drug education for young people has led Parker (1994) to argue that key government departments have backed away from funding research into this topic. Perhaps the absence of positive evidence for the effectiveness of drugs education should be taken as an indication that drugs education alone cannot address problems which are social in origin (HEA/NEFR, 1993). Such findings reinforce the need for research that sets drug use within its social context. Such research is necessary to formulate a drugs education policy that is designed to enhance social well-being, rather one that seeks to create a moral crusade.

Conclusions

The many positive developments in school health education in recent years have taken place in spite of the National Curriculum and the framework of legislation and official guidance, rather than because of it. Most practitioners regard government views on 'moral frameworks' and 'the value of family life' as unacceptably judgmental and therefore unhelpful in attempts to educate and empower young people in the area of personal, social and health education. Excellent work has been undertaken at a local level by education authority advisory services and health authorities in developing policies, local guidance documents, resource packages and the provision of training to support this area of the curriculum. Innovative and participatory educational strategies, using, for example, theatre and drama in education companies and peer education have been used increasingly in school health education. Evaluations of these initiatives show that they are effective, and suggest that they should be utilized more widely and more often in schools (see Clift and Stears, 1992, for a review). These examples of participative and active learning in social education in schools actively engage young people, and are relevant to their interests and needs.

Teachers generally favour a holistic health education philosophy in which learning about health, sex and drugs occurs within a whole-school approach. Unfortunately, official attitudes often appear inimical to such developments in the area of personal and social education. Governments throughout the 1980s and 1990s have displayed a dislike of social subjects. The former Senior Chief HM Inspector, Eric Bolton, has criticized government policy as dominated by right wing pressure groups (Chitty and Simon, 1993). Black has attacked the way that membership of bodies responsible for the control of the curriculum and of assessment has been filled by right-wing individuals:

> It is now clear that the membership of the national councils for the curriculum and for assessment give each of these an increasing bias towards that particular element in our governing party. Because of this, the teaching profession is rapidly losing any serious respect for these councils. The hopes of many that the government would exercise its sole power to appoint to the councils in an impartial way have been sharply disappointed. (Black, 1993, p. 59)

It is difficult not to agree with Bolton and Black, that Conservative education policy has been ideologically driven by the party's right wing, and that a result of this domination has been the weakened position and low status of the social subjects within the school curriculum. The government has pursued a three-fold strategy towards social subjects: firstly, by censoring a critical social perspective within National Curriculum core and foundation subjects; secondly, by excluding social subjects from the National Curriculum; and thirdly, by garrisoning social subjects into a variety of cross-curricular themes which suggests they lack the credibility of 'real' subjects within the curriculum proper. This chapter has shown how this has happened in the specific context of aspects of health education. The 'social' in the social subjects is seen by pupils as a mechanism imposed on them by the school, in an attempt to regulate their values, ideas and behaviour. This creates a problem for educationalists and teachers, in that young people often perceive social subjects as disempowering rather than empowering. Inevitably this works against schools developing into recognizable health promoting institutions.

Notes on Contributors

John Ahier is a Lecturer in the Sociology of Education at the Open University, and previously lectured at Homerton College, Cambridge. His current research interests include contemporary developments in educational policy and the relationship between domestic financial life and national economic understanding.

Shane Blackman previously worked at the University of Greenwich, the University of London Institute of Education and the University of Surrey. He is currently Senior Lecturer in Applied Social Science in the Centre for Health Education and Research at Christ Church College, Canterbury. His current research interests are youth underclass, popular music, and drugs education and the National Curriculum.

Stephen Clift is a Reader in Health Education in the Centre for Health Education and Research at Christ Church College, Canterbury and has been active in research and training activities in the area of young people and HIV/AIDS education since 1986. Co-Director of the Health Education Authority's Secondary Schools HIV/AIDS and Sex Education programme, he is also directing a project exploring the health dimensions of international travel and tourism.

Anna Craft began her professional life by teaching 4–11-year-olds in inner London and has now worked for over ten years with children and teachers in primary and secondary schools. Her current interests include social aspects of learning and empowering both teachers and children to make real choices in their personal and professional lives. She is Director of the Open University's Certificate Programme (short, applied, postgraduate courses for teachers).

Keith Crawford is a Lecturer in Education at Edge Hill College of Higher Education, Ormskirk, Lancs where he coordinates curriculum courses in social studies and history.

Rob Gilbert is an Associate Professor in the School of Education at James Cook University, Queensland, Australia. His chief interests are in the sociology of the curriculum and social education.

Alistair Ross joined the University of North London, where he is now Professor of Education, after ten years teaching in primary schools in inner London. As well as research interests in children's social and economic learning, he is Director of the Primary Schools and Industry Centre and is Faculty Research Director for Humanities and Teacher Education.

David Stears is a Principal Lecturer in Health Education and Director of the Centre for Health Education and Research at Christ Church College, Canterbury. He has developed health education and promotion courses for the College for more than ten years, and is Course Director of the MSc programme in Health Education and Health Promotion. He is a member of the Institute of Health Education and a founder member of the Health Education Lecturers' Forum.

Jeff Vass is a Lecturer in Education Studies at the University of North London and was previously co-Director of the IMPACT project, involving parents in the primary curriculum. He has research interests in discursive analyses of curriculum practice and in education in relation to cultural studies.

Bibliography

ACMD (Advisory Council on the Misuse of Drugs) (1993) *Drug Education in School*, London, HMSO.

Ahier, J. (1988) *Industry, Children and the Nation*, Lewes, Falmer Press.

Ahier, J. (1994) 'Caring in an enterprise culture? Some implications of a survey of student teachers' economic and professional attitudes', *British Journal of Education and Work*, 7, 1, pp. 33–42.

Alexander, R. (1984) *Primary Teaching*, London, Cassell.

Alexander, R. (1992) *Policy and Practice in Primary Education*, London, Routledge.

Allen, I. (1987) *Education in Sex and Personal Relationships*, London, Institute of Policy Studies.

Allen, I. (1992) 'The role of parents in sex education for young people', in *HIV/AIDS and Sex Education for Young People*, London, All-Party Parliamentary Group on AIDS, Paper No. 3.

Amis, K. (1969) 'Pernicious participation', in Cox, C. and Dyson, A. (Eds) *Fight for Education: A Black Paper*, London, Critical Quarterly Society, pp. 9–10.

Anderson, B. (1983) *Imagined Communities: Reflections of the Origins and Spread of Nationalism*, London, Verso.

Anderson, D. *et al.* (1981) *The Pied Pipers of Education*, London, Social Affairs Unit.

Anglesey, K. and Hennessy, R. (1984) 'Social sciences in primary schools', *Social Science Teacher*, 13, 3, pp. 83–4.

Ashton, P., Kneen, P., Davies, F. and Holley, B. (1975) *The Aims of Education: A Study of Teacher Opinions*, London, Macmillan.

Backhouse, J. (1969) 'Social Studies', in Schools Council *The Middle Years of Schooling from 8 to 13* (Schools Council Working Paper 22), London, HMSO.

Ball, S. (1990) *Politics and Policy Making in Education*, London, Routledge.

Bantock, G. (1986) 'The attack on the culture of quality', in O'Keeffe, D. (Ed) *The Wayward Curriculum*, London, Social Affairs Unit.

Barcan, A. (1986) 'English: Two decades of attrition', in O'Keeffe, D. (Ed) *The Wayward Curriculum*, London, Social Affairs Unit.

Barker, F. (1984) *The Tremulous Private Body: Essays in Subjection*, London, Methuen.

Barthes, R. (1973) *Mythologies*, London, Paladin.

Baudrillard (1983) *Simulations* (trs P. Foss, P. Patten, P. Beitchman), New York, Semiotext.

BENAVOT, A., CHA, Y-K., KAMENS, D., MEYER, J. and WONG, S-Y. (1992) 'Knowledge for the masses: World models and national curricula, 1920–1986', in MEYER, J. *et al.* (Eds) *School Knowledge for the Masses: World Models and National Primary Curricular Categories in the Twentieth Century*, London, Falmer Press.

BENNETT, N. *et al.* (1984) *The Quality of Pupil Learning Experiences*, London, Erlbaum.

BERNSTEIN, B. (1971) 'On the classification and framing of educational knowledge', in YOUNG, M. F. D. (Ed) *Knowledge and Control: New Directions for the Sociology of Education*, London, Collier Macmillan.

BERTI, A. and BOMBI, A. (1988) *The Child's Construction of Economics*, Cambridge, Cambridge University Press.

BIRCHENOUGH, F. (1938) (3rd Edition) *History of Elementary Education in England and Wales*, London, University Tutorial Press.

BLACK, P. (1993) 'The shifting scenery of the National Curriculum', in CHITTY C. and SIMON B. (Eds) *Education Answers Back*, London, Lawrence and Wishart.

BLACKMAN, S. (1994a) *Youth at Risk*, London, Central Drugs Prevention Unit.

BLACKMAN, S. (1994b) *Drugs Education and the National Curriculum*, London, HMSO.

BLAIR, A. (1994) *Drugs: The Need for Action*, London, Labour Party.

BLYTH, W.A.L. (1969) (2nd Edition) *English Primary Education* (2 vols) London, Routledge and Kegan Paul.

BLYTH, W.A.L. (1990) *Making the Grade for Primary Humanities*, Buckingham, Open University Press.

BLYTH, W.A.L. (1993) 'Subsidiarity in education: The example of British primary humanities', *The Curriculum Journal*, **4**, 2, pp. 283–94.

BLYTH, W.A.L. (1994) 'Beyond economic and industrial understanding: An economic perspective in the primary curriculum', *British Journal of Education and Work*, **7**, 1, pp. 11–17.

BLYTH, W.A.L., COOPER, K., DERRICOTT, R., ELLIOT, G., SUMNER, H. and WAPLINGTON, A. (1976) *Place, Time and Society 8–13: Curriculum Planning in History, Geography and Social Science*, Bristol, Collins/ESL.

BLYTH, W.A.L., RUDD, A., DERRICOTT, R., COOPER, K. and WENHAM, P. (1978) 'Aspects of power in the genesis and development of one curriculum project', in RICHARDS, C. (Ed) *Power and the Curriculum: Issues in Curriculum Studies*, Driffield, Nafferton Books.

BMRB (British Market Research Bureau) (1994) *Young People's Attitudes Towards Sex Education*, London, Family Planning Association.

BOYD, W. (1956) *Emile for Today: The Emile of Jean-Jacques Rousseau — selected, translated and interpreted by William Boyd*, London, Heinemann.

BOYSON, R. (1975a) 'Maps, chaps and your hundred best books', *Times Educational Supplement*, 17 October.

BOYSON, R. (1975b) *The Crisis in Education*, London, Woburn Press.

BREAKWELL, G. and FIFE-SCHAW, C. (1992) 'Estimating sexual behaviour parameters in the light of AIDS: A review of recent studies of young people', *AIDS Care*, **4**, pp. 187–201.

BRIGGS, A. (1985) *The Collected Essays of Asa Briggs, II: Images, Problems, Standpoints, Forecasts*, Brighton, Harvester.

BROWN, A. (1990) 'From notional to national curriculum: The search for a mechanism', in DOWLING, P. and NOSS, R. (Eds) *Mathematics Versus the National Curriculum*, London, Falmer Press.

BROWN, A. and DOWLING, P. (1993) 'The bearing of school mathematics on domestic space', in MERTTENS, R., MAYERS, D., BROWN, A. and VASS, J. (Eds) *Ruling the Margins: Problematising Parental Involvement*, London, University of North London Press.

BROWN, C. (1991) 'Continuities in education for citizenship', *Social Science Teacher*, **20**, 3, pp. 90–8.

BROWN, M. and PRECIOUS, N. (1968) *The Integrated Day in the Primary School*, London, Ward Lock Educational.

BROWNE, G. (1969) 'Notes from a junior school headmistress', in COX, C. and DYSON, A. (Eds) *Fight for Education: A Black Paper*, London, Critical Quarterly Society, p. 50.

BRUNT, R. (1989) 'The politics of identity', in HALL, S. and JACQUES, M. (Eds) *New Times: The Changing Face of Politics in 1990s*, London, Lawrence and Wishart.

CACE (Central Advisory Committee for Education (England)) (1963) *Half Our Future* (Chair: Sir John Newsom), London, HMSO.

CACE (Central Advisory Committee for Education) (England) (1967) *Children and Their Primary Schools* (Chair: Lady Bridget Plowden), London, HMSO.

CALLAGHAN, J. (1976) 'Speech on 18 October at Ruskin College, Oxford', *Times Educational Supplement*, 22 October.

CANNON, C. (1964) 'Social studies in secondary schools', *Educational Review*, 17 November, pp. 18–30.

CARRINGTON, B. and TROYNA, B. (1988), 'Children and controversial issues', in CARRINGTON, B. and TROYNA, B. (Eds) *Children and Controversial Issues: Strategies for the Early and Middle Years of Schooling*, Lewes, Falmer Press.

CHESNAUX, J. (1987) 'Information society as civic mutation', *Arena*, **81**, pp. 26–34.

CHITTY, C. (1988) 'Central control of the curriculum, 1944–1987', *History of Education*, **17**, 4, pp. 321–34.

CHITTY, C. (1992) 'From great debate to great reform act: The post-war consensus overturned, 1976–88', in RATTANSI, A. and REEDER, D. (Eds) *Rethinking Radical Education*, London, Lawrence and Wishart.

CHITTY, C. and SIMON, B. (Eds) (1993) *Education Answers Back*, London, Lawrence and Wishart.

CHOMSKY, N. (1980) *Rules and Representations*, Oxford, Blackwell.

CLIFT, S. and STEARS, D. (1991) 'Moral perspectives and safer sex practice: Two themes in teaching about HIV and AIDS in secondary schools', in AGGLETON, P., DAVIES, P. and HART, G. (Eds) *AIDS: Responses, Interventions and Care*, London, Falmer Press.

CLIFT, S. and STEARS, D. (1992) *AIDS: The Secondary Scene*, Horsham, AVERT.

Bibliography

COHEN REPORT (1964) *Health Education, A Report of the Joint Committee of the Central and Scottish Health Services*, London, HMSO.

COHEN, J. and WILSON, P. (1993) *Taking Sex Seriously*, Liverpool, Healthwise.

COHEN, P. (1990) *Really Useful Knowledge: Photography and Cultural Studies in the Transition from School*, Chester, Trentham.

COLLEY, L. (1992) *Britons: Forging the Nation 1707–1837*, New Haven, CT, Yale University Press.

COLQUHOUN, D. (1993) 'Economic rationalism, healthism and school health education', *Health Education Journal*, **49**, pp. 15–17.

COMMISSION ON CITIZENSHIP (1990) *Encouraging Citizenship*, London, HMSO.

CONNELL, R. (1989) 'Working class curriculum', in McCRAE, D. (Ed) *Imagining the Australian Curriculum*, Woden, ACT, Curriculum Development Centre.

CONQUEST, R. (1969) 'Undotheboys hall', in COX, C. and DYSON, A. (Eds) *Fight for Education: A Black Paper*, London, Critical Quarterly Society, pp. 17–20.

CORBETT, A. (1990) 'French curriculum reform', in MOON, B. (Ed) *New Curriculum, National Curriculum*, London, Hodder and Stoughton.

COTGROVE, S. (1982) *Catastrophe or Cornucopia: The Environment, Politics and the Future*, Chichester, Wiley.

COTGROVE, S. and DUFF, A. (1980) 'Environmentalism, middle class radicalism and politics', *Sociological Review*, **28**, 2, pp. 333–51.

COURTHOPE BOWEN, H. (1903) *Froebel and Education By Self-activity*, London, Heinemann.

COX, C. and DYSON, A. (Eds) (1969) *Fight for Education: A Black Paper*, London, Critical Quarterly Society.

COX, C. and DYSON, A. (Eds) (1970) *Black Paper Two: The Crisis in Education*, London, Critical Quarterly Society.

CRAFT, A. and CLAIRE, H. (1993) *Planning Learning Across the Curriculum* (OU Course E624) Milton Keynes, Open University Press.

CRAWFORD, G. (1970) 'The primary school: A balanced view', in COX, C. and DYSON, A. (Eds) *Black Paper Two: The Crisis in Education*, London, Critical Quarterly Society.

CRESSY, D. (1989) *Bonfires and Bells: National Memory and the Protestant Calendar in Elizabethan and Stuart England*, London, Weidenfeld and Nicolson.

DALZELL-WARD, A. (1975) *A Textbook of Health Education*, London, Tavistock Publications.

DAWSON, G. (1981) 'Unfitting to teach: Sociology in the training of teachers', in FLEW, A. (Ed) *The Pied Pipers of Education*, London, Social Affairs Unit.

DEARDEN, R. (1968) *The Philosophy of Primary Education*, London, Routledge and Kegan Paul.

DEARDEN, R. (1969) 'The aims of primary education', in PETERS, R. (Ed) *Perspectives on Plowden*, London, Routledge and Kegan Paul.

DEARDEN, R. (1971) 'What is the integrated day?', in WALTON, J. (Ed) *The Integrated Day in Theory and Practice*, London, Ward Lock Educational.

DENI (Department of Education (Northern Ireland)) (1992) *Educational (Cross-Curricular) Themes* (Circular 1992/20), Belfast, HMSO.

DES (Department of Education and Science) (1977a) *Educating Our Children: Four Subjects for Debate*, London, HMSO.

DES (Department of Education and Science) (1977b) *Education in Schools: A Consultative Document* (Cmnd 6869), London, HMSO.

DES (Department of Education and Science) (1978) S*pecial Educational Needs: Report of the Committee of Enquiry into the Education of Handicapped Children and Young People* (Chair: Lady Mary Warnock), London, HMSO.

DES (Department of Education and Science) (1981) *The School Curriculum*, London, HMSO.

DES (Department of Education and Science) (1983) *Teaching Quality*, London, HMSO.

DES (Department of Education and Science) (1985) *Better Schools*, Cmnd 9469, London, HMSO.

DES (Department of Education and Science) (1986) *Draft Statement of Principles on the Teaching of Politically Controversial Issues in Schools and Colleges*, London, DES.

DES (Department of Education and Science) (1987) *Sex Education at School*, Circular No. 11/87, London, HMSO.

DES/WO (Department of Education and Science/Welsh Office) (1987) *The National Curriculum, England: A Consultation Paper*, London, HMSO.

DES/WO (Department of Education and Science/Welsh Office) (1989) *History Working Group: Interim Report* (July 1989), London, DES/WO.

DES/WO (Department of Education and Science/Welsh Office) (1990) *History Working Group: Final Report* (April 1990), London, DES/WO.

DES/WO (Department of Education and Science/Welsh Office) (1991) *Science in the National Curriculum*, London, HMSO.

DEPARTMENT OF HEALTH (1992) *The Health of the Nation*, London, HMSO.

DERRICOTT, R. (1975) *Working With Teachers*, HGSS Working Paper 1, University of Liverpool.

DERRICOTT, R. (1984) 'Place, time and society 8–13: Retrospect and prospect', *Social Science Teacher*, **13**, 3, pp. 81–3.

DERRICOTT, R. (1993) 'Place, time and society, and the Schools Council 8–13: Breadth of view and balance of interests', in CAMPBELL, R.J. (Ed) *Breadth and Balance in the Primary Curriculum*, London, Falmer Press.

DFE (Department for Education) (1993) *Draft Education Act 1993: Sex Education in Schools* (proposed circular to replace Circular 11/87), London, HMSO.

DFE (Department for Education) (1994a) *Religious Education and Collective Worship*, Circular 1/94, London, HMSO.

DFE (Department for Education) (1994b) *Education Act 1993: Sex Education in Schools*, Circular 5/94, London, HMSO.

DOWLING, P. (1991a) 'Gender, class and subjectivity in mathematics: A critique of humpty dumpty', *For the Learning of Mathematics*, **11**, 1.

DOWLING, P. (1991b) 'A touch of class: Ability, social class and intertext in SMP 11–16', in PIMM, D. and LOVE, E. (Eds) *Teaching and Learning Mathematics*, London, Hodder and Stoughton.

DOWLING, P. (in press) 'Discursive saturation and school mathematics texts: A strand from a language of description', in ERNEST, P. (Ed) *Mathematics, Education and Philosophy: An International Perspective*, London, Falmer Press.

EDWARDS, G. (1991) *Living Magically*, London, Piatkus.

EDWARDS, G. (1993) *Stepping into the Magic*, London, Piatkus.

EMLER, N., OHANA, J. and DICKINSON, J. (1990) 'Children's representations of social relations', in DUVEEN, G. and LLOYD, B. (Eds) *Social Representations and the Development of Knowledge*, Cambridge, Cambridge University Press.

ENTWISTLE, H. (1970) *Child-Centred Education*, London, Methuen.

ESLAND, G. (1971) 'Teaching and learning as the organisation of knowledge', in YOUNG, M.F.D. (Ed) *Knowledge and Control: New Directions for the Sociology of Education*, London, Collier Macmillan.

EVANS, R. and O'CONNOR, L. (Eds) (1992) *Drug Abuse and Misuse: Developing Educational Strategies in Partnership*, London, David Fulton.

FLEW, A. (1986) 'Education against racism', in O'KEEFFE, D. (Ed) *The Wayward Curriculum*, London, Social Affairs Unit.

FOREMAN, N. (1991) 'Viewpoint', *Social Sciences: News from the Economic and Social Research Council*, 12, November, Swindon, ESRC.

FOUCAULT, M. (1970) *The Order of Things*, London, Tavistock.

FOUCAULT, M. (1980) *Power/Knowledge*, Sussex, Harvester Press.

FROEBEL, F. (1887) *Education of Man*, Appleton Press.

FROEBEL, F. (1895) *Pedagogies of the Kindergarten*, Appleton Press.

FROOME, S. (1970) 'The mystique of modern maths', in COX, C. and DYSON, A. (Eds) *Black Paper Two: The Crisis in Education*, London, Critical Quarterly Society.

GALTON, M. and SIMON, B. (1980) *Progress and Performance in the Primary Classroom*, London, Routledge and Kegan Paul.

GALTON, M., SIMON, B. and CROLL, P. (1980) *Inside the Primary Classroom*, London, Routledge and Kegan Paul.

GARDNER, H. (1993 edition) *Frames of Mind: A Theory of Multiple Intelligences*, London, Fontana.

GAWAIN, S. (1993) *The Path of Transformation*, Mill Valley, CA, Natraj.

GIBBINS, J. (1989) 'Contemporary political culture: An introduction', in GIBBINS, J. (Ed) *Contemporary Political Culture: Politics in a Post-modern Age*, London, Sage.

GIDDENS, A. (1981) *A Contemporary Critique of Historical Materialism*, London, Macmillan.

GIDDENS, A. (1990) *The Consequences of Modernity*, London, Macmillan.

GILBERT, R. (1984) *The Impotent Image: Reflections of Ideology in the Secondary School Curriculum*, Lewes, Falmer Press.

GILBERT, R. (1992) 'Citizenship, education and post-modernity', *British Journal of Sociology of Education*, **13**, 1.

GIROUX, H. (1989) 'Schooling as a form of cultural politics: Toward a pedagogy of and for difference', in GIROUX, H. and McLAREN, P. (Eds) *Critical Pedagogy, the State, and Cultural Struggle*, Albany, NY, State University of New York Press.

GOODSON, I. (1987, 2nd Edition) *School Subjects and Curriculum Change: Studies in Curriculum History*, London, Falmer Press.

GOODSON, I. (1989) 'Curriculum reform and curriculum theory: A case of historical amnesia', *Cambridge Journal of Education*, July, pp. 131–41.

GOODSON, I. (1994) *Studying Curriculum: Cases and Methods*, London, Falmer Press.

GOODSON, I. and DOWBIGGIN, A. (1990) 'Curriculum history, professionalization and the social construction of knowledge', *Curriculum and Teaching*, summer 1990.

GRAHAM, D. (1992) 'Beware hasty changes', *Times Educational Supplement*, 3 January, p. 10.

GRAHAM, D. (1993) *A Lesson For Us All: The Making of the National Curriculum*, London, Routledge.

GREAT BRITAIN (1988) *The Education Reform Act*, London, HMSO.

GREIG, S., PIKE, G. and SELBY, D. (1987) *Earthrights*, London, World Wildlife Fund and Kogan Page.

GREIG, S., PIKE, G. and SELBY, D. (1989) *Greenprints for Changing Schools*, London, World Wildlife Fund and Kogan Page.

GROSSBERG, L. (1989) 'Putting the post back into post-modernism', in ROSS, A. (Ed) *Universal Abandon? The Politics of Post-modernism*, Edinburgh, Edinburgh University Press.

GRUNSEIT, A. and KIPPAX, S. (1993) *Effects of Sex Education on Young People's Sexual Behaviour*, Macquarie University, Australia: National Centre for HIV Social Research (Commissioned by Youth and General Public Unit, Office of Intervention, Development and Support, Global Programme on AIDS, World Health Organisation).

GUARDIAN (The) 6 September 1989.

HALL, S. (1989) 'The meaning of new times', in HALL, S. and JACQUES, M. (Eds) *New Times: The Changing Face of Politics in the 1990s*, London, Lawrence and Wishart.

HALSEY, A. (1981) *Change in British Society*, Milton Keynes, Open University Press.

HANSON, J. (1969) 'Social studies 11–13', SCHOOLS COUNCIL, *The Middle Years of Schooling from 8 to 13* (Schools Council Working Paper 22), London, HMSO.

HARGREAVES, A. (1994a) 'Critical introduction', in GOODSON, I. (Ed) *Studying Curriculum: Cases and Methods*, London, Falmer Press.

HARGREAVES, A. (1994b) *Changing Teachers, Changing Times: Teachers' Work and Culture in the Postmodern Age*, London, Cassell.

HARRIES, E. *et al.* (1983) *The New Approach to the Social Studies: Continuity and Development in Children's Learning through First, Middle and High Schools*, London, London Borough of Merton/Schools Council.

HARVEY, D. (1989) *The Condition of Post-modernity: An Enquiry into the Origins of Cultural Change*, Oxford, Blackwell.

HARVEY, I. (1993) *Condoms Acros the Curriculum*, Cambridge, Daniels Publishing.

HASSAN, I. (1985) 'The culture of post-modernism', *Theory, Culture and Society*, **2**, pp. 119–31.

HEATER, D. (1990) *Citizenship: The Civic Ideal in World History, Politics and Education*, London, Longman.

HEA/NFER (Health Education Authority/National Foundation for Educational Research) (1993) *A Survey of Health Education Policies in Schools*, London, NFER.

HILL, D. (1986) 'Urban studies: Closing Minds?', in O'KEEFFE, D. (Ed) *The Wayward Curriculum*, London, Social Affairs Unit.

HILLGATE GROUP (1986) *Whose Schools? A Radical Manifesto*, London, Hillgate Place.

HIRST, P. (1965) 'Liberal education and the nature of knowledge', in ARCHEMBAULT, R.D. (Ed) *Philosophical Analysis and Education*, London, Routledge and Kegan Paul, pp. 113–38.

HMI (Her Majesty's Inspectorate of Schools) (1977) *Curriculum 11–16*, London, HMSO.

HMI (Her Majesty's Inspectorate of Schools) (1978) *Primary Education in England: A Survey by HM Inspectors of Schools*, London, HMSO.

HMI (Her Majesty's Inspectorate of Schools) (1980) *A View of the Curriculum*, London, HMSO.

HMI (Her Majesty's Inspectorate of Schools) (1982) *Education 5 to 9: An Illustrative Survey of 80 First Schools in England*, HMI, London, HMSO.

HMI (Her Majesty's Inspectorate of Schools) (1983) *9–13 Middle Schools: An Illustrative Survey*, London, HMSO.

HMI (Her Majesty's Inspectorate of Schools) (1985a) *Curriculum Matters 2: The Curriculum from 5 to 16*, London, HMSO.

HMI (Her Majesty's Inspectorate of Schools) (1985b) *History in the Primary and Secondary Years*, London, HMSO.

HMI (Her Majesty's Inspectorate of Schools) (1985c) *Education 8 to 12 in Combined and Middle Schools: An HMI Survey*, London, HMSO.

HMI (Her Majesty's Inspectorate of Schools) (1986) *Curriculum Matters 7: Geography from 5 to 16*, London, HMSO.

HMI (Her Majesty's Inspectorate of Schools) (1988) *Curriculum Matters 11: History Curriculum from 5 to 16*, London, HMSO.

HMI (Her Majesty's Inspectorate of Schools) (1989) *An Inspection Review: Aspects of Primary Education: The Teaching and Learning of History and Geography*, London, HMSO.

HMI (Her Majesty's Inspectorate of Schools) (1991) *Economic and Industrial Understanding 5–11*, London, HMSO.

HOBSBAWM, E. (1983) 'Introduction: Inventing traditions', in HOBSBAWM, E. and RANGER, T. (Eds) *The Invention of Tradition*, Cambridge, Cambridge University Press.

HOBSBAWM, E. and RANGER, T. (Eds) (1983) *The Invention of Tradition*, Cambridge, Cambridge University Press.

HUNT, L. (1984) *Politics, Culture and Class in the French Revolution*, Berkeley, CA, University of California Press.

HUTCHINGS, M. (1989) 'Children's ideas about the world of work', in ROSS, A. *et al.* (Eds) *The Primary Enterprise Pack*, London, PNL Press.

HUTTON, C., DIBB, L. and LEWIS, J. (1992) *Living for Tomorrow: National AIDS Trust Youth Initiative*, London, National AIDS Trust.

HUYSSEN, A. (1986) *After the Great Divide: Modernism, Mass Culture, Post-modernism*, Bloomington, IA, Indiana University Press.

INNER LONDON EDUCATION AUTHORITY (1978) *People Around Us: Families*, London, ILEA LMS.

INNER LONDON EDUCATION AUTHORITY (1979) *People Around Us: Friends*, London, ILEA LMS.

INNER LONDON EDUCATION AUTHORITY (1980a) *People Around Us: Work*, London, ILEA LMS.

INNER LONDON EDUCATION AUTHORITY (1980b) *Social Studies in the Primary School (Curriculum Guidelines)*, London, ILEA LMS.

ISAACS, S. (1930) *Intellectual Growth in Young Children*, London, Routledge.

JACOBS, M. (1991) *The Green Economy*, London, Pluto Press.

JAMESON, F. (1984) 'Post-modernism, or the cultural logic of late capitalism', *New Left Review*, 146, pp. 53–92.

JAMIESON, I. and HARRIS, A. (1992) 'Evaluating economic awareness, Part I: Management and organisation issues', *Economic Awareness*, **4**, 3, pp. 17–21.

JOHNSON, C. (1969) 'Freedom in junior schools', in COX, C. and DYSON, A. (Eds) *Fight for Education: A Black Paper*, London, Critical Quarterly Society, pp. 48–50.

JOHNSON, R. (1992) 'Radical education and the new right', in RATTANSI, A. and REEDER, D. (Eds) *Rethinking Radical Education*, London, Lawrence & Wishart.

JOHNSTON, R. (1989) *Environmental Problems*, London, Bellhaven Press.

JONES, E., FORREST, J., GOLDMAN, N., HENSHAW, S., LINCOLN, R., ROSOFF, J., WESTOFF, C. and WULF, D. (1985) 'Teenage pregnancy in developed countries: Determinants and policy implications', *Family Planning Perspective*, **17**, 2, pp. 53–63.

KAMENS, D. (1992) 'Variant forms: Cases of countries with distinct curricula', in MEYER, J., KAMENS, D. and BENAVOT, A. (Eds) *School Knowledge for the Masses: World Models and National Primary Curricular Categories in the Twentieth Century*, London, Falmer Press.

KAUFFMAN, L. (1990) 'Democracy in a post-modern world?', *Social Policy*, **21**, 2, pp. 6–11.

KELLNER, D. (1992) 'Popular culture and the construction of post-modern identities', in LASH, S. and FRIEDMAN, J. (Eds) *Modernity and Identity*, Oxford, Basil Blackwell.

KUHN, T. (1962) *The Structure of Scientific Revolutions*, New York, Harper Row.

LASCH, C. (1991) *The True and Only Heaven*, New York, W Norton.

LAWRENCE, E. (Ed) (1952) *Friedrich Froebel and English Education*, London, University of London Press.

LAWTON, D. (1969) 'Social studies', SCHOOLS COUNCIL *The Middle Years of Schooling from 8 to 13* (Schools Council Working Paper 22), London, HMSO.

LAWTON, D. (1975) *Class, Culture and the Curriculum*, London, Routledge and Kegan Paul.

LAWTON, D. (1981) 'Foundations of social science', in MEHLINGER, H. (Ed) *UNESCO Handbook for the Teaching of the Social Sciences*, London, Croom Helm.

LAWTON, D., CAMPBELL, J. and BURKITT, V. (1971) *Social Studies 8–13* (Schools Council Working Paper 39), London, Evans/Methuen Educational.

LAWTON, D. and DUFOUR, B. (1973) *The New Social Studies*, London, Heinemann.

LAYTON, D. (1973) *Science for the People*, London, Allen and Unwin.

LEAHY, R. (1981) 'The development of the concept of economic inequality: I — Descriptions and comparisons of rich and poor people', *Child Development*, **52**, pp. 323–52.

LEAHY, R. (1983) 'The development of the concept of economic inequality: II — Explanations, justifications and concepts of social mobility and change', *Developmental Psychology*, **19**, pp. 111–25.

LECA, J. (1992) 'Questions on citizenship', in MOUFFE, C. (Ed) *Dimensions of Radical Democracy: Pluralism, Citizenship, Community*, London, Verso.

LEITNER, M., SHAPLAND, J. and WILES, P. (1993) *Drug Usage and Drug Prevention: The Views of the General Public*, London, HMSO.

LEWIS, D. (1993) 'Oh for those halcyon days! a review of the developments of school health education over the last 50 years', *Health Education Journal*, **52**, 3, pp. 161–71.

LGDF (Local Government Drugs Forum) (1993) *Health Education Co-ordinators, LGDF Circular 1/93*, London, LGDF.

LILLEY, I. (1967) *Friedrich Froebel: A Selection from his Writings*, Cambridge, Cambridge University Press.

LINCOLN RALPHS, F. (1969) 'Foreword', SCHOOLS COUNCIL *The Middle Years of Schooling from 8 to 13* (Schools Council Working Paper 22), London, HMSO.

LUKE, T. and WHITE, S. (1985) 'Critical theory, the informational revolution, and an ecological path to modernity', in FORESTER, J. (Ed) *Critical Theory and Public Life*, Cambridge, MA, MIT Press.

LYOTARD, J-F. (1984) *The Post-modern Condition: A Report on Knowledge*, Manchester, Manchester University Press.

MACKENZIE, W. (1978) *Political Identity*, Harmondsworth, Penguin.

MARRIOTT, S. (1994) 'Curriculum review in Northern Ireland', *Education 3–13*, **22**, 2, pp. 8–12.

MARSDEN, W. (1993) 'Recycling religious instruction? Historical perspectives on contemporary cross-curricular issues', *History of Education*, **22**, 4.

MARSHALL, T. (1950) *Citizenship and Social Class*, Cambridge, Cambridge University Press.

MATZA, D. (1964) *Delinquency and Drift*, New York, John Wiley.

MEHLINGER, H. (1981) *UNESCO Handbook for the Teaching of the Social Sciences*, London, Croom Helm.

MERTTENS, R. and VASS, J. (1989) *Plan and Assess the National Curriculum in the Primary Classroom*, Oxford, Heinemann.

MEYER, J. (1992) 'Background: A perspective on the curriculum and curricular

Research', in MEYER, J. *et al.* (Eds) *School Knowledge for the Masses: World Models and National Primary Curricular Categories in the Twentieth Century*, London, Falmer Press.

MEYER, J., KAMENS, H. and BENAVOT, A. (Eds) (1992) *School Knowledge for the Masses: World Models and National Primary Curricular Categories in the Twentieth Century*, London, Falmer Press.

MIDWINTER, E. (1971) 'Curriculum and the EPA community school', in HOOPER, R. (Ed) *The Curriculum: Context, Design and Development*, Edinburgh, Oliver and Boyd.

MINISTRY OF EDUCATION (1957a) *A Handbook of Health Education*, London, HMSO.

MINISTRY OF EDUCATION (1957b) *Primary Education*, London, HMSO.

MONTESSORI, M. (1914) *Dr Montessori's Own Handbook*, London, William Heinemann.

MORGAN, R. (1983) 'From a death to a view: The hunt for the Welsh past in the romantic period', in HOBSBAWM, E. and RANGER, T. (Eds) *The Invention of Tradition*, Cambridge, Cambridge University Press.

MORT, F. (1989) 'The politics of consumption', in HALL, S. and JACQUES, M. (Eds) *New Times: The Changing Face of Politics in the 1990s*, London, Lawrence and Wishart.

MORTIMORE, P., SAMMONS, P., STOLL, L., LEWIS, D. and ECOB, R. (1988) *School Matters: The Junior Years*, London, Open Books.

MURRAY, R. (1989) 'Benetton Britain', in HALL, S. and JACQUES, M. (Eds) *New Times: The Changing Face of Politics in the 1990s*, London, Lawrence and Wishart.

NCC (National Curriculum Council) (1989) *The National Curriculum and Whole Curriculum Planning: Preliminary Guidance — Circular No 6*, York, National Curriculum Council.

NCC (National Curriculum Council) (1990a) *Curriculum Guidance 3: The Whole Curriculum*, York, National Curriculum Council.

NCC (National Curriculum Council) (1990b) *Curriculum Guidance 4: Education for Economic and Industrial Understanding*, York, National Curriculum Council.

NCC (National Curriculum Council) (1990c) *Curriculum Guidance 5: Health Education*, York, National Curriculum Council.

NCC (National Curriculum Council) (1990d) *Curriculum Guidance 6: Careers Education and Guidance*, York, National Curriculum Council.

NCC (National Curriculum Council) (1990e) *Curriculum Guidance 7: Environmental Education*, York, National Curriculum Council.

NCC (National Curriculum Council) (1990f) *Curriculum Guidance 8: Education for Citizenship*, York, National Curriculum Council.

NCC (National Curriculum Council) (1991) *Managing Economic and Industrial Understanding in Schools*, York, National Curriculum Council.

NCC/SEAC (National Curriculum Council/School Examinations and Assessment Council), (1993) *The National Curriculum and its Assessment: An Interim Report* (The Interim Dearing Report: Sir Ron Dearing), York and London, NCC/SEAC.

NIAS, J. (1989) *Primary Teachers Talking: A Study of Teaching as Work*, London, Routledge.

O'KEEFFE, D. (1981) 'Labour in vain: Truancy, industry and the school curriculum', in ANDERSON, D. *et al.*, (Eds) *The Pied Pipers of Education*, London, Social Affairs Unit.

O'KEEFFE, D. (Ed) (1986) *The Wayward Curriculum: A Cause for Parents' Concern?*, London, Social Affairs Unit.

OLDFIELD, A. (1990) *Citizenship and Community: Civic Republicanism and the Modern World*, London, Routledge.

O'RIORDAN, T. (1981) (2nd Edition) *Environmentalism*, London, Pion.

PARKER, H. (1994) 'Clear cut statistics', *The Guardian*, 22 February.

PEARCE, I./EEA (Educating for Economic Awareness) (1987) Letter to 'All initiatives and projects economic awareness/understanding field', 28 July, London, Educating for Economic Awareness.

PEPPER, D. (1984) *The Roots of Modern Environmentalism*, London, Croom Helm.

PHELPS, F., MELLANBY, A. and TRIPP, J. (1992) 'So you really think you understand sex?', *Education and Health*, **10**, 2, pp. 27–31.

PIERREPOINT GRAVES, F. (1936) *A Student's History of Education*, London, Macmillan.

PLANT, M. and PLANT, M. (1992) *Risk-takers — Alcohol, Drugs, Sex and Youth*, London, Routledge.

PLASKOW, M. (Ed) (1985) *The Life and Death of the Schools Council*, London, Falmer Press.

PORRIT, J. and WINNER, D. (1988) *The Coming of the Greens*, London, Fontana.

PRENDERGAST, S. (1992) *Girls' Experiences of Menstruation in School*, Cambridge, Health Promotion Trust.

PRESTON, B. and WILKINSON, P. (1994) 'Patten seizes on school sex row in moral crusade', *The Times*, 24 March.

PRING, R. (1972) 'Focus of knowledge and general education', *General Education*, **19**.

PRING, R. (1976) *Curriculum Design and Development*, Milton Keynes, Open University Press.

QUICKE, K. (1992) 'Individualism and citizenship: Some problems and possibilities', *International Studies in Sociology of Education*, **2**, 2.

RANSOM, N. (1990) 'From 1944 to 1988: Education, citizenship and democracy', in FLUDE, M. and HAMMER, M. (Eds) *The Education Reform Act 1988: Its Origins and Implications*, London, Falmer Press.

RAWLING, L. (1990) 'The right attack on sociology', *Social Science Teacher*, **19**, 3, pp. 74–5.

REGAN, D. (1986) 'Sociology and politics: Unsuitable subjects for schools', in O'KEEFFE, D. (Ed) *The Wayward Curriculum*, London, Social Affairs Unit.

RITZER, G. (1993) *The McDonaldization of Society: An Investigation Into the Changing Character of Contemporary Social Life*, Newbury Park, CA, Pine Forge Press.

ROBERTS, Y. (1994) 'Old-fashioned values', *New Statesman and Society*, **7**, 306, 10 June.

ROGERS, V. (1968) *The Social Subjects in English Education*, London, Heinemann.

ROLLS, I. (1969) 'Environmental studies: A new synthesis', *Education for Teaching*, spring.

ROMAN, L., CHRISTIAN-SMITH, L. and ELLSWORTH, E. (Eds) (1988) *Becoming Feminine: The Politics of Popular Culture*, London, Falmer Press.

ROSS, A. (1982) 'In-service and curriculum development: A case study of social studies in primary schools in the ILEA', *British Journal of In-Service Education*, **9**, 2, pp. 126–36.

ROSS, A. (1990) 'Primary school social studies in the new curriculum', *Social Science Teacher*, **19**, 3, pp. 82–3.

ROSS, A. (1993) 'The subjects that dare not speak their name', in CAMPBELL, R.J. (Ed) *Breadth and Balance in the Primary Curriculum*, London, Falmer Press.

ROSS, A., AHIER, J. and HUTCHINGS, M. (1991) *Student Primary Teachers: Their Economic and Industrial Background, Understanding and Attitudes* (EATE Research Report 2), Bath, Enterprise Awareness and Teacher Education.

ROWE, G., AGGLETON, P. and WHITTY, G. (1993) 'Subjects and themes in the school curriculum', *Working Papers on the ESRC Project, Assessing Quality in Cross Curricular Contexts*, London, Institute of Education (mimeo).

ROWLAND, S. (1987) 'Where is primary education going?', *Journal of Curriculum Studies*, **19**, 1.

RSA (Royal Society for the Encouragement of Arts, Manufactures and Commerce) (1985) *Education and Industry: Industry Year 1986*, London, RSA.

RUDAT, K., RYAN, H. and SPEED, M. (1992) *Today's Young Adults*, London, Health Education Authority.

SAHLINS, P. (1989) *Boundaries: The Making of France and Spain in the Pyrenees*, Berkeley, CA, University of California Press.

SCAA (Schools Curriculum and Assessment Authority) (1994a) *The National Curriculum and its Assessment*, ('The Dearing Report', Sir Ron Dearing), London, SCAA.

SCAA (Schools Curriculum and Assessment Authority) (1994b) *History in the National Curriculum: Draft Proposals*, London, SCAA.

SCAA (Schools Curriculum and Assessment Authority) (1994c) *Geography in the National Curriculum: Draft Proposals*, London, SCAA.

SCDC (Schools Curriculum Development Council) (1986) *Planning Conference on Economic Awareness, 21/22 July 1986, Conference Report*, mimeo, London, SCDC.

SCDC/EEA (Schools Curriculum Development Council/Educating for Economic Awareness) (1987) *Educating for Economic Awareness: Information Briefing (1)*, June, mimeo, London, Schools Curriculum Development Committee.

SCHOOLS COUNCIL (1969) *The Middle Years of Schooling from 8 to 13* (Schools Council Working Paper 22), London, HMSO.

SCHOOLS COUNCIL (1981) *The Practical Curriculum* (Schools Council Working Paper 70), London, Methuen.

SCRUTON, R. (1980) *The Meaning of Conservatism*, London, Macmillan.

Bibliography

SCRUTON, R., ELLIS-JONES, A. and O'KEEFFE, D. (1985) *Education and Indoctrination*, Harrow, Middlesex Education Research Centre.
SELLECK, R. (1972) *English Primary Education and the Progressives, 1914–1939*, London, Routledge.
SHOTTER, J. (1993a) *Conversational Realities*, London, Sage.
SHOTTER, J. (1993b) *The Cultural Politics of Everyday Life*, Milton Keynes, Open University Press.
SIMON, B. (1988) *Bending the Rules: The Baker 'Reform' of Education*, London, Lawrence and Wishart.
SKIDMORE, W. (1975) *Sociology's Models of Man*, New York, Gordon and Breach.
SMART, B. (1993) *Postmodernity*, London, Routledge.
SMITH, S. (1994) 'Is four too early to be told about the facts of life?', *The European*, 8–14 April.
SOCIAL SCIENCE TEACHER (1980) *Social Studies in the Primary School* (special edition), **9**, 4/5.
SOCIAL SCIENCE TEACHER (1984) *Primary and Middle Schools Social Studies* (special edition), **13**, 3.
SOCIAL SCIENCE TEACHER (1988) *In Defence of School Social Studies* (special edition), **17**, 2.
SOED (Scottish Office, Education Department) (1993) *Guidelines for Environmental Studies*, Edinburgh, SOED.
STAUTH, G. and TURNER, B. (1988) 'Nostalgia, post-modernism and the critique of mass culture', *Theory, Culture and Society*, **5**, pp. 509–26.
STEADMAN, D. et al., (1978) *Schools Council Impact and Take-up Project: First Interim Report*, (mimeo), London, Schools Council.
STEADMAN, D. et al., (1980) *Schools Council Impact and Take-up Project: Second Interim Report*, (mimeo), London, Schools Council.
STEARS, D. and CLIFT, S. (1992) *A Survey of AIDS Education in Secondary Schools*, Horsham, AVERT.
STOKER, P. (1992) *Drug Prevention: Just Say No*, London, David Fulton.
SUTHERLAND, I. (1979) *Health Education: Perspectives and Choices*, London, Allen and Unwin.
TAWNEY, R. (1923) *Secondary Education for All: A Policy for Labour*, London, Labour Party/Allen and Unwin.
THOMSON, R. and SCOTT, L. (1992) *An Enquiry into Sex Education: Report of a Survey into Local Education Authority Support and Monitoring of School Sex Education*, London, Sex Education Forum.
TIZARD, B., BLATCHFORD, P., BURKE, J., FARQUAHAR, C. and LEWIS, I. (1988) *Young Children at School in the Inner City*, London, Laurence Erlbaum.
TONES, K. (1987) 'Health promotion', in DAVID, K. and WILLIAMS, T. (Eds) *Health Education in Schools*, London, Harper and Row.
TONES, K., TILFORD, S. and ROBINSON, Y. (1990) *Health Education: Effectiveness and Efficiency*, London, Chapman Hall.
TREVOR-ROPER, H. (1983) 'The invention of tradition: The highland tradition of

Scotland', in HOBSBAWM, E. and RANGER, T. (Eds) *The Invention of Tradition*, Cambridge, Cambridge University Press.

TURNER, B. (1989) 'From post-industrial society to post-modern politics: The political sociology of Daniel Bell', in GIBBINS, J. (Ed) *Contemporary Political Culture: Politics in a Post-modern Age*, London, Sage.

VASS, J. (1985) 'Personhood and pedagogy: The social production of "special" identities', paper given to the Intercollegiate Seminar, Department of Anthropology, University College, London.

VASS, J. (1993a) 'Apprenticeships in the absence of masters: Authority and canonical texts in pedagogical communication', in MERTTENS, R., MAYERS, D., BROWN, A. and VASS, J. (Eds) *Ruling the Margins: Problematising Parental Involvement*, London, University of North London Press.

VASS, J. (1993b) 'Marginal dialogues, social positions and inequity in rhetorical resources', in MERTTENS, R. and VASS, J. (Eds) *Partnerships in Maths: Parents and Schools*, London, Falmer Press.

VASS, J. (1993c) 'Translating economic mythology into primary curriculum discourse', paper given at the Third Primary Schools and Industry Conference, September, University of North London.

VASS, J. (in press) 'The dominance of structure in "post-structural" critiques of mathematics education', in ERNEST, P. (Ed) (in press) *Mathematics, Education and Philosophy: An International Perspective*, London, Falmer Press.

WALKERDINE, V. (1984) 'Developmental psychology and child-centred pedagogy: The insertion of Piaget into early education', in HENRIQUES, J. *et al.*, (Eds) *Changing the Subject: Psychology, Social Regulation and Subjectivity*, London, Methuen.

WALKERDINE, V. (1988) *The Mastery of Reason*, London, Routledge.

WALTON, J. (Ed) (1971) *The Integrated Day in Theory and Practice*, London, Ward Lock.

WELLINGS, K. *et al.*, (1993) *Sexual Behaviour in Britain: The National Survey of Sexual Attitudes and Lifestyles*, Harmondsworth, Penguin.

WEXLER, P. (1987) *The Social Analysis of Education*, London, Routledge.

WEXLER, P. (1990) 'Citizenship in the semiotic society', in TURNER, B. (Ed) *Theories of Modernity and Post-modernity*, London, Sage.

WHITE, H. (1978) *The Tropics of Discourse: Essays in Cultural Criticism*, Baltimore, MD, Johns Hopkins University Press.

WHITEHEAD, D. (1980) *The Dissemination of Educational Innovation in Britain*, London, Hodder and Stoughton.

WHITEHEAD, M. (1989) *Focusing Upstream*, London, King Edward Hospital Fund.

WHITTY, G. (1985) *Sociology and School Knowledge: Curriculum Theory, Research and Politics*, London, Methuen.

WHITTY, G. (1992) 'Lessons from radical curriculum initiatives: Integrated humanities and world studies', in RATTANSI, A. and REEDER, D. (Eds) *Rethinking Radical Education: Essays in Honour of Brian Simon*, London, Lawrence and Wishart.

WIENER, M. (1981) *English Culture and the Decline of the Industrial Spirit 1850– 1980*, Cambridge, Cambridge University Press.

WILLIS, P. (1990) *Common Culture*, Milton Keynes, Open University Press.

WONG, SY. (1991) 'The evolution of social science instruction, 1900–86', *Sociology of Education*, **64**, 1, pp. 19–32.

WOOD, D. (1988) *How Children Think and Learn: An Introduction to Cognitive Development*, Oxford, Blackwell.

WOODCOCK, A., STENNER, K. and INGHAM, R. (1992) ' "All these contraceptives, videos and that . . ." young people talking about school sex education', *Health Education Research*, **7**, 4, pp. 517–31.

WOODHEAD, M. (1991) 'Psychology and the construction of children's needs', in WOODHEAD, M., LIGHT, P. and CARR, K. (Eds) *Growing Up in a Changing Society*, Milton Keynes, Open University Press.

WRONG, D. (1964) 'The oversocialized conception of man in modern sociology', in COSER, L. and ROSENBERG, B. (Eds) *Sociological Theory*, London, Collier-Macmillan.

WRONSKI, P. (1981) 'Social studies around the world', in MEHLINGER, H. (Ed) *UNESCO Handbook for the Teaching of the Social Sciences*, London, Croom Helm.

WYNESS, M.G. (1992) 'Schooling and the normalization of sex talk within the home', *British Journal of Sociology of Education*, **13**, 1, pp. 89–103.

YEARLEY, S. (1991) *The Green Case*, London, Harper Collins.

YOUNG, I. (1990) *Justice and the Politics of Difference*, Princeton, NJ, Princeton University Press.

YOUNG, J. (1971) *The Drugtakers*, London, Paladin.

YOUNG, M.F.D. (1971) *Knowledge and Control*, West Drayton, Collier Macmillan.

Index